"A timely book written with compassion, wisdom and devotion. It provides the reader with gentle wise council of how to find our way back to the simple miracle of living, while discovering a renewed affection for our life. You will begin to feel good about the miracle of being truly who you are, instead of trying to be something you are not."

-Robert A. Johnson
Author of *He, She, We, Inner Work,* and *Balancing Heaven and Earth*

"Ever Flowing On is a helpful guide for the soul's journey. Full of insights and markings on the trail of life for the serious seeker. I highly recommend this book."

-Angeles Arrien, Ph.D.
Anthropologist and Author of *The Four-Fold Way*

"Michael DeMaria is a rare, loving wisdom teacher who has befriended the human psyche and traveled to its depths. He knows how to extract the psyche's sacred treasures that lead to our full awakening as spiritual beings in human bodies. I love this book! It is profound! It will guide you and transform you if you will follow its gentle trail to wholeness."

-Jacquelyn Small
Author of *Becoming Naturally Therapeutic,* and *Transformers*

"Ever Flowing On is a wake up call to those who live at the edge longing and yearning for harmony and connectedness. Brimming with gems of wisdom it is priceless to those who are committed to living simply. This timely book is a valuable contribution to consciousness. I highly recommend it."

-Malidoma Patrice Some', Ph.D.
Author of *Of Water and Spirit,* and *The Healing Wisdom of Africa*

This powerful book describes in detail and with great clarity the process of 'being and becoming oneself'. Drawing from rich personal experience as well as varied cultural background ranging from Aztecs to Zen, Michael DeMaria offers a most useful map for our spiritual journey.

-Piero Ferrucci
Author of *What We May Be,* and *Inevitable Grace*

Michael DeMaria's book...points our way back to wholeness in the most genuine and natural way. In this way our everyday life is seen for the magnificent and sacred adventure it truly is.

-STUART MILLER, PH.D.
Author *Hot Springs,* and *Understanding Europeans*

"Michael DeMaria gives us the gift of a skillful and beautiful interweaving of existential psychology, cross-cultural symbolism, the vision quest, autobiography, and therapeutic case vignettes. He provides a gentle guidebook for our journey with life and shows "how the agony of the quest blossoms into the joy of the dance." This book will be, for many, the most useful and inspiring description of this domain."

-WILLIAM F. MIKULAS, PH.D.
Author of *Taming the Drunken Monkey* and *The Way Beyond.*

"Ever Flowing On is a spiritual guidebook for our post modern age. In our rapidly moving world of technology, globalization and materialism, one loses the inner connection with oneself thus a loss of true intimate relationships with others. We feel isolated, depressed, driven, and lack a sense of well being. This work describes the passage back to reclaiming our core nature, the essence of one's being. This absorbing, well designed book is about becoming friends with one's soul. And it is soulfully written. I find it to be a true contribution to understanding the processes of self-development.

-NANCY QUALLS-CORBETT, PH.D.
Author of *The Sacred Prostitute*

In the tradition of Sam Keen and Robert Johnson, soul doctor Michael DeMaria has brought a fresh and discerning voice to psychological and philosophical thought. Here you will find a response to our inner yearning for a model of the self and life journey which is at once elegant and authentic. Ever Flowing On is a heart centered approach to living and being.

-BARRY ARNOLD, PH.D.
Author of *In Pursuit of Virtue* and *Essays in American Ethics*

Ever Flowing On is a wonderful achievement! This is what the world needs: a book by a psychologist who understands and knows the terrain of the soul's journey and brings it to life in intimate detail. Dr. DeMaria urges us to meet and kiss the dragons in our lives, identify the myths we are currently living and embrace our uniqueness and individuality, letting go of our desire for things and lovingly embrace our yearning for Spirit.

-TREBBE JOHNSON
Author of *The World is a Waiting Lover*

EVER
FLOWING
ON

On being
and becoming
oneself

By
MICHAEL BRANT DeMARIA, PH.D.

FOREWORD
ROBERT A. JOHNSON

To my daughter
Danielle
And
To my grandmother
Elizabeth

TABLE OF CONTENTS

Acknowledgments

There is no way to thank everyone who has contributed to the birth of this work. Except perhaps to begin at the beginning. I would like to first humbly thank the Oneness that connects us all in the grand pattern of Being. Although, I know those intellectual readers will see the paradox, I have found the paradox is necessary, helpful and centering. I sit first and foremost in humble gratitude to my Creator for opening a window for me and helping bring this work to life out of the intimate knowing and loving that ever so slowly grows day after day. I would like to thank my parents, Jacqueline and Francesco for their ever present love and support, and for teaching me to follow my heart AND keep my feet planted firmly on the ground. To my grandparents, who are all gone now, for making the sacrifices they made and the guidance I continue to experience from their spirit. To my precious wife, Kathy and daughter, Danielle, for giving me the greatest gift - family and belonging, even when I am and at my worst. I would also like to thank my brothers Brian and Randy, for giving me once again great stories to share! I love you guys.

I owe a very special thank you to Stuart Miller, who has been a godfather to this work and to me. His encouragement, love, support and wisdom is on every page. Stuart you truly have been a fixed star to steer by, thank you. Another special thank you to Bill Plotkin, who not only helped me find the courage to speak my own truth, but modeled how to do so. To my students, clients, friends and fellow journeyers, you have given me so much - You continue to

ACKNOWLEDGMENTS

be my greatest teachers and I sit in humble gratitude for all of our times of growing, crying, laughing and celebrating this mysterious, crazy and miraculous life. I would like to thank Jacquelyn Small, Malidoma Patrice Some and Piero Ferrucci not only for their early reading of the manuscript, but their input and suggestions. You have each been teachers of the first order in a truly Being level path of healing. A sincere thank you and a warm embrace to Bill Mikulas and Barry Arnold who remain ever present sources of brotherhood and friendship that lasts a lifetime. I would like to thank Michael O'Donovan and Terra Nova publishing for believing in this work and to helping shepherd it into publication. Other's who reviewed and gave support, insight, hand holding, editing are Lindsey Kelly, Michael Beck, Laura Colo, Patricia Crumly, Trebbe Johnson, Sara Halprin, Victor Farr, and MaryAnn Fournier. A special thank you to Patti Rieser for bearing witness to the unfolding and for kicking me into gear when I needed it. To Donna Freckman, thank you for doing a wonderfully thorough job copy editing of the manuscript and your insightful and most helpful input. A thank you to my life long spiritual brothers, Bill Schulz, Richard Sneider, Bob Brennen and Dan Fitzsimmons - you each are by my side every day and to "the posse" you know who you are.

Any omissions, errors, inconsistencies, are purely my fault and I apologize for any oversights that the astute reader might find. In true organic fashion if you do find any and let me know, they will be corrected in future editions.

FOREWORD

There is an ancient parable about how *truth* came into the world. In this myth there are four wise beings who have taken turns creating all things. After the earth has been filled with every kind of animal, plant, tree and human they must decide where to hide *truth*. Since this will be the ultimate goal of existence, they do not want to place it in an easily accessible place. After pondering this question for a long time, the first wise being spoke, "I have an idea, let us hide *truth* on the highest mountain, the humans will never find it there." The second almost immediately responded, "No, no, they will easily find it there. We must make it much more difficult to discover, let us hide it in the deepest part of the ocean, they will most assuredly drown before finding it there." The third after thinking about the first two ideas, then said, "These are good ideas, but not the best. Let us hide *truth* in the farthest reaches of outer space, the humans will take forever to find it there." The first two immediately realized this could be the answer. However, the fourth wise being, who was the oldest and also most quiet of the beings sat silently with his eyes closed. He always waited until the end to speak. Finally, speaking in a serene and tranquil voice he said, "These are all good ideas, but you know human beings, constantly moving and doing, they will most assuredly search for it on the mountain, in the seas, and even on the farthest star all before they will sit still and be quiet long enough to look in the most obvious of places. Let us hide *truth* in the very last place they will look, in their own hearts." They looked at each other and smiled, yes *truth* shall be placed in the very heart of the human being. This is a poignant story for our time. The world is in desperate need to reconnect with the *truth* that is only found through a reconnecting with the heart. I can not over emphasize the peril humanity faces if we are not able to bring a feeling dimension into our world. Without it we will most certainly perish. However, with it, all things become possible. It is amazing how people work together and for the good of the whole when the heart is the place they work from. This is a book from and about the heart.

Michael's dream of his grandmother begins the book, where she asks him a simple question, "If you died tomorrow what of value have you left your daughter?" This is a heart question. A question that is often not asked in our culture until it is too late. It is the kind of question which inevitably leads to a journey. This book literally grew out of Michael's answering of this question. Michael discovered, as we all do, that before we come to our own hearts we are destined to take endless journeys climbing mountains, swimming oceans and trying to reach the stars. In the process, we inevitably will become lost, stuck or trapped. We take hopelessly wrong turns, try to fly too close to the sun or drown in our own sea of projections. Then somehow, mysteriously our individual lives through the slender threads of fate return us to the source from which we come and find what turns out to be buried treasure in our own back yards, the truth that resides in our own hearts, the golden world. This is the stuff of life. The journey Dr. Jung called the process of individuation. It is a process that is given new life in Michael's able hands.

Michael takes us on this journey as a wise and competent guide of the soul. Here is a map, a spiritual guide book that charts not only the "big picture" of the life journey, but also the "intimate details" of the terrain of our never ending adventure of self-discovery. This vast perspective then unfolds into rich poetic detail, without which any conceptual discussion falsifies human truth. Reliable maps afford the discerning journeyer with details of the difficult terrain, the trails off the beaten path, the hidden springs to quench your thirst, the dangers and the treasures. Faithful maps like these are priceless. *EVER FLOWING ON: On Being and Becoming Oneself* is such a map. A book of wisdom for the soul's journey home. There is an elegant structure underlying these sections - *The Source, The Abyss, The Quest and The Dance* - which mirrors the essential movement of life itself most profoundly revealed in the analogy of child birth.

The Source can be seen as the oneness of the child in the womb, prior to the contractions that will announce life, our mythic Garden of Eden, what Michael calls amness. Once the contractions of life begin, the child is in the stage of the *Abyss,* pain but without moving. This is the mythic fall from grace, being expelled from the Garden. It is here the world is split and duality begins. The third, is the child moving down the birth canal, pain, but with movement, this is *The Quest* stage of the journey, this is pain with purpose. Finally, upon birth itself, when the infant enters a strange and wondrous new world, he is ready for *The Dance.* Michael reveals throughout the book how this process is undergone over and over again. Similar to the medicine wheel of so many indigenous cultures, we live out this mythic cycle every day, every year and in every lifetime. These are perennial, archetypal patterns that Michael makes readable and understandable. The essential points of the world's great wisdom traditions are here brought to life and expressed simply through stories culled from his 20 years of experience working with himself and others, bringing a remarkable balance of feeling and thinking, being and becoming, masculine and feminine.

The reason the balance is so important is that our world has been horribly out of balance. The verb of masculine experience is *to move*, the verb of the feminine is *to be*. It is easy to see that we have been in the grips of almost an entirely masculine form of experience in the last two thousand years, with its most extreme and painful consequences becoming obvious in the last century. Everything is "moving" and "doing" today. There is very little "being" in our lives, and it's killing us. It is our Being that is in such terrible shape. When we ignore the truth of our hearts, we destroy our connection to Being. We murder the feminine daily in our culture. Every Westerner refuses Being 50-500 times a day, that is *the feminine feeling function*. In this work Michael helps redeem these lost parts of our world, being and feeling, through our reconnecting with our heart and soul. These faculties are our most simple and direct ways of whole-making, which is the sacred function of life.

When a heart connection is made the world comes alive and glows. The miracle occurs through feeling, for that is when the world begins to mean something to us. It speaks to us. This is what we long for. This is a book that explores deeply this longing for Being, our inmost yearning for oneness and it does so by braiding together being and becoming. It is a timely book written with compassion, wisdom and devotion.

It is refreshing to find a book that is not promising to help "perfect" your life, a promise that is always false and empty. Dr. Jung made it clear the goal of individuation was not to become a "perfect" person, but rather a whole one. Framed between the birth of his daughter and the death of his grandmother, Michael takes us on a journey towards self-discovery and oneness, not only within ourselves, but with the world. Michael does not promise to help you lose weight, regain your youth or find your perfect soul mate. He provides something much more precious, the gentle wise council of how to find your way back to the simple miracle of living and being, while discovering a renewed affection for your life. You will begin to feel good about the miracle of being who you are, instead of trying to be something you are not. This is to learn to love and belong to your life in an intimate, authentic and genuine way.

~ROBERT A. JOHNSON
Jungian Analyst
Author of *He, She* and *We,*
Owning Your Own Shadow,
and *Balancing Heaven and Earth*

PRELUDE

Imagine...a landscape of old growth forest: thousand year old trees, a silence deep enough to wash all thoughts away, leaving nothing in its vastness, but your beholding the present moment. The moist moss covering the ground scents the air, dawn breaks through the stand of trees, beckoning the world to wake out of its night slumber. The first rays glitter through the dewy pine branches, revealing a mist not visible moments before. The breeze dancing leaves whisper through the shafts of light filtering in from the east. Mystery is palpable. The forest is alive: breathing and inviting the day into being.

As the sun rises anew each day, so we too have the opportunity to awaken each moment of every day. Sometimes our numbness makes us blind to the stark miracle of existence rising ever around us. The blessing remains, however, that no matter how long we have slept, waking up is possible. Vastness lies perpetually around us on our never ending journeys. In every pain and joy lies the makings of our next awakening.   All that we require is an open mind and a thirsty heart.

It was such a day that I knew I had to write this book. I had stayed the night under the forest canopy and as I began to stir a dream played in my mind. It had already awakened me once in the middle of the night. In this nighttime visitation my grandmother came and asked me this question, *"If you died tomorrow what have you of real value to leave your daughter?"* I woke in panic. I could not answer her question.

I imagined over and over my daughter as a young adult trying to understand who I was through old pictures, a few academic papers, or personal belongings, but nowhere had I put down what I knew to be of real value for one to know in living a life. The only way I could get back to sleep was committing myself to write a book that in some way would be my answer to that question. It turned out to be more difficult than I ever imagined. My grandmother died half way through the writing, which only added more gravity to my need to finish it. This book is dedicated to her and to my daughter, with gratitude for the meaning they both give to my life as I try to live in the balance between the worlds they define for me.

As I wrote I became aware that I was writing what I wished someone had told me as I began my life journey. The book began to emerge as a psychospiritual guide book of the soul's journey. I write not as an observer, but as a fellow traveler, who has been keenly interested in what the Native Americans call our "Earthwalk". These are markings on the way for other travelers, word cairns that hopefully will help those who understand the life journey understood as a spiritual quest.

My grandmother I have realized has become more present to me through her physical absence. Since her death it has become so vividly clear how crucial it is for us to speak our truth while we are here. I have at times included personal accounts of my own journey with the hope that truly what is most deeply personal resonates with what is most universal, that is, they hopefully will serve as touchstones to your own journey, in this way serving as part of the pattern that connects all experience with the grander themes we are all touched by. The structure of this book proceeds in a spiraling fashion. Therefore, although the most useful way of reading it is front to back, there is an implicit structure that allows the reader to start virtually anyway in the text and then proceed. The themes in this way circle throughout the text. If you find yourself drawn to a particular section, *"The Source"*, *"The Abyss"*, *"The Quest"* or *"The Dance"* feel free to start there and it will no doubt lead you to the other sections in the order that is right for you.

In the end, I feel peace now with the dream. I ask the reader that if you are willing to take this journey with me you read the words written within with the eyes of your heart AND that you be willing to dance!

PART 1:

THE SOURCE

"Grandmother, how do I begin?"

"Tell her a story.
The most important story for every child to hear,
the story of how she came into the world...
Tell it simply, with heart,
for within her birth is etched the very story of Creation."

CHAPTER 1:

THE MYSTERY OF BEING

I am that I am...
~God

"It's time!" The words rang out like a mantra summoning me to awaken from a thousand year sleep. Having been up for the past 36 hours I could barely keep my eyes open. "Hello? Are you listening to me? It's time!" My wife shouted, finally shaking me out of my trance. We were in the hospital. She had gone into labor and we were on the verge of witnessing the birth of our first and, as it turned out, only child. My wife had gone into the hospital a day earlier because of high blood pressure. We both worried through the night about complications. We were filled with anxiety, and yet, already, there was something more: waiting for the birthing. We were experiencing an incredible feeling of foreboding; half exhilaration, half terror. What we knew above all else was that we had become part of something much grander than anything we had previously imagined, part of a process much vaster then ourselves. This being had been growing within Kathy for 9 months, but now, in the middle of the rushing through of our everyday lives, the grace of the present moment began to knock at our door, waking us up. The time had come.

Never having witnessed a birth before, we were being led along a path by others who had gone before us. We tried simply to trust what we had been told. It wasn't easy. We had seen Lamaze films, and to be quite honest had been scared by them. The images on the screen of blood, sterile room, and masked strangers had seemed impersonal, even gruesome. Yet, all that earlier repugnance had faded away now in "our" room, with "our doctors" and "our baby" about to be born. With all my stress and my wife's painful labor, we had finally begun to feel as if we were on a river that was now taking control, taking over, if we would just let it. I did my best to help my wife breathe, relax and stay focused on the little teddy bear we had chosen as her focus object. I coached her with her breathing, and paying close attention to the monitor, told her when the contractions would begin to peak. Then without fail, the little green blip on the monitor would skip and become worse for a few seconds and she would scream, "Like hell it's peaking, what do you know, you're not a real doctor!" Our anxiety intensified.

Finally, over what seemed like days, they wheeled us into the delivery room. The room and the people became a blur as I focused on Kathy's breathing. Holding her hand, I watched her face contort with pain when I told her to push. Then my attention turned to the doctor, and I heard his words, "There's the head," then in a flicker of a moment, "You've got a little princess!". A girl, a baby girl, and a sudden pure joy filled the room. The room came alive with laughter, joyous tears, and a brightness I have seldom experienced, as I whispered to Kathy, "We have a little princess." As I did, her eyes filled with indescribable relief and tears welled up and proceeded to roll ever so gingerly down the sides of her cheeks.

The following hours were enchanted as this newborn filled our world with an experience that even the word awe fails to capture. Danielle. She just "was." We basked in her presence, in her just being, her pure Danielleness, an experience no words could ever capture. As the nurses and doctors carried on with their business, I felt a glow over my body. I experienced every moment as profound, almost as if everyone in the room moved in slow motion. Unlike the films we had seen, nothing seemed gruesome in the actual delivery; rather, we felt ourselves immersed in a living, breathing, ongoing process that gave this birthing freshness, grace and richness: *amness.*

I share this experience with you because it is such a stark reminder for me of the quality of what I like to call *"amness"* that is missing from most of our moments of living. Simply stated, the experience of amness is the experience of "I am" without the I. Amness has no bounds. Amness is the felt sense, the experience of oneness. Amness is everywhere, is everything, the alpha and the omega. Amness is profoundly the ground, the soil from which we emerge, our source out of which we are born and to which we return upon death.

All-That-Is

Where did you come from, baby dear?
Out of the everywhere into the here.
                    ~George McDonald

There is a powerful fact that is true for each and everyone of us. We all have spent 9 months (give or take a few weeks) completely within another human being. Take pause to think on this for a moment. We were encased within the abdomen of another human being. Wholly dependent upon this other. The womb bathed us in its warmth and nurturance and we were completely at one with this other. We grew out of another being, who in turn grew out of another being, and so on, and so on... The great parade of being marches onward in this way. Can we really ever say when we came to be? Let yourself imagine for a moment, your grandmother giving birth to your mother. Now imagine your grandmother's mother giving birth to her, and go further back to her mother, and her mother's mother. All the way back, back in time, there is a connection with life that has never ceased. From one living source to another the flame has been burning forever. We are all of the same fire. When the Native American's say the Spirit-that-moves-in-all-things they are referring to this inmost truth - People of the One Fire. Where did it start? One can never pinpoint it in time and space. It defies reason, logic and analysis. It is similar to the question of what existed before the Big Bang? Or, why is there a Universe at all, instead of nothing? **The deepest mystery is that there is something eternal about who we are.** The subatomic particles that make up the blood that courses through our veins have always been, and at the same time are always reborn every moment. Through every living thing runs this thread of amness that unites us and if we follow this golden strand far enough, it will bring us to the insight that all creation is related to us. We are all part and parcel of this fabric of *all-that-is* and are not only related to each other, but also to the galaxies and stars that fill the night sky. *Amness* is a return to the source of who we are and *all-that-is*. In this way, all of creation, the millions of years of plant life, animal life, and the billions of years of rock life all in some amazing way are etched into the very fabric of our cells, blood and very being.

The word *source* comes from the Latin *surgere*, meaning to rise, spring up, and surge forth. It usually is used to refer to a fountain, a stream, from which something comes into existence, develops or derives its very being. Our daily moments of amness nourish us like refreshing, crystal clear spring water rising up from the great reservoir of *amness*. Einstein spent the last half of his life searching for what he called, the Unified Field Theory, which would conceptually and mathematically describe that which underlies and interpenetrates all phenomena in the cosmos. In quantum physics we now realize that consciousness itself and all phenomena that consciousness experiences occur in one grand field of Being. We may imagine ourselves separate from this field, the source of *all-that-is,* yet the separation is illusion. Every experience of amness in a very real way is one of being at the *source,* from which *all-that-is* perpetually arises and to which it returns. To use Einstein's famous analogy, Amness is a circle whose circumference is no where and whose center is everywhere. Therefore, when we are in the grips of amness we are actually experiencing the Unified Field. Amness is the unified field.

THE VITAL CONNECTION

This fact helps us understand further why the infant is such a powerful example of *amness,* of what we might call an *immediate living-ness.* An infant, for instance, is immersed in pure be-holding. No sense of self or "I" separates the baby from whatever it senses and experiences. The infant's eyes take in everything, holding onto nothing, no conceptualizations, no rationalizations or differentiating, just sheer be-holding. This is the condition we all started from as sentient beings upon this planet. It is what I like to call our *vital connection* to all-that-is. Unfortunately, from a tender age in our society we all too quickly become educated out of this *vital connection*. Of course, it is crucial that we learn to differentiate, categorize, and name the world around us. It is through this process that we develop an ego, that is, the social self that helps us maneuver in the world. Yet, underneath our sophisticated well developed masks of civilized competence and solidity lies that infant-like core of pure be-holding. This is our original face, our true inheritance. The core of our psyche is that softness of pure Being...*amness,* where we feel ourselves in the unbroken web of *all-that-is.* It is here in the vital connection with the present moment that we re-connect with existence and ourselves and re-member who we truly are, beyond and beneath all the differentiation of names and roles, fears and duties. Here we can rest in the here-and-now and breathe in the synergy of feeling integrated with the seamless field of *all-that-is.* Many years later I shared my experience of Danielle's birth with a Native American Elder. He responded in a matter of fact tone of voice, "Yes, the world glows as a new soul enters the world and as an old soul leaves." This is *amness:*

> *Those of you who have been present at a birth know*
> *that a numinous face fills the room - Creation and the*
> *Great Mystery overflow. No matter how messy the*
> *child may be from the birth, a radiance glows from that*
> *little being. The newborn is almost total spirit, coming*
> *awake in unknown flesh. Those wings of spirit...flutter*

and open, flap and stretch in a brief display, and are
then quiet again.[1]

I have found it exceedingly helpful and rich to have people who in workshops or in psychotherapy spontaneously recall times they have *experienced* amness in their lives. They inevitably begin to speak of *the* most profound, moving and intimate moments of their lives. Their eyes light up, their skin glows, and something about their whole presence relaxes as they simply begin to remember these experiences. Sometimes they smile, other times they laugh, and more often then not their eyes well up as they recall the joy of the connection and the bittersweet pain of disconnection. Like Serena:

> *When I am dancing, I am alive. I am the dance,*
> *the music flows through me, is me! I know what you*
> *mean by "amness". I can't try to get there, I just find*
> *myself...there... all of a sudden letting go...then, some*
> *melting deep inside begins to happen, and...it's as if*
> *all my usual inhibitions, painful self-consciousness, and*
> *awkwardness fall away. "I" fall away. Then there is*
> *just dancing, or maybe being danced! No, even more*
> *subtle....dancing happens...Sometimes I wonder if I live*
> *just for those moments. How I wish I could live in*
> *those moments always.*

One woman talked of watching thunderstorms move over the Gulf of Mexico and feeling as if the thunder rolling off the water came from "inside" of her. In those moments she "felt alive and connected to the ocean, the sky, and the rain." One young man shared how listening to a particular piece of music always brought a sense of both tears to his eyes and food to his soul. He would put on his ear phones, lie down, tie a bandanna around his eyes and literally, "lose" himself in the music. He would feel the usual boundaries of his body give way. Others spoke of out-of-body experiences. Not only did the psychological boundaries of an "I" disappear, but so did the actual bodily sense of "I." People often describe feeling as if they are "floating" or "melting." In the midst of a profound amness experience, one's usual physical, emotional, psychological, and spiritual boundaries give way to an oceanic oneness. This is both its joy and, to some, its terror. I have had others describe amness experiences occurring while long-distance running, playing soccer, skiing, playing with their children and perhaps most frequently of all making love. It is this particular quality of *amness* that is the root experience of being alive in all of its vividness and richness. I have found working over the years with people that helping them learn to re-connect and re-discover *amness* leads them back to an abiding immediacy with their experience of themselves and the world around them. The more we invite *amness* the more our bodies and our very beings become more fluid, relaxed and open to deeper levels of tranquility and serenity.

This form of experience does not involve a value judgment such as, "Boy, I'm enjoying this sunset. This sunset is just beautiful. I am so lucky to be looking at this sunset right this moment." In this example, there is a distance between the sense of "I" and the sunset. The sunset is seen as an object in the world upon which the "I" is making a value judgment. Whereas, in a dynamic *amness* experience there is simply pure *be-holding* where subject and object dissolve into a unitary experience of Being. Children know this experience much more intimately than adults. They only recently left the unselfconscious, even unconscious experience of *amness*. They easily immerse themselves in the moment, particularly in play. Adults who have lost touch with their inner child often have lost touch with *amness*. It is no wonder that there has been such a powerful movement over the last decade towards reclaiming one's inner child. Re-embracing the child that dwells within us is one way back to the *vital connection* between self and the greater life from which we come. As Jesus said, "Unless you change your life and become like a child, you cannot enter the kingdom of heaven."

There is a powerful story in the *Gospel of Thomas* which gives us a deeper appreciation of the intimate relationship between the archetype of the infant, amness, and the Kingdom of Heaven:

> *Jesus saw some infants nursing. He said to his disciples, "These infants are like those who enter the kingdom of heaven." They said to him, "How then can we enter?" Jesus said to them, "When you make the two one, and when you make the inside like the outside, and the upper like the lower, and when you make male and female into a single one, then you will enter the kingdom."* [2]

This simple story vividly draws the connection between the infant and this *vital connection* of *amness*, a wisdom we all possess, but usually only in its latent form. The infant bestows upon us the re-membering of amness, the wisdom of just being. This remarkable passage also gives us a deeper glance into the profound nature of amness. It is beyond duality. Most of our lives are lived in a black and white duality, it is the rare soul who transcends the opposites of existence, however, we all have moments of transcendence. It is in these moments that we re-member a place that in its natural state exists beyond such duality. It is the dwelling place all mystics have known exists as the precious aim of a long spiritual journey. It is the place of oneness. Life is a journey towards *amness,* a quest for reconnecting with this unitary experience of body, mind, and soul, which opens up the possibility of living most fully and loving most deeply.

Some may ask, "If amness is beyond duality, then why use the word vital connection, since connection implies duality? What is being connected to what?" This is a good question and moves us ever further into the territory of amness. The word connection comes from the Latin connectere, meaning to fasten or come together; to couple, to link. So the vital connection is the connection between human being and Being. In an organic sense we might imagine a tree pulled from it's roots. Often today we have lost our essential rootedness in our first person experience of the world. We might imagine the vital connection as a tap root. It is this root that sinks us into the vast field of Being that is our true vital connection. It appears a duality only to the degree that there has been a severing of a previous unity.

Another useful metaphor is an electrical connection. There are two wires. One is connected to the source current. The other is dead wire, no current. When they are "connected" the current flows freely. No duality. Often a question comes up in therapy that suggests this metaphor, "Do you feel plugged in?" The person usually immediately, intuitively knows what I mean by this. If not, I will go further and say, "Do you feel plugged into creation, into Being, being alive?". Do they feel plugged into life, into the senses, feelings and texture, nuance and smell of life?

Unfortunately, most people today suffer from depersonalization and derealization, which means they feel disconnected, out of touch. It is as if they are watching their life like a movie, they are not "in" their bodies and therefore, they are not "in" their life. They have lost their vital connection.

In both analogies there is a sense that the cut off part is dead, either dead wire, or a dead tree. The images of the rootedness of a tree as well as an electromagnetic current also denote the need for a flow - in one a flow of current, in the other a flow of nutrients, minerals and water. Finally, both analogies also imply a "vitality" at the root of the connection; one electrical, one biochemical. Another way of talking about the vital connection is through what has been tradition-ally called the "connected breath." This is a deep diaphragmatic breathing that infants and many tribal people naturally breathe. In predominately white, civilized, Western culture we breathe shal-low breaths. We breathe from the chest, not the diaphragm. The connected breath refers to the out breath being connected to the in breath, but further it means that one is "connected" to the breath of all things. To breathe in this way is to realize that you and the trees are one organism. In fact, to some Native American tribes God is spoken of as the Master of The Breath, it is our most basic rootedness in Being. One of the characteristics they saw in the "white man" that scared them was they seemed to be unaware of their breath. They were not "connected" to the breath of creation in a conscious way. What do I mean by this?

In helping my daughter with the "Carbon-Dioxide - Oxygen Cycle," I was reminded how clearly this amazing cycle display's a quality of amness and the vital connection. For those not familiar with this cycle, it simply refers to the fact that in photosynthesis plants and trees take in sunlight, water and carbon dioxide and then give off oxygen and food (in the form of hydrogen, sugar, such as in roots or fruit); then in respiration, animals/humans take in oxygen and food and give off carbon dioxide, water and fertilizer for the plants. There is a profound reciprocity here. It is no accident that trees produce oxygen and food for us and we produce carbon dioxide, water and fertilizer for them. Of course not, it is a fact that most of us completely ignore. Otherwise, whenever we looked at trees we would see part of own lungs. Is it just me or is there something incredibly awesome about that? Science had simply led us back to the vital connection with everything around us...amness. Now the challenge is to experience this as a tangible, palpable reality, not just as idea, but as a living breathing actuality, we and the plants are connected in this grand web of Being. Now we are invoking amness.

The Miracle

There are two ways to look at the world, one that almost nothing is a miracle, or two, that everything is a miracle.

~Einstein

Why is there something instead of nothing? This has been an ancient riddle since the beginning of recorded time. We can love life or hate it, but the fact that it exists at all continues to be a miracle. The awareness of this miracle reaches into the core of each and every one of us, of everything we touch, love and wish for. It also has to do with everything we cannot see, that which dreams are made of, the stuff of reality, the stuff of fantasy, where ideas come from, how anything happens, appears, is contemplated, witnessed or simply is. Until we can stand back enough to let "what is" dazzle us in a blaze of glory, meeting us in a resounding, joyous chorus that chants, "I am you, you are me, we are all one," we will feel cut off. For Being is our mother and our father, our sister and our brother, BEING is *All-That-Is*.

BEING...Let yourself say the word out loud. Being with a big "B". B-E-I-N-G. I never tire of saying Being, as long as I allow myself the delicious miracle of this word. In this way, it is more than a word, it is an incantation to *all-that-is*. Therefore, allow yourself to close your eyes, breathe deeply and fully, and as you exhale simply say BEING. Let yourself resonate with everything around you as you utter this deeply felt, deeply sacred word. For "it" denotes *all-that-is*.

When we fully grasp the statement, "It's a miracle anything is at all," we are led to a greater appreciation of all facets of our world. For one, we begin to realize that it is a miracle anything gets *done* at all. So often we spend our time regretting what we have not done or anticipating what we need to do. Even when we think about what we have done, we incessantly judge it according to impossible standards.

Imagine how freeing it could be to really be amazed each time you accomplish anything. Even waking up in the morning, going to the bathroom, drinking a glass of water takes on mythic proportions.

Children are immersed in this reality. If I ask my daughter to go brush her teeth, this seemingly mundane affair takes on all the drama of an adventurous journey. In the middle of finding her toothbrush, she turns on the water and begins running her hands through it. She notices the feel of the water, giggles just at the sheer fact of the miracle of running water, how it feels and how it flows. She finds my shaving cream and plays with the texture of it then notices the funny designs she can make with it on the sink. Then she takes small drops of water and slowly dissolves the intricate designs she made the moment before. Next thing I know she's been "brushing her teeth" for the last 20 minutes but still has no toothpaste on her toothbrush. Frustrating from a parent's perspective trying to simply "get the job done". But this simple story illustrates that most adults have learned how to "get the job done" at the expense of feeling vitally connected to our experience the way my daughter is connected to the moment as she plays in the water in the sink. From this perspective it truly is a miracle anything ever gets done!

Going further into this understanding we confront perhaps the inmost level of the miracle, that is, "it is a miracle I am at all." To *truly* view our own individual and unique life as a miracle in its moment to moment unfolding, is to see consciousness as a form of grace. In this way life becomes a practice of gratefulness. It is when we are able to profoundly appreciate the sheer fact of existence that the mystery and depth of Being can truly move us and even redeem us if we allow it. As soon as we are lulled back to sleep and forget the miracle, the incessant complaints and blaming begin about why this is this way, or so and so isn't more thoughtful, kind and appreciative. Here is the birth place of conflict, dissatisfaction and thus, suffering. Yet, even if we follow suffering and pain to their logical conclusion - death, they too will forever put the miracle of existence back into perspective. All of a sudden, upon the death of a loved one, we see the miracle that they "were" at all and now will never "be" again.

It is so important to be gentle and merciful with ourselves. No matter how "bad" things become, well below the surface, in the silent recesses of ourselves are the seeds of our becoming are growing and germinating. Our awareness can blossom then into witnessing the unfolding panorama of Being. The silence and darkness are our mother and father. They are the deepest mystery of Being. Remember, Being is a verb, pointing to the process itself, which includes the unseen, the unheard and the unknown.

As we deepen our ability to live in the awareness that, "it is a miracle that anything is at all," the more we nurture our "vital connection," the more we can appreciate this one, particular, unique, never to be repeated instant in creation, the more we experience the nourishing waters of *amness*. For many this is the experience of the spiritual, of the Creator, for some it is Love. Whatever different people and cultures have "named" it, these various signs are always and forever pointing towards the *e'lan vital*, the vital impulse of life itself, which vibrates and pulsates with the blood of Being, animating all Creation.

We are born of *all-that-is,* which is forever a mystery, yet we catch glimpses of the source of all we are in our moments of amness.

THE MYSTERY OF BEING

The mystical is not how the world is, but that it is.
~Wittgenstein

To better understand how we have become separated from the ground of being we must dig deeper into the soil of our cultural heritage. We can trace part of our "vital roots" back to Aristotle. Until his time (400 B.C.) the question "what is?" or "what is reality?" was not asked. Reality just "was" -- a miracle, supernatural. Aristotle decided the question "what is?" could never be answered, at least not logically; therefore, it became more important to begin to describe how things were. This approach led inevitably to the quest for knowledge and certainty being more to do with counting how many things there were, describing how they function, taking them apart and putting them back together. As a result, the elaborate march of "progress" became caught up in classifying, dividing, analyzing what is, into "it's": how "it" is, how many "its" there are, what "it" is made of, how "it" all goes together, what "it" can do, when "it" happens, why "it" happens, when "it" started, when will "it" end, etc. etc. etc. This move into analysis was a new playground for the "mind" (another "it".)

"It" ("all-that-is" or Being) came to be seen as a noun, a thing. Even today most of us live as though Being is a noun. When we try to talk about Being or grab hold of "it," we are treating "it" as a thing, and when we do, we lose "it."(One can see we are limited by our language, because here I am having to refer to reality as an "it" while trying to evoke the deeper truth of Being as the grand process of all-that-is). In actuality, there is no "it" to get hold of. Being is the proliferation and never ending unfolding of reality "itself." Being is...

Being is with us, is us every moment. There is no other word used more than "is." For those who have ever learned a foreign language you know that when you begin to study the verb "to be" you are in for a fun time, or frustrating one, depending how you like chaos. The verb "to be" winds itself in and out of every utterance. Every time we speak, or write, "it" is there. We cannot avoid "it." However, we have lost the joy in the sheer fact of being. Being Is!

Children reveal to us the innate curiosity we all share concerning Being, as they drive us crazy with such juicy questions as; "What is God made of? Why are we here? What is this world? What happens when we die? What is anything really?" No amount of scientific or pat religious answers quench the thirst with which these questions are asked. Unfortunately, as a result, we hide or even worse, deny our thirst as we grow up, telling ourselves there is no water that could ever quench such thirst. Whenever I read philosophers or spiritual teachers ancient or modern, or for that matter clients or friends who admit that their thirst remains, I am always moved. That level of honesty profoundly touches me, as it continues to when I meet people on their own search and they have come to the very real place of not knowing and have the courage to say so.

More akin to the consciousness of children, most indigenous peoples do not have a word for "it." The impersonal pronoun that makes everything that is alive, into something inert, dead, inanimate is nowhere to be found for example, in the root language of the Lakota Sioux. They knew, as we did as children, that everything is alive!

It is something of another miracle itself that science, in the findings of quantum physics, has actually helped all of us re-discover this childlike awareness of the miracle - "what is." It is almost as if, in trying to count and describe the "its" we see, hear and feel, we have come face to face with the enormous wonder at existence our ancestors knew. For example, every breath you take contains 10 to the 30th atoms. The equation $E=MC2$ describes the energy of each and every one of these atoms. Energy is equal to mass multiplied by the square of the speed of light. Simply put, this means that even a very minute amount of matter contains a vast amount of energy. Say, for instance, if you broke off a small piece of this page you are reading, perhaps the size of a dime; now multiply the weight of that piece of paper, times the speed of light (186,000 miles per second), now square that number. You get an incredibly large number. Now imagine that in every cell of your body there are literally millions of atoms, and there are millions of cells in your body. You are one powerful being. You are on fire! You breathe fire! The world is made of this fire-light-energy! We *are* that energy. These discoveries re-ignite our curiosity concerning truly "what are we?" and "what is this phenomenon called reality?"

Unfortunately, we are usually taught in school not to have too much enthusiasm. We are taught cold, hard facts. Not that we are on fire! Over time, the mystery, wonder, and miracle of being alive are relegated to the scrap heap. We become machine-like, going through the motions, taking our cues of who we are, what to do, how to think from others to the point that we become separated from our childlike wonder of "wow, being alive is so totally awesome!" Instead we become bored to tears.

PARADISE, AMNESS AND NATURE

All cultures have their myths of Paradise. The Garden of Eden in the West, Nirvana in the East - no matter the name, they all point to Amness. Paradise is whenever we are in a state of *amness*. We drink of the infinite elixir of just pure Being: no place to go, nothing to have to be - no regret, no anticipation, just be-holding the moment, the precious present. Ahhh! that is paradise.

The main theme in all mythic Paradise stories is human beings living in an unselfconscious harmony with Nature. So it is no wonder that the natural world provides endless opportunities for amness for children and adults alike. In the left front corner of our yard when I was a child, there grew a maple tree I loved dearly. Our house sat atop a hill, so I could roll and tumble down the hill until I came near my good friend, my sacred maple tree. This maple had smooth bark that even in winter felt warm to my touch. I always referred to the tree as "her." As most children, I intuitively understood the meaning of "Mother Nature." I knew she was a living being who helped me feel real and substantial, safe and secure. When the impinging adult world became too much, when parents were arguing, brothers were fighting, or friends left, I would go to her. In Native American culture she would be considered a "medicine place," to our Celtic ancestors she would have been a "guardian spirit": a place in nature where one goes to heal and become centered within oneself. I can still picture those moments and the excitement I would feel just thinking about being with her. I would begin by rolling down the hill, almost bumping into her, then jump up and climb into her branches. As I did, I could feel the comfort of her branches wrapping around me. She just was. She was a being, and is a being. A pal of mine from my childhood days in Connecticut recently sent me a picture of our house and I felt a glowing over me as I recognized my friend, the maple, peeking out at me from the corner of the picture.

Trees can communicate a profound sense of the reality, the being or amness of their place to us. They live out their lives moving downward towards the molten core of the earth, upward towards the vast sky, and outward just enough to radiate from the core of their own being. If we could only learn that lesson: *for every inch upward and outward, we must dig our roots in an equal distance downward and inward.* I recall experiencing vividly as a child, the sense of place my friend the maple had. Her joyous experience of simple AMNESS! She filled me with the mystery, the bliss, of pure being.

It didn't matter what time of the year, spring, summer, fall or winter. With each season she changed her mood. In winter I would climb her after dark and as the snow fell gently to the ground find that "just right" feeling between her two largest branches that felt like two arms holding me. There was a light from our house that would cast

39

shadows through the branches. The darkness and silence became a slice of eternity. As the snow fell, in those silent nights, there was a contentment and something more, completeness. No place to go. Nothing to do. No anticipation. No regret. So, too, we can imagine that during the aboriginal times when the tree provided the central metaphor for Being, human culture was in its childhood, and our sense of place was keen as a bright morning.

My sacred maple's sheer presence communicated that abiding truth, "I am that I am." Is it any coincidence that God spoke these words to Moses in the form of a "burning bush?" Everyone of us from our early years is in search of this experience. This deep affirmation of Being. I remember when I began to examine my own life's journey more intently, someone asked, "What did you want to be as a child?" I felt strange when I heard those words. I tried asking the little boy within me. As I sat with the question, that little boy inside began showing me old images of wanting to be a film maker, a doctor, a surgeon, a forest ranger, an actor, an artist, a drummer. The images came faster and faster and I found myself recalling earlier and earlier experiences until that little boy showed me the most lucid clear image I could recall. An image of moments where I was completely present, when I was a beholder, a witness. I was simply be-holding the world around me, entranced with the sight of trees, grass, and clouds moving above me, the wind caressing my hair, and the sun playing chase with the moon. Being and beholding. That's what I wanted to be, the sun, moon and stars. No, it would be more accurate to say, that is who I felt myself to be. I came to realize this truth I had instinctively known and desperately, now, needed to re-member.

Re-membering became the beginning of much healing for me. The more I reconnected with those vivid moments of gazing out onto the world and beholding the unfolding of nature, the more I felt myself able to do the same in my present life. I recalled hours of beholding, just beholding; whether out the school bus window or laying on the grass watching clouds appear and disappear. I remember simply reclining into the moment, witnessing *all-that-is* and truly feeling connected to all things. When it rained, it was as a miracle, the landscape changed and I soaked up the changes like the changing colors of a kaleidoscope.

Amness and Beholding Visualization

Beholding is a melting into amness, flowing with the river. Holding is grasping at the water, trying to trap the waves. Cultures have many different terms for beholding and for the experience of amness. In some cultures it is considered a particular place that only a privileged few ever have the opportunity of entering - variously called "nirvana", "enlightenment", "samadhi", or "the pure land." My experience tells me differently. All of us have had spontaneous experiences with amness, though we do better when we learn how to make such awareness part of the fabric of our everyday living. Because most people I work with do not have such a practice I find the following visualization very helpful. My openness to re-experiencing my daughter's birth and recalling my sacred maple tree *both came from my practicing such an exercise.* Now, this is an opportunity for you to explore this terrain yourself.

Take a moment now before reading on to close your eyes and begin by taking a few very deep breaths. Imagine that these are the first real conscious breaths of your life. As you breathe in imagine that you are stoking a fire inside with each breath, that you are re-connecting with the air around you, the space around you, and ultimately with all being. Now let yourself visualize a time or a place in your childhood where you felt a deep sense of "Amness." No where to go. Nothing to do. Nothing to *have* to be. Nothing to buy. Nothing to sell. Just pure being. When you have the image, allow yourself to dwell with it. Notice the feeling in your body as you allow yourself to journey to that time, that place where you were able to just be.

Try to allow somewhere between 10 and 15 minutes to explore this experience in as much detail as possible. If you have difficulty, do not push yourself but simply let the idea of imagining a time when you felt a deep sense of Amness incubate within you for a few days or even weeks. You may find your time in a dream, or have it in a sudden unexpected image or in a memory. It will come when you are ready. After you have your image write it down, providing as much detail as you can. Pay particular attention to describing what the experience was like for you. As you write keep the following questions in mind:

What circumstances led up to the experience?
How did you feel in your body?
Who else was there?
How did the experience change you?
How often do you remember this moment in time?
How can bringing this memory back into your present life help you?

Secondly, try to symbolically bring the experience into your present existence. This may take the form of writing a poem, drawing a picture or creating something else that reminds you of the experience. For the more daring, you may draw a picture using children's crayons and paper, drawing it the way you would have as a child. One way to foster this is to use your non-dominant hand to do the drawing and coloring. Finally, ask yourself, *"How might I nurture this experience in my life?"* In this way you will begin to "seed" the lawn of your life and slowly but surely amness will germinate and grow. You will find yourself having more and more amness experiences. Of course this is a life long process that cannot be rushed. The key is patience. It is, in essence, the most natural process. A monk once described the movement of the soul towards God as analogous to one dropping a ball. We desire and naturally move towards *amness* if given the chance. Whether we try or not the gravity of the whole fabric of Being is drawing us ever closer to amness our whole life-long until at death we merge perfectly, imperceptibly back into the source from which we came.

PART II:

THE ABYSS

"Grandmother, how do I tell my child about
the great pain that is inevitable in every life, that her path will
not always be easy or enchanted, as it is now?"

"Tell her the truth. Tell her your first wound, how it made
you grow and how you are now thankful for that which you
once cursed. Let her know, that her father does bleed and
grieve. It is a strong man who can do that..."

CHAPTER 2:

PARADISE LOST:
I AM NOT ENOUGH

*My story is not a pleasant one; it is neither sweet nor
harmonious, as invented stories are; it has the taste of
nonsense and chaos, of madness and dreams - like the
lives of all...who stop deceiving themselves.*[1]
~Herman Hesse

For the first 23 years of my life, my earliest memory was being in
the hospital. I had a number of surgeries as a child. Two were for
congenital defects: one on my genitals, and one at the core of the
inner tissues of my body. From very early in my life I had a feeling
that I was not enough. I believed that something about the very basis
of me - my body, my felt sense of self - required fixing. I had become
a broken machine. I had ceased to drink of the blissful state of *amness*.

The memory goes something like this: I am around six years of
age. The nurses are preparing me for surgery in a strange room with
masked strangers all around me. They begin looking more like monsters than humans. I lie there wondering, "What is this? Where am
I? What is going to happen to me?" In particular, before they put me
in the operating room I become aware of the cold metal gurney I am
on, the stench of chemicals, one of which stands out from the rest, the
smell of ether. I feel more alone and scared then I ever have. I begin

to panic, feeling as if I am going to die, that I am about to "not be."

Today, I am convinced that as much of a curse as this experience might have been it also made me, at a very young age, question what it meant "to be." Through a long process of reflecting on this experience, it has become ever more clear to me how we all must face non-being in sentient form: death, plain and simple. Only then can we begin to see our life as figural against the background of death.

After I remember being wheeled into the operating room, the memories become even more powerful. I am lying down, vulnerable, looking up at these masked men and women. I hear one of them say in a muffled voice, "Now, when I put this over your nose and mouth begin to count backwards from ten." I had enough trouble counting forward at that age, much less backwards. One of them, begins to put a translucent green plastic cover over my nose and mouth. I resist the growing urge to scream, run, "find my mommy." I freeze, paralyzed with fear. The ether begins to flow. The gas smells awful. I don't want to breathe it. I try to hold my breath and pray that maybe I'll just die and this nightmare will just disappear. The voice speaks again, "Well, we will count for you." "Great," I think, "some help you are!". Realizing I am going to have to take another breath at some point, I truly feel I've reached my end. That for some horrible reason my parents have given me over to these people to be tortured and killed. My imagination is running now: I will never see my parents and my brothers again. My body begins to shudder, then suddenly out of breath I surrender, as my mouth opens gasping for a breath. The last thing I hear is, "Ten." I recall feeling my whole body and being spiraling away. As I lose consciousness I enter a kaleidoscopic world of lights and turning images, a vast mind-scape with no familiar landmarks. A dream scape with its full share of bewilderment, chaos and an odd mixture of joy.

After that, my memory becomes vague. All I know is that I believed I had died. And, in reality, a part of me had. The next thing I remember is awakening in a children's hospital ward. Kids screaming, children with broken limbs, or no limbs. We were all in what seemed like cold steel cribs, a children's jail cell. As I lay there looking through the bars, my head ached, I felt drugged and everything looked blurry.

I had a confrontation with death. In experiencing the trauma of anaesthesia and surgery, I came in contact with something radically "not me." The world had inflicted a wound. The blissful un-self-conscious world I had lived in had ruptured. I had been expelled from the Garden of Eden. No longer bathed in simple amness, I was plunged head first into a stark nothingness of pain and fear. But, I also made a quantum leap in growing a self. From one surgery I had a scar with over 200 stitches inside and out of my body which left a 5 inch long scar on my abdomen. I used to enjoy telling others in college that I had a baby through a caesarean-section before my sex change. After the laughs I would show them the scar. Their look of shock and curiosity was always worth it.

My wife, of course, is not impressed with the birthing implications of my pseudo-caesarean scar. She enjoys reminding me that I have no idea what *giving* birth is really like. *I* did not go through the excruciating pain that led to the miraculous sense of amness. Certainly, I did feel the anguish, uncertainty, and powerlessness a father feels in such a situation; yet, ultimately she is right. I did not experience the depths of my being coming apart at the seams to give birth to another. Yet, my pseudo-caesarean section scar tells of another birth I experienced, one that was fraught with similar dimensions of joy and terror. These trauma's polish the soul even as they turn us upside down and inside out.

Each one us, at some level, is symbolically giving birth every moment. In fact, we might go as far as to say, the pain of childbirth is also at the core of each waking moment of existence. What do I mean by this? The incredible relationship between profound, abiding amness as experienced in the womb; or the infant suckling at the mothers breast is contrasted with the forever dual reality of separation and abandonment - traveling down the birth canal, leaving the mother's breast. To be alive *is* truly agony and ecstasy. Not one or the other but both. To truly live, be creative, and deal with the adversity of life requires effort, pain, and endurance. If we are to discover the eyes of a new born infant in every moment of every day, we must be able to embrace the pain of the death of the preceding moment. If we are to learn to let go of rusted and calcified perceptions and assumptions about the world and who we are, our arrogance that we *know* what the world is really like, how it works, and why we are here, we must be willing to let the pain of change enter our very being. In so doing we can then be led to the beholding of new horizons and new possibilities. As Kahlil Gibran says:

*Your pain is the breaking of the shell that encloses
your understanding. Even as the stone of the fruit must
break, that its heart may stand in the sun, so must you
know pain.*[2]

My grandfather used to say in his Italian accent, *"Quel che non amazza
ingrassa,"* literally, that which does not kill you strengthens you and
will allow you to grow and develop more than you ever thought possible. (He used to like to play on the word *ingrassa* which literally means
to "fatten" you.) Indeed, there is much that will not kill us but *will*
cause great pain. At the center of life there lies the image of the Grim
Reaper holding his scythe. The image of the scythe symbolizes death
as well as recalling the more benign figure of Father Time. Father
Time is just an old man with a scythe, the Grim Reaper, however, is a
skeleton like, hooded demonic figure with his scythe. Both have to do
with us: our lives, hopes and dreams being like wheat, and the scythes
of time and ultimately death constantly, unceasingly cutting us down.
This is the work of non-being, and its teaching is the impermanence
of everything. When we dwell deeper with this double image of the
scythe we begin to realize that the scythe has a purpose. It is not cutting wheat just to "kill" the wheat, it is harvesting. So the wheat can
be put to good use. We are like wheat that is ultimately transformed
to flour, baked into bread, eaten, and then given back to the earth to
nurture new seeds. If we could only see death as a harvesting, how
much more we could learn. Perhaps we would not resist change and
be open to life and love more completely. In cultures that understand

that time is a wheel, death is seen as a harvesting, and people reap wonderful gifts of perspective and serenity that come with such wisdom. In cultures that see time as linear progress, however, death can only be seen as a monster to be conquered. For these cultures the only way to deal with the great grief is to invent neurotic fantasies of immortality and intricate denials, and a loving wise Father Time is eclipsed by the hideous Grim Reaper.

Me and Not-Me

As children we slowly begin to differentiate the world into what we consider "me" and "not-me." That which is labeled "not-me" is the part of the world from which we feel disconnected, alienated, cut-off. That which is identified as "me" is that which brings us security, support and wholeness. The world of "not-me" is expanded every time we are confronted with non-being, nothingness, and negation. To better understand this initial primary split, the revolutionary psychiatrist Ronald Laing suggested a very simple exercise. Take a moment and swish around the saliva in your mouth. You feel connected to it. The saliva is part of you. The experience is located in the sensations of your own mouth. Now spit in a clean cup, the kind of cup you would not think twice about drinking from. Look at the spit in the cup. A moment ago it was part of you. Now, all of a sudden, it is separate. Out in the world, looking back at you. It has become "not-you." Now, put the cup to your mouth and slide the spit back into your mouth. Notice the emotions, the bodily sensations you're feeling right now. When I have students and workshop participants do this, even in imagination, most become nauseated. There is a built in repulsion. Yet, all that has changed is the spit has left the confines of what you consider "me."

There is an even more vivid example that is best done only in imagination. Imagine your finger is bleeding. Now put the bleeding finger in your mouth and attempt to clean off the blood. For most, this is not such a bad experience, or I should say this is not a "not-me" experience. The blood is flowing immediately from your finger into your body through your mouth. Now, imagine a clean, sterile bandage. Take the bandage, put it on the bleeding flesh then imagine licking the bandage, or sucking on it. Same blood, same sterile pad, but the image, the feeling, is repellant.

These are examples of the long process of ego differentiation. An infant has no problems with the previous exercises; spit or bandage. Infants have been known to play with feces with no sense of disgust, which of course intensifies our own feelings of repulsion. Certainly there is a good reason for some levels of such disgust. Throughout life we naturally develop survival responses which signal us that certain aspects of the world of "not-me" can be a danger to survival. So there is a functional aspect to this process of differentiation.

Our difficulty arises when we lose the link with our vital experience of amness, the innocent feeling of being rooted in *all-that-is*. The intrusion of the world of trauma and non-being gives rise to a two-sided process. On one hand we begin to differentiate ourselves practically from the world around us and "grow an ego." At the same time we begin our process of building walls, creating emotional, physical, and intellectual armor to ward off the world which separate us from our essential unitary "amness" experience leading us to feel as though we are "not enough." It is a paradoxical loss, for we must be separate to "grow up"; but if we do so, without being grounded in "amness" we forget to "grow down" at the same time. This is what we have not achieved in our culture. This dual process benefits and limits us in a variety of ways.

The Emotional Umbilical Cord

Experience follows a law that logic
knows nothing of.

~Eisenbud

We are all born attached to an umbilical cord. This tough, cord-like structure connects us to the placenta, to our mother. It is our vital rootedness for the first nine months of our existence. It provides all of our physical nurturance while also removing all of our waste. The umbilical cord contains two umbilical arteries and one umbilical vein which pump blood to and from the placenta and the fetus so an exchange of nutrient and waste materials with the circulatory system of the mother takes place. We would die without it. It is crucial and absolutely necessary for our survival. Yet, at the moment of birth, this life sustaining cord must be clamped and then cut, radically severed, if we are to survive. That otherwise, same cord which brought us life and sustenance, can become a cord of death, wrapping around our fragile necks and choking us. When the cord is cut, there is a confrontation with non-being that is also a freeing.

Here is the key: *At the very moment we are confronted with non-being/death we are aware that we are separate at some level. We then over time interpret this separation as indicating in some fundamental way we are not enough.* Of course, non-being, trauma, and death are not evil or bad, they are part of the turning wheel of life which every time leads to decay, but in the end a rebirth. Many aboriginal cultures plant the placenta and umbilical cord of the child with the seeds of a new tree. They become vivid symbols of death bringing life. That tree is then considered to be connected spiritually with the soul of the child. The child will have a kinship with that tree throughout its life. (I wonder if my parents planted my placenta under that maple tree in front of my house, hmmm.) At the very moment the physical umbilical cord is cut, another takes its place. This is the moment of psychological bonding, the most crucial aspect of our first hours of life. This bonding is nothing less than an emotional and psychospiritual grounding between a child and the child's primary care giver. Just like the physical umbilical cord, this psychological one provides the nurturance and sustenance which helps the child deal with emotional waste and provides emotional, moral, and soulful food all through childhood. In this way the relationship is an umbilical cord to the greater social world. We know that without this emotional sustenance an infant will begin to refuse food, become sickly, wither and eventually die. To change metaphors, it is almost as if parents must create a psychospiritual space, just as much as a physical one, for the child to grow and thrive.

Yet, at the center of the birthing process there has already been severing, pain and suffering. We may imagine the child in the womb before the birth canal has opened sufficiently to be able to pass as a "no exit" experience, a crushing sense that there is no way out - suffering without a purpose or end. At the moment of emergence, the infant enters an utterly new world which is both unimaginable, bewildering, and terrifying, yet, also an eternity away from the cramped, convulsing universe where he/she was trapped moments before. Now there is movement, the pain has led somewhere, suffering has had a purpose. This we can bear.

As we have seen this is a process we repeat over and over again in life: from infant to toddler, from toddler to child, from child to adolescent, from adolescent to adult, from adult to elder. A connection always implies at some time in the future a need for differentiation. It is a central lesson. We find ourselves in "no exit" situations and suffer greatly. Just when we think we cannot tolerate it anymore, something shifts, we change. ***Change occurs when the pain of where we are overcomes the fear of where we are going.*** Living is painful. However, from the moment of birth onward there is something about this pain that is like a persistent voice that wants to be heard and we ignore it over and over. What is this voice of pain telling us? Is it a voice we can learn to hear? Can we cultivate a compassion and mercy vast enough to hear it fully speak? Or will we incessantly silence it by externally avoiding it? Grier was moving through a transition from young adulthood to mature adulthood. He heard the voice loud and clear:

*It was early morning when I awoke in my own apart-
ment in the new city I had moved to with my new wife.
A feeling of panic began to come over me as I began to
realize it was all up to me. Mom and Dad were 1500
miles away. I had a new job and a new wife, and for
the first time I realized whether we ate, had shelter, had
a problem, it was up to me to solve it, take care of it.
There were no more safety nets. AAAGGHHH!!! I
thought, "I don't want to grow up yet. It's too much
responsibility." I longed for the safety and security of
my old life. I felt like I was suffocating as I began to
feel heart palpitations and sweating.*

Parents go through their own passage during these times of death
and rebirth as Gloria, a mother with her daughter going off to school
for the first time, attests:

*I had a hard time sleeping just worrying about her.
My little girl had left me, gone off to a strange city over
a thousand miles away. I couldn't give her a hug, hold
her, see her. I missed her smile, her smell, everything
about her. I would see her pictures and just start to
cry. I never knew letting go would be so hard. I would
think about where she was, what she was doing. For 18
years I saw her virtually everyday of her life or talked
to her. She was the light of my life. I hurt. I mean
I was proud of her, very proud and excited for her,
it's just that she had become the center of my world.
And without her I felt alone, abandoned, I had to find
something else to focus on just to survive.*

When the familial/parental umbilical cord is severed then another
one that has been growing for a long time takes its place: a cultural/

56

social umbilical cord. We must find our place in society. This process lasts through decades of further growth until we reach mid-life and cry for something more. This is when we have climbed the ladder of success and discover, in horror, that it is leaning against the wrong wall. We then must give less attention to our social/cultural umbilical cord, put it in second place and see who we are apart from our connection to society. In this way we once again taste death and learn anew about slow rebirth and transformation.

GROWTH, DEATH, AND IMPERMANENCE

To be alive means to be always dying. This awareness of our constant decay is felt profoundly in the flow of time and experience. With every triumph there is a sadness, within every blossoming there is a withering. We are deeply part of this ecological rhythm of rising and falling. We all know about and want to embrace that part that grows, the "tree of us," however, within the eco-system of the psyche there is also the "tree mold of us," that is, that part of us which is not tall and grand, but small and ugly and even desires to break us down, moving us ever towards disintegration and death.

One of the central reasons we do not feel enough is that we know we are not immortal. One day we will die. How can we ever hope to be enough with this truth staring us in the face? At the same time, to live with the awareness of the eventual termination of this bodily reality is the essential catalyst to genuine psychospiritual growth. Unfortunately, it is our greatest fear, our ultimate "no exit" experience and what we run from culturally and individually almost everyday of our lives. How we deal with the reality of death determines to a large degree how we deal with life. The existential fact of death can serve as an impetus for growth because it confronts us with the unresolvable fact that all things change, even our most preciously held beliefs, our greatest loves, hopes and dreams, even the intimate fact of our own body, our own life.

The experience of dying and the possible journey after death is the deepest mystery that confronts us as human beings. It is Shakespeare's "undiscovered country." We are as rivers flowing to the sea who, when we come to the end of our journey, become unrecognizable as individuals as we pour our small, humble, fragile human being out into the ocean of Being.

There is an intimate relationship between our perceived "not being enough" and the fact of change. One of the reasons we never feel like we are "enough" is that no matter who we are or where we are it is impermanent, always changing. Practically, on a daily basis, or even a moment-to-moment basis, this awareness of perpetual change is powerfully felt. Everything is moving. No moment lasts forever. We learn this powerful fact very early on, and it haunts us the rest of our lives. Try to hold onto a moment and before one knows it, it is gone. In fact, trying to hold onto it only makes it pass away more quickly. This truth lies at the heart of one of William Blake's best known poems entitled *Eternity:*

> *For he who tries to grasp to himself a joy*
> *Does the winged life destroy*
> *But to he who kisses the joy as it flies*

Part II: The Abyss

Lives in eternity's sunrise [3]

Perpetual movement in life is the source of our most acute pain and greatest joy. A young man I worked with, John, talked about the experience of trying to grasp to himself a joy when he had lost his wife:

> *I recall the day it hit me that I had lost her. I became overwhelmed with the need to hang on to the past, obsessing about it, thinking about how we could be back together, all the time a tightness in the core of my body would feel like holding onto the pain, not letting it go, a gut-wrenching pain. I went through the weeks and months half dazed, living in the past. It was hard to imagine a future. The grief was overwhelming. Things would never be the same. I felt that part of me had died with her. It was painful just to **be** without her. I hadn't realized how intertwined our souls had become.*

I had a very hard time reconciling myself to this truth as a child that everything passes away, no experience remains forever. I remember it bothered me greatly that every moment ended and all too soon I would begin to forget the depths of joy or the fun I had just days ago. It is similar to the wish most of us had as kids, "I wish everyday was Christmas," because no matter how much fun one was having Christmas day, we were always aware that it was perpetually drawing to a close. In some way, I also felt as if "I" must not have really felt those deep emotions if they were so easily replaced by others. No moment existed that felt solid, there was nothing in the grand march of time to hold onto anywhere. Even my body itself perpetually changed and transformed, year after year. So as children do, I invented a plan.

One particularly boring day I decided to implement my scheme. We were in the family Chevrolet Chevelle which my mom called, "Old Suzabella," our beloved station wagon. It had a striking, even loud metallic blue paint job which was very popular in the 60s. I was sitting far in the back where I could gaze out the window and watch the world go by. Then the large outgrowth of the car that housed the spare tire caught my eye. This was it. This was the moment that would not end. I decided until the day I die I would remember that moment. I stared into that bump on the side of the car with the spare tire and concentrated as hard as I could, telling myself, "I will not let this moment pass!"

Years, later I wondered why I had picked such a flat boring moment. Why not a beautiful sunset or a glorious moment of love? No, this 9-year-old picked a spare tire holder. To this day I think of that moment often. It is a memory that always reminds me that there exists nothing in life that can stop time. The real challenge for all of us is to continue to learn to kiss the moment as it flies.

In a very real way, we face death in every moment, for always we are re-experiencing the grand drama of birth and death. The moment begins, and then slowly dies. In our experience of this paradox of birth and death, of movement and time, we know that every moment is enfolded, impregnated with non-being.

For a child, the growing awareness of impermanence is at the root of his interest in movement. With the awareness of impermanence comes a deeper recognition of death. When death is better known the question of "what to be" takes on more importance. However, many times in our incessant search for "what to be," we forget the reality of amness we have known which teaches that "we are," always and already, "who we are":

> *The child is constantly confronted with the nagging question, "What are you going to be?" Courageous would be the youngster who could look the adult squarely in the face and say, "I already am". We adults have forgotten, if indeed we ever knew, that a child is an active, participating, and contributing member of a society from birth. Childhood isn't a time when he is molded into a human who will then live life; he is a human who is living life. No child will miss the zest and joy of living unless denied by adults who have convinced themselves that childhood is merely a period of preparation.*[4]

This quote by David Elkind can help us recall how a child, in a radical way, "already is" immersed in *amness*. We must remember what we can learn from the child about Being and *amness*. I had a friend from Europe, who had been all around the country and commented, "It's the oddest thing, whenever I go to a party, or any gathering the first thing I am asked in America is, 'what do you do,' as if that is what is most important about me. Almost as if that is who I am." I certainly could identify with his observation. I had been on both sides of that question, many times.

I had a very sobering experience recently concerning this "what do you want to be when you grow up?" self-questioning. I had been hiking in the mountains of Wyoming when I met a back country ranger. This is what I wanted to do from about the age of 12 to 15. I wanted to be a forest ranger in the Grand Tetons of Wyoming, communing with the power and passion of the high country. Living in the wild. Here was this man, living my childhood dream. We talked of the passions and wonders of his job. He spoke of the solitude, the wild, and the majesty of the mountains. Then after awhile he asked me about what I do. I talked about my life as a psychologist, my family and home in Florida. After some time, he confided in me that he never had the stability in his job to have a family and that he had to keep odd jobs to finance anything extra in his life. He also said the winters were becoming more and more difficult to weather year after year and often imagined what it was like to live in Florida. He had also always dreamed of going to graduate school and "really making something of himself!" He also mentioned that as much as he loved the solitude, he missed a deeper communion with others.

The point here is that we both experienced our lives as "not enough." Although we each had much in our lives we loved and cherished, we also experienced a voice within that taunted us and kept whispering, "something is missing." We begin to then dream the impossible dream that the "grass is always greener." I always like to tell people, "the grass is never greener, but it is sometimes a different shade of green and of course it also may be brown." We spend so much time wondering and wishing what might have been that we end up letting the miracle of the precious present moment pass us by. Whatever road we choose, by necessity, we will have to have not chosen an infinite number of other paths. For every doctor who dreams of pursuing an acting career or music career, there is a actor or musician that dreams of having pursued a medical career. Of course, then there is the extreme cases where the inner voice of "not being enough" becomes a scream that silences all other voices. We contemplate surrendering all of who we are to non-being, literally.

Suicide, Terminal Illness and Non-Being

To be or not to be? That is the question.
~Shakespeare

My first contact with an existential philosophy professor taught me the universality of this contemplation. In class he asked boldly, "Who here has thought about killing themselves?" Everyone in the room was stunned. "You mean us? Are you serious?" said a student. "Yes, I am," replied the professor. There was a brash girl in the back row, who wore a purple tie-dyed summer dress. She proudly, raised her hand. While she looked at the rest of us with contempt. I thought to my self, "Do I dare raise my hand? I *have* thought about it. But, here I am a college student and psychology major. I'm supposed to have it all together." Whatever that meant. Could I allow myself to be so vulnerable? Something in me, slowly started raising my hand. Another part of me began shouting inside, " NO." The deeper, stronger force inside said, "YES! Be honest, be truthful, this is the time." We were the only two raising our hands. He nodded towards me in a knowing way. He then said, "At least we have two honest people here."

Of course, suicide is all too real. There is the case of Albert. He had lived his life from the outside-in. Doing what others said he ought to, becoming the doctor his parents wanted him to be, marrying the woman his friends said he should, wearing the "right" clothes, buying the "right" car, and even playing the games that magazines, television and friends told him he should. At the height of his outward image of success with money, prestige, and good looks, he shot himself in the woods on a Sunday morning. Unfortunately, Albert never even entered a therapist's office for fear it would not go with his "image" of who he thought he "should" be. The irony is that the tyranny of the image he took to be his essential self killed him.

Ultimately, all that we truly have is our own soul. Perhaps, all we are is our soul. The shiny apples tempt us, the winning of fame, fortune. There is nothing intrinsically wrong with such fruit, but their origins are deep inside us. As Muhammad Ali used to say, "The fight is won or lost far away from witnesses - behind the lines, in the gym, and out there on the road - long before I dance under those lights." For him, the fight took place within the inner sanctum of his own solitude in his long hours of training, focusing, and being committed to God in his own profoundly personal and private way.

Psychologists talk about the difference between "process" and "product" being like an iceberg. The tip of the iceberg is what the world sees, like Muhammad Ali's successful fights. What we do not see is the immense structure beneath the surface of that smaller tip. As much of

Part II: The Abyss

90 percent of our lives is about the process, usually hidden from the rest of the world, that gives rise to the visible 10 percent.

And what is the source of our underlying structure if not our sacred connection to amness, to Being. All else is our playing with surfaces. We hunger and long for a taste of truth, depth in life, a tangible rootedness.

Camus, the French writer and philosopher, enjoyed saying that the only true philosophical question was whether or not to kill yourself. Perhaps he was half right, that is, it is the question of non-being that truly puts our life, our being in perspective. For some that is the contemplation of suicide, for others it is the profound confrontation with a near death experience or severe trauma. Do we really know the value of something until we contemplate or experience not having it? How often have you heard the phrase, "you don't know what you've got until it's gone?" Most of us have come to know that timeless truth. Whether its about a mother, a father, a brother, a sister, a child, an arm, a leg, or a job. A young woman, Ginny, related how she had no idea that she loved her husband until she had decided to leave him. The divorce papers were signed, then all of a sudden she saw him with another woman on a date one evening and it hit her for the first time what he had meant to her:

> *The pain and disorientation were overwhelming. What had I done! Suddenly, my images of a boring, unfulfilled marriage and husband were transformed. Now I felt the pain he had felt all those years that I threatened to leave him. I never felt like staying and then suddenly, all I wanted was him, to be with him, to hold him, to touch him to make love to him. But, now it*

*was too late. It would never be again. If I only could
turn back the clock knowing what I know now.*

Losing a relationship gives us just a taste of the greatest loss of all, death. Few of us receive the opportunity to catch a glimpse into losing our life, or get close enough to losing it to find out how truly precious it is. Stephen did:

> *When I received the diagnosis of terminal cancer I felt
> the life just begin to be sucked right out of me. It was
> like a huge vacuum or black hole at the core of myself.
> I was dying, there was no cure. No pleading, no beg-
> ging, no bargaining would change that. I was helpless
> and felt a pervasive hopelessness surround me like a
> dark cloud. No more plans, no more future goals, no
> more of any of that, I was bereft, and felt abandoned
> by God, goodness, wholeness, the rest of humanity. It
> was marching on, while I wrestled alone with the demon
> of death.*

Whether we contemplate taking our own life or a doctor pronounces an impending death, we gaze sometimes for the first time into the abyss, non-being. The contemplation of not-being, or more exactly the confrontation with not-being, leads us to really wake up to the life we are living. It's value. It's worth.

SOMETHING IN YOU NEEDS TO DIE

*Verily, verily I say unto you,
except a corn of wheat fall into
the ground and die, it abideth*

alone: but if it die, it bringeth
forth much fruit.

~John 12.24

The first thing I tell people who come to me talking about suicide is," Well, there is something in you that needs to die, but not all of you. What needs to die within you?" They usually begin to talk about the pain, the guilt and the shame they carry with them. I then ask, "Now, there is something in you that wants to live, or perhaps even that wants to be born, bloom and grow. What might that be?" They may say, "No, I just want to disappear, to not be anymore, to not do it anymore, I just can't go on." Then I ask, "Do you want the joy you feel at the beach to die? Or the taste of a juicy red delicious apple on a spring day to die? Or the smile on your daughter's face on Christmas morning to die?" Usually, the reply, sometimes with a tear and the most subtle smile, is, "Well, no, of course not". Then I say, "Well, that is part of you, that you carry with you always. To end your life is to end those parts of you that want to live, as well as those that do not."

The darkness and the pain is much like the black on some pictures. If it were not for those areas of darkness, the whole work of art would not be what it is. It sets the colors in relief. Perhaps, it provides needed shadowing and depth. D.H. Lawrence wrote a poem that speaks to this important need for darkness:

THE END, THE BEGINNING

If there were not an utter and absolute dark
of silence and shear oblivion

67

at the core of everything,
how terrible the sun would be,
how ghastly it would be to strike a match, and make a
light.

But the very sun himself is pivoted
upon the core of pure oblivion,
so is a candle, even as a match.

And if there were not an absolute, utter forgetting
and a ceasing to know, a perfect ceasing to know
and a silent, sheer cessation of all awareness
how terrible life would be!
how terrible it would be to think and know, to have
consciousness!

But dipped, once dipped in dark oblivion
the soul has peace, inward and lovely peace.[5]

It is the need to confront non-being, death, and impermanence that Lawrence reminds us is crucial. It is the importance of our revering the profound mystery surrounding every scientific discovery, every little fact we learn. No matter how much we think we know, ultimately, it leads us to how much we do not "know." Ultimately, we are always bathed in mystery, in the unknown, and if we do not learn to befriend the darkness we will never learn of its blessings.

One needs the darkness to see the stars. The sun's light can blind us. We lose the vastness of the universe during the day. The darkness carries a mysterious illumination with it that we can use to plumb the depths of the world and of ourselves. In this way, the dark sky is not blackness as much as it is openness, a clearing to see more deeply.

Part II: The Abyss

Perhaps, this is the teachings of the abyss, that for us to see deeply into ourselves we need the abyss, that becomes like a great yawning opening in being to glimpse our vaster selves. When we walk into these dark places within ourselves and bring consciousness to them something remarkable happens. Instead of seeing darkness as "depression" it reveals itself to be a world with its own wisdom. This poem came to me during such a time in my own life:

Presence of the Night

Lonely nights...
Dark abyss...
Sometimes I curse you and
this life...

Then like some strange and wondrous
visitation in the night...between
the cries, the shouts and tears...

There is a sound, so silent, so sweet,
That I realize the "something more than me"
quietly moving through the rapids of this night...

It is then I reach my hand out
into the dark...
I call your name...

There, abiding presence
you touch me..
and embrace me...
though..without hands,
without body...
and it is then...that I realize...

The place I have been absent from,
all the time I have been here...
in this place..
this space..
called Life...

Deliver me...home
dear presence of the night...
safely upon the shores of that which
I have always been, but so easily
have denied....

Carl Jung also learned to appreciate pain, tragedy, and non-being like few others. When someone came to him saying something like, "I'm getting married," "I got a new job," or " I just received a promotion," Jung would look over his glasses, and say, "Well, if we keep our heads about us we might just be able to get through this." But, when someone would tell him of a great tragedy, such as, "I'm getting divorced," "My wife just died," or "I lost my job," he would reply with a knowing grin, "Let's open some champagne and celebrate, now we might really learn something about ourselves." In fact, when an American came to him and said, "I can't go on anymore. I just can't do it, I've come to the end of my rope," he would reply in his Swiss accent, "Yah, gut! Now something will happen!" His insight into the darkness of the human psyche contained this kernel of truth: ***It is precisely when our lives have become unmanageable and tragic that the ego can finally be knocked out of the controlling center of our psyche.***

The precious ego that we have worked so hard to forge in youth, later in life becomes the mask which separates us from an immediate

70

vital connection with the world. Up until this point the ego had been serving as the center of gravity for our lives telling us what is true, valuable and important - namely, security, belonging, power and status. Finally, when the ego is knocked out of the center of our psyche, then and only then, can the soul begin to emerge with its awareness of the synthesis of Being. We can then learn to follow the flow of life, instead of incessantly and vainly trying to control it. This ability to appreciate what tragedy and true confrontation with not-being can provide is not only the beginning of opening up to the wonder, awe, and mystery of life, it is also the hallmark of living soulfully.

Matthew Fox has gone so far as to say that after the Enlightenment, we now need an Endarkenment. The Enlightenment promoted the values of reason, logic and cool rationality. We have gained much from it, learned a great deal, succeeded in knowing all lands and oceans of the earth. We feed more people then ever thought possible. We explore space, walk on the moon. However, we have lost the ability to feel awe, wonder and mystery at the miracle of our own unique fragile life. Our faculty of intuition has atrophied to being simply a play thing, a curiosity, nothing more then a "gut instinct" not to be trusted. We have also lost our ability to enter, appreciate, and understand the depths of the mysteries that still lie all around us. The subtle rhythm of honoring lightness *and* darkness has been lost. Instead of dancing a silent arabesque in the flickering shadows between the two; most of our lives are spent simply swinging from one extreme to the other like a pendulum. How do we rediscover the dance? We begin by acknowledging that the darkness of the abyss has a place within our lives.

This is the great challenge when we encounter, day after day, week after week, the wounds, disillusionment, crushing self-doubt - all forms of not-me, nothingness, the void, that screams out, "You don't belong, you're not worthy. You are worthless. Your dreams don't matter, your being doesn't matter. Just give up now." Something intimate is happening in these moments. The voice of doubt is the voice of the abyss calling us to something greater if we can let our ego die and find in our brokenness new life. We then can move from our small melodramas to our greater story. Can we have the courage to get to know the terrain of the dark aspects of ourselves and each other, in all of its subtlety, richness and depth. If we don't, our faces will turn into those of our enemy as we invariably will project our own darkness on others, refusing to make peace with the dark figure in the mirror.

BEFRIENDING THE DARKNESS

Be patient with everyone, but above all with yourself...
do not be disheartened by your imperfections, but always
rise up with fresh courage...How are we to be patient in
bearing with our neighbor's faults, if we are impatient
in bearing with our own? He who is fretted by his own
failings will not correct them; all profitable correction
comes from a calm and peaceful mind.[6]

~St. Francis de Sales

Death comes to us in many forms. In a way, every illness we have, every pain, ache and fever is a little taste of death. The contingent nature of life looms at our door when we are ill. Many physicians will tell you how stress lowers the psycho-immune system and renders us susceptible to becoming ill. In this way the body "forces" us to pay attention to the life we are living, to slow down or stop us, to give ourselves a chance to reflect and rejuvenate.

The point is, we are usually so obsessed with reducing pain, with spending millions of dollar's to make an aspirin relieve our headache two minutes faster, that we may be medicating ourselves out of stopping and reflecting. An analogy may be helpful here.

Think for a moment about the athlete who has a damaged knee. It's hurting but everyone is depending on him to keep playing. So the doctor gives him a shot of cortisone to numb the pain. All of a sudden he can go out, ignoring the injury that his body is telling him he has, and wound himself further.

In an analogous way, the pearl is created in the oyster in its effort to heal itself. To rid itself of sand, or mend a puncture in the shell, the inner layers slowly give rise to the pearl. The "mother of pearl" on the inside of the shell truly functions as the mother, layer by layer, creating the pearl as a result of it's inner healing. When a foreign particle penetrates the shell's mantle, cells from the "mother" attach to the particle and build up more or less concentric layers of pearl around it. Metaphorically, the soul is the pearl and the "mother of pearl" is amness. The puncture is the wound. In time the innocence is reborn in the pearl, the soul, while gaining the experience through the deepening and development of one's life. Even those in the grips of overwhelming grief, pain, and loss appear to be comforted with the words, "Your soul is growing as it becomes ever more polished and strengthened by the pain you're experiencing," like raw stones put in a jewelers tumbler, the tumbling, friction and wearing away of the snags and rough edges create the soft, supple, smoothness of the true gem.

The "I" That Resides in the Eye of the Hurricane

One thing that comes out in myths is that at the bottom of the abyss comes the voice of salvation. The black moment is the moment when the real message of transformation is going to come.[7]
~Joseph Campbell

As we journey from *amness* to non-being and back again, the development of the I, of a self continues. Every time we cycle through the pattern, we enhance our awareness, as in a grand cross-stitched fabric, adding texture, color and depth with each new experience. Of course, from our perspective it is similar to a child sitting on the floor by grandmother's rocking chair while she is doing her embroidery. All the child see 's from his peculiar vantage point is a big mess; threads going every which way, making no discernable pattern. However, once the child crawls up on grandmother's lap they then have the opportunity to behold what beautiful work she was creating. The pattern from her perspective is plain to see. So it is between us and Being. It is when we feel our life has become an irrevocable tragedy that we might just discover who we really are. For example, there is nothing like a good old fashioned hurricane to provide some crucial life lessons.

"Find the eye of the hurricane" used to be just a useful saying for me until my house received two direct hits by hurricane Erin and Opal, between the months of August and October 1995. Both times, the eye walls crashed right into our back yard, spawning tornadoes and destruction as they went.

We woke up late that first morning, feeling sure Erin would pass us by and head away from Florida toward the Louisiana coast. Having evacuated for false alarms over many years, and not having had even a close call for almost a decade, we felt it unlikely we would be hit. I lay resting in my warm comfortable bed with the air conditioning protecting me from the scorching, humid heat of a Florida summer, when I heard my wife's voice, "Oh, my God, it's coming straight for us." She turned up the TV and the announcer said, "The eye wall will be making land fall somewhere around Pensacola Beach in just a few hours". Up until that point I had made no preparations for a hurricane. My daughter, still at a tender age, said, "Daddy will we have to evaporate," although we knew she meant to say, "evacuate," we appreciated the irony, and as adults we wished we could evaporate, unfortunately, there was no time. Considering we live right on the coast, there was a great deal to do, so I spent the few precious hours we had readying the house. When I finally had time to catch my breath, it started raining and then storming. So we huddled downstairs in the hallway in a cave I made of mattresses, our animals, blankets, snacks, the TV, and a portable radio. Not long after the howling wind the power went out. The last map images we saw on the TV showed the eye wall heading literally right over our house. The wind kept picking up strength creating an eerie crying sound which became louder and louder. Then the doors and windows actually began to bend and bow from the wind.

We burrowed into the mattresses. Each time a limb or pine cone would pelt the window, my chest tightened and my breathing stopped. I thought silently to myself, "They just aren't going to hold much longer." My dog whimpered and my daughters eyes widened in disbelief, amazement, and terror. She whispered, "Daddy, will we be alright?"

"Yes, sweetheart. We will be just fine."

I squeezed her hand a little tighter trying to reassure her, though I knew how unsure I was myself. All of a sudden, a harsh ripping sound began and then a tremendous crash. We realized that part of the roof was coming off. I tried to make my way to a side window that was not bowing in the wind. Shingles everywhere -- flying, circling, hitting the ground. Water began pouring through the now gaping holes in the roof. The sheet rock began to be soaked and slowly water began seeping in everywhere. The seals on the sliding glass door gave way as they did on most of the windows. The water was spraying upwards 5-10 feet in the air cascading into the dining room. As the winds picked up, and the rain seeped in so did the fear spread in the recesses of my body.

I had to remind myself a number of times to breathe as the storm continued to rage outside. Then as I looked out the window an immense swirling of debris in the wind and the sound of a freight train. A tornado. I had been taught what to listen for, what to do, but never did I imagine one would come this close.

On the Gulf Coast one can often see water spouts over the water, spawned by the many thunderstorms. It is one of the thunderstorm capitals of the world. To see the thunderstorms start to brood over the water and the dark ominous clouds move closer had never ceased to bring chills up my spine and make me feel very much alive! Now, here I was with one visiting me in my own territory. The roaring increased and the awesomeness of the experience bordered on the awful.

Awful and awesome have the same root word, awe. Being so confronted with the raw indiscriminate power of nature fills us with something that can only be termed "awe." It is that pure intense beholding, the giving up of any attempt to control, grasp, or hold. Like a flower blooming or a prisoner surrendering you open to what is, in all of its might, grandeur, majesty and terrible intensity. One has no choice but to behold. Awe is when the great prophets drop to their knees. When Jesus wept. When Moses beheld the burning bush. And here I sat, crouched in what I thought was my fortress of a house, feeling puny, small and insignificant, yet at the same moment feeling connected, somehow to "all-that-is"; feeling like crying one moment, and saying, "wow" the next! In the midst of chaos I found myself drinking the waters of *amness* once again. Less than two months later as we were still recovering from the first hurricane, we suffered another direct hit, Hurricane Opal. I went looking for that book, *When Bad Things Happen to Good People* by Rabbi Kuschner. I found myself depressed, agitated, grumpy, yelling at a lot of people, things I do not do on a regular basis. I felt like the Gods of Karma had punished me, sent me a mortal blow. Definitely a blow to my ego. I felt as if I had done something wrong. I began looking at all the things I had felt guilty about over the last 10 years, no 20 years. I reviewed every choice I had ever made. Well, if I had done this, or done that, or took that job, or gone to that school, or married that person, or not even gotten married, or was a monk, a priest, a surgeon, or maybe a hermit living somewhere north of the Arctic circle then...*then* this would not have happened!

Even as I was writing about these events in my journal, often the same day they happened, I was able see, briefly, how foolish these mind games were. But, when one is in the throes of self-damnation, self-recrimination, self-punishment, folly can seem all too real. Such is a time when that tree branch of logic can be a friend to cling to, not to mention taking some healthy doses of self-acceptance! I did my best to exercise my reason and to talk to myself about the inevitability of experiencing non-being.

The bare fact is, whether we like it or not, no matter how spiritually evolved or emotionally stable we are "Shit happens." And sometimes, if not most of the time (all of the time when it's Mother Nature at work) it's nobody's fault. Watching people during the days and months after the hurricanes was an incredible lesson even for a seasoned psychologist. How people handle adversity is a wonderful projective personality test. There are those who keep their sense of humor and agency and those who grumble, complain and blame everybody and everything. People either act or re-act. Most of us spend our lives vacillating between the two. Also, the world, when we are in the throes of adversity, is much like a mirror that reflects our face. The more we grimace at it, the more it will frown back. But if we have the presence of mind to contemplate and even laugh at it, it will be a friend who will help steady and love us.

During this pregnant time I had a dream. I was on my knees on the grass outside the back of our house. The house had been destroyed even worse than in actuality. I looked up at the heavens and asked, "God, why are you punishing me," and to my amazement I heard a voice answer back, "My son, I am not punishing you, I'm polishing you." The next day I awoke feeling a sense of peace, and it transformed much of my attitude towards the devastation. I could bear the pain if it was not a punishment but a gift of transformation for my soul. A few lines from a poem by David Whyte came to mind:

> *Like the moment you too saw, for the first time, your*
> *own house turned to ashes.*
> *Everything consumed so the road could open again.*[8]

Seeing my "house turned to ashes" became a challenge to new life, so the "road could open again!" Though it took two years of continuous struggle to put our lives and home back together, it provided invaluable grist for the mill of growing and being more human. So, when any of us allow ourselves to enter the "house of sorrow," we begin to learn the truth of Ecclesiastes 7, "The heart of the wise is found in the house of mourning." I had begun to find the "I" of the hurricane, the wisdom that could only be reached by traversing the interior depths of my own grief and loss. The "eye" was a much strengthened ability to witness the chaos around me, without judging myself or others. The "I" had become an "eye" that was seeing more clearly, more fully, more completely and instead of controlling, was learning better to behold.   I had another lesson in learning to befriend the abyss and find that the darkness of a "no exit" situation could be a clearing, an opening in Being, that far from dying I was about to wake up.

Death Visualization

It is said that a Shaman's greatest ally is death. In Asia and many aboriginal cultures they say that to truly live one must "*keep death over one's shoulder.*" When I first heard these words I thought, "how morbid!" Over the years, however, I have become more and more aware of their precious meaning. "To keep death over one's shoulder," refers to the inmost existential truth that death is the ultimate measure, that allowing ourselves to live each day, even each moment as if it is our last, is to wake us up to the life we are living. So many of us live and act as if we will live forever. Seen against the great background of the universe though, we are here merely for a split second. If we can find the courage to wake up everyday with the Shoshone words, "It is a good day to die," on our lips we will appreciate that our life journey is ever drawing to a close, and we live on the wings of grace with each breath we take.

Unfortunately, not only do we deny death in our culture, but when touched by it, we tend to pathologize the grief reaction. "Oh, get over it," is the cry if we go on "too long" with our tears and mourning.

PART II: THE ABYSS

People who are in the grips of immeasurable grief are hidden away. We are embarrassed by their depth of feeling, the rawness of their emotions. Yet, the grief itself is the well-spring of love. There is so much collective grief today, we have become numb to it. If grief could make a single sound, we wouldn't be able to hear anything else. I always like to imagine the sound of grief when allowed to be heard always resonates with and will bring forth a resonating chord of love. For it is at the crossroads of death and sorrow that we discover a deeper love and life. If we are afraid of death and grief, so too we will be afraid of life and joy. Where the great rivers of sorrow and joy come together, the energy of true spirituality springs forth. A powerful way to bring this truth to the surface and know it personally is to do the following meditation/visualization:

Meditate on the following questions. Answer them in your journal trying to write as freely as possible without editing:

> *How many years do you think you will live?*
> *If you could write your own epitaph what would it say?*
> *If you were told you only had 30 days to live what*
> *would you do with your remaining time left?*

Now close your eyes and take a deep breath. Allow yourself to let death appear to you in any image that your unconscious mind wishes to clothe it. It may be anything: a person, an animal, an abstract design, a landscape. The language of the soul is imagery, so simply let it appear. Now, when the image is clear in your mind, allow it to ask you this, "Imagine you have just died, you are in the tunnel

81

leading to the light you so often hear about at the end of the tunnel you hear a voice and it says, are you happy or unhappy with the way you lived your life? Why? Now if I allow you to go back and live the rest of your life from your present age, what do you need to do differently so that next time we meet you will answer the first question with a "Yes." Now go and really live until next time we meet!"

After the visualization give yourself plenty of time once again to write down the experience in your journal as fully and completely as you can.

CHAPTER 3:

DESIRE:
LONGING TO BE ENOUGH

Love bade me welcome,
yet my soul drew back,
Guilty of dust and sin.
But quick-ey'd Love,
observing me grow slack
From my first entrance in,
Drew nearer to me,
Sweetly questioning
If I lack'd anything
~George Herbert

Desire. That magical, mystical something that drives us, propels us, pulls us, taunts us, blesses us, and drowns us. Desire. When oneness and amness recede; and we become aware the inescapable and painful reality of separateness, we begin the drama of desire. Since I no longer feel connected to *all-that-is* in a tangible vital way, I *desire* to be connected to at least something, somebody or somewhere; a parent, a lover, a guru, alcohol, sex, chocolate, the list is infinite. We move from the womb of the world to being shipwrecked on the island of life. We need food from outside us to feed us: Clothes to warm us and rocks and wood to shelter us. We need hugs and affection to help us know we have a place here and that we belong and are loved. Desire is set in motion.

In most spiritual traditions, the loss of oneness and the rise of desire are crucial subjects of myth and theology. In the West, we have seen, humanity is expelled from the Garden of Eden. In Buddhism desire is the grand culprit that leads to ceaseless suffering. What these great traditions seem to be saying is that prior to being born we live in pure Spirit where every need is met before one even has it. Once we are born into a body our every need is not met. We now live a temporal and corporeal existence which by definition leads to desire for needs being met, which leads to suffering. Each of us live out being ousted from the Garden of Eden.

In the individual human being desire presses more urgently as we move out of the age of childhood. At no other time do the power and pain of the phenomenon of "I" become more pronounced than in adolescence. Desire literally begins to flow into our bodies and minds as the centers of our being are ignited by the flames of desire. Breasts grow, genitals mature, hormones are unleashed, and we become intoxicated with a general wanting to become. Being is not enough, becoming is our guide, the outlines of who we can be. Gone is the easy grace of losing oneself in solitary play where the world laughs in the starlit night, comforts itself in midsummer sunlight and whispers in the spring rain. We are grown and the primal etchings on our being, no matter how civilized we have become, rise to the surface: we must find a mate. In a most fundamental way we, even in our very potency, feel painfully inadequate, powerless, and lacking. Moreover, all that we want is forbidden: We can't drive, can't drink, can't have sex, can't run naked in the rain, can't cut school, can't fingerpaint aimlessly, can't cry in public, can't love our parents in the old way, can't scream in church and say, "It's all bull #&*@$." Can't, can't, can't. At the very moment we feel life in all its wonder and power crying out, " I AM," we also feel cut off from the silent miracle of "amness." It's a miracle any of us survive our teenage years!

All these lacks are most powerfully experienced in our need for someone of the opposite sex to bless our new "being in the world." Though we know we are no longer the world, we sense that in merging with another we can taste that oneness again.

We each move forward through adolescence as the world closes in. As in all genuine, real and loving relationships the other fails us eventually, and so, too, does the world. The world has a harsh need to change us. It is almost as if desire is the world's way of tantalizing us into jumping into it, and then when we do, it embroils us in the inevitable wounds and injuries that growing a self requires. As we suffer through our failures, the confrontations with non-being, we begin to make promises and assertions to ourselves which we hope will protect us from further injury. I like to use the analogy that in the inner most recesses of our souls, when we are in our youth, there is wet cement: then slowly but surely the world begins to make imprints in that cement and these imprints become the myths and expectations by which we live.

We are supported through much of childhood by these mythic structures that end up being written in the "wet cement" at the core of our souls. Expectations then harden and become rigid templates through which we experience the world such as, "everyone should

like me," "one who loves me will always and unfailingly be my cooperative partner," "the world is fair," "I deserve to be happy," "evil
people are out there and will be punished by God, in a way that I
see fit," "our country, and grownups know what they are doing," "the
legal system is fair," "Good things happen to good people; bad things
happen to bad people," These myths can become even more toxic
such as, "I'm evil," "I'm made of bad stuff," "I don't deserve the air
I breathe." More often than not these myths are beneath conscious
awareness, and it feels as if they truly assert the way life is. Yet,
through searching self-reflection these myths can be seen for what
they are, so many filters that cloud our perceptions of reality and
our ability to simply see "what is." As we do so, we can also begin
to know how splits have been created between what we feel, what we
think, and what we do. Before long we come face to face with the
universal symptom in modern life.

THE UNIVERSAL SYMPTOM

> *Patients...did not talk straight. They were never com-
> pletely, never wholeheartedly behind their words...Listen-
> ing to them caused some inner struggle, almost as if one
> had to listen to two speakers talking simultaneously....
> There were words and sentences and whole stories
> which were quite understandable and made sense in
> themselves; but the accompaniment of the tone of voice,
> facial expression and gestures interfered subtly and
> sometimes grossly with the total communicative effect...
> It also seemed that (there)...was a lack of unity...the
> pheonenon of "duplicity" as a true universal symptom.*[9]
> ~ *Hellmuth Kaiser*

Part II: The Abyss

As we begin to be more and more cut off from our vital connection to the world, our duplicity grows. We are increasingly at odds with ourselves. Therefore, we are no longer connected to our words and actions. The Native American phrase, we speak with "forked tongue," is appropriate. An internal civil war brews beneath our surface calm. In this sense of not being enough, the voice of desire and the voice of denial weave a web of deception with our words. We become a divided self. One client, Joshua, described it this way:

> *I started ever so slowly to become aware as our work progressed that who I thought I was, my mind and my beliefs were really not "me". At least not all of me. My words were hollow. Although I felt emotions within, somehow I was trapped in this body, in these roles that other people expected me to play. Then through speaking my pain, my wounds, what I always thought would be unspeakable, I learned to soak my words in blood, sweat and tears. It was then that others started to listen, and probably more importantly, I started to listen and hear, spellbound, who I was.*

We would all do well to learn to soak our words in blood, sweat, and tears. It is in those moments when our words are palpable, truly capable of touching another soul, that we discover our own enoughness. Unfortunately, as the years march on, we become more and more convinced that we are not enough. We are not good enough. We are not worthy enough. Enough for what? For unconditional love and acceptance. We then go so far as to even believe in the extreme idea that we may be made of bad stuff, unlovable stuff. The contrary forces of the fact of our existence and the sense that we are somehow not quite all here, create a fundamental problem, expressed in the universal symptom.

Yet, fundamentally, we are open, loving beings. The child in a state of amness is radically open. Sure, he/she is not yet differentiated enough to maneuver well through social reality, but it is his openness that allows him the vital connection to all-that-is. This inborn ability to be loving, however, becomes compromised through his simply living, as desires are frustrated. The open innocence that underlies his experience of amness is cut into, injured, over and over and ever more deeply by repeated confrontations with non-being. Then we begin to bleed in the world and duplicity arises.

Duplicity always has the universal injury - wounded innocence - as its core. The forms our duplicity can take are infinitely varied, depending on the type of wound to our innocence and our specific reactions. Duplicity in essence makes us incapable of being truly present in the moment. Subsequently, the clearest manifestation of the universal symptom is not living and being in the moment. Likewise, although the infant is not able to maneuver through social reality, he or she is fully present - hiding nothing.

In our loving state of amness in the world we became connected, bonded to people, places, things, animals and inevitably these bonds begin to give way. We move, someone leaves us or dies, a precious stuffed animal is lost, mistakenly thrown away. Our favorite tree is destroyed in a hurricane. Our house is devastated in a fire, destroyed in a flood. We are in a terrible accident and lose an arm or a leg. The list is infinite, the teaching is clear - loss is inevitable. Every trust bears the seeds of its own betrayal, every connection bears the mark of separation. But, accepting the teaching intellectually is not enough. We must come to the reality of this *through* allowing ourselves to grieve. If we do not, we become atrophied, stopped up, frozen. This may occur in many ways. Children who experience severe trauma, for example, from emotional, physical or sexual abuse, may suffer a splitting of their experience of self. The full robust self is no longer present, only parts of it are, while other parts remain in hiding, concealing the deep pain, injured innocence and grief. Duplicity. In other cases, we may simply deny that a loss had any meaning to us: "Oh, I never really liked grandpa anyway, I hated going over there, I'm glad he's dead." All the while the child is looking at the ground. Duplicity. We may cover our hurt with cynicism and sarcasm: "That's life, no big deal, who cares, you move, you make new friends, you carry on, doesn't bother me." Duplicity. Each of these ways of dealing with the inevitable losses of one's life leads to a sealing off of one's full *vital connection* to one's whole heart and soul. The lines of a poem by Oriah Mountain Dreamer provides a glimpse into this possibility:

> *All I want to know is if you have touched the center of*
> *your own sorrow. If you have been opened by life's*
> *betrayals or have become shriveled and closed from*
> *fear of further pain.*[2]

As we increasingly avoid the inevitable grief of being human and being alive, duplicity slowly gains ground. For every confrontation with non-being results in an injury to our *perceived* innocence. The word "perceived" is key here, because ultimately amness, Being with a capital "B" is incapable of being destroyed or injured. It is the vastness in which all injury to beings-in-the-world float. This experience is difficult to reach, this level of transcendent *amness,* but it is the golden elixir that transforms injury into a new openness. Such healing allows one to be injured AND innocent.

William Blake had keen insight into this injured innocence. In his *Songs of Innocence* and *Songs of Experience,* he describes what he calls the twice-born human. Our initial birth is into amness, which allows for openness of the heart and soul. Yet there is no experience and thus, no learning. When we begin to experience and learn, we simultaneously begin to close off heart and soul. For Blake, the real challenge became, accumulating more and more experience without shutting off our innocence. This he called the marriage of heaven and hell. This is nurturing the *vital connection* while also being able to learn the wisdom of the world. The Chinese word Tzu which is added to such great names as Lao Tzu and Chaung Tzu, refers to both the wisdom of a master and innocence of a child. Nietzsche expressed this by saying that in the end the lion of wisdom ultimately is transformed once again into the infant. This is the golden paradox.

This new innocence can only be found to the extent we are able to stop deceiving ourselves, hiding our injuries, and refusing to follow the river of grief down to the sea. To merge with our brokenness requires great courage and trust. The emotional river keeps flowing. That is why time is the great healer, it flows on, the rapids become calm water again ultimately flowing home to the sea. We become duplicitous when we get lost in an eddy, a whirlpool of self-denial, self-blame and self-hatred. The injuries become unspeakable, unsayable, and we seal them off from awareness, from others. We then play a game of emotional hide-and-seek. This concealment seals us off from having any genuine connection and communication with others.

One of the most profound ways, perhaps the only way, to keep the river of experience flowing is to accept and take responsibility for everything we say, do, and feel as part of us. To walk our talk. This means not only those aspects of ourselves we *desire* to identify with (our ego), but also those parts of us we abhor and want to disown (the shadow). When we separate these aspects from conscious awareness, the insidious process of duplicity again takes hold of us. One way of overcoming this duplicity is to remember that all parts of us, even our shadow, has potential and value. This is the attitude of a shaman when he says, *"All is Sacred"*.

In this way we begin to view our pains, disappointments, and losses as fruitful. We let go of pathologizing who we are and begin to spiritualize our situation, creating meaning from the seemingly meaningless. It is totally within one's own hands to create one's life, no one else will do it for us - not a therapist, the government, organized religion, science, technology or even a mentor. They can guide, provide challenges, input, and reflection, but, ultimately it is up to each one of us.

I see clients struggling with both the universal injury and the symptoms of the inner civil war of duplicity daily. One particular young man comes to mind, his name was Jonathan.

Jonathan

*People say that [what] we're all seeking is a meaning
for life. I don't think that's what we're really seeking. I think that what we're seeking is an experience
of being alive, so that our life experiences on the purely
physical plane will have resonances within our own
innermost being and reality, so that we actually feel the
rapture of being alive.*[11]

~Joseph Campbell

Jonathan was a young man who came to see me in the midst of a
spiritual crisis. He had great difficulty dealing with the fact that
there seemed to be so many paths to choose from in his life; both
in what he wanted to be, and what he wanted to believe. He visited
all kinds of churches; Lutheran, Methodist, Pentecostal, a Jewish
Temple, Buddhist, Taoist, etc. He found meaning in each of them,
yet he still felt lost. The absolute spiritual dimension he was seeking
was looking more and more like mere cultural artifacts of particular
groups. The Divine became increasingly out of reach.

Jonathan, having been raised a Catholic, had been engrossed by
the mass at a very young age. He still would cry when he went to
communion, feeling the presence of Jesus in the bread and wine. He
would feel Jesus at the last supper as he would walk up to the altar.
He could sense Jesus' pain of knowing he would die the next day.
Jonathan felt these feelings so acutely that he had even considered
becoming a priest during his adolescence. But, he discovered drinking and sexuality and then felt too impure to enter on such a path. He
acutely felt his injured innocence. However, he could not talk about

it to anyone. His family knew one side of him, his nighttime friends another. He was living a divided life and it was strangling him. In his mind, having had pre-marital sex, drinking, experimenting with smoking and lying to his parents he had become just a step away from being the devil himself. He had fallen from grace and he was sure there was no way for him to be redeemed. Thoughts of suicide filled his mind.

From this pain, he began the adventure of self-discovery. His sense of non-being impelled him to search for a way home. In our work together we began to explore what elements spoke to him in each of these different paths. I was asking him to identify resonances that might be so strong as to bring rapture, joy and bliss. I explained Novalis' saying, "The seat of the soul is where the inner world and the outer world meet. Where they overlap, it is in every point of the overlap." Another way of saying this is the meeting point of the internal and the external is the eternal. Jonathan and I also talked about Joseph Campbell's observation, "We're so engaged in doing things to achieve purposes of outer value that we forget that the inner value, the rapture (the resonation) that is associated with being alive, is what it's all about."

I asked Jonathan to tell me which of the experiences he had in these many churches resonated with him most, where was a vital connection. He responded it was the charismatic Episcopal church he attended. At the same time he said, "But I thought the sermon sucked." Previously, Jonathan would have rejected what moved him in this experience because his mind found an aspect of the setting intellectually inadequate. Duplicity. He denied his feelings and even his soul because that was one way he had learned to cope with the pain of his wounded innocence.

His rather cool and even rigid parents, not to speak of social authorities like teachers, had reinforced the split. Over and over we discussed how he continually felt pulled in different directions. His friends said one thing, his parents another - all the while his heart would have a profound experience his mind would continually try to belittle and even deny. It is no wonder he had chronic colitis and a knot in his stomach much of the time. His mind kept trying to find the one "right," "correct" path based upon only logic and analysis instead of his following the one that "felt" right. In this way, he would swing like a pendulum, being the good, perfect altar boy on Sunday morning and then by Friday night of the following week, being as bad as he could be. Over time he realized that by trying to get in touch with his whole being he could have his heart, mind and soul dialogue like people in a meeting to come up with a consensus on the path to choose. More duplicity being healed! In this way, he could engage his whole being. He realized he did have to take into consideration his very powerful analytic mind, but he also needed to temper it with his equally strong, empathic heart. He described becoming more fully involved in the decisions in his life when he took time to consult "all" the many parts of himself. He found a church he felt comfortable in and realized it did not have to be perfect and therefore neither did he. The more compassionate he became with himself, ironically the less he felt the compulsion to act out in self-destructive ways.

Divine Discontent

Ralph Waldo Emerson had an eloquent phrase to describe Jonathan's original predicament: his need to search for a way home. He called it, "*divine discontent.*" Many of the millions that are suffering from depression and spend annually 12.4 billion dollars a year on treating it, could better be said to suffer from "divine discontent." A profound spiritual hunger, a lack of meaning grips them. People are hungry and there is nothing to eat. Their souls are thirsty and there is precious little water to drink.

The number one factor in many life-threatening diseases is a lack of meaning and purpose in one's life. This is divine discontent. When one does not address and pay attention to this divine discontent, one can begin to experience the empty self, many times experienced as a vacuum at the core of one's body. Many people describe this vacuous feeling as being located right around the navel. A true sign of the loss of the vital connection.

Divine discontent occurs whenever we exchange internal value for external. To me this is a litmus paper test. In chemistry there is a simple test to see if a liquid is acidic or basic. The strip of paper turns red if acid and blue if base. If you have a decision to make, you can ask yourself simply is this based more on internal values (living from the inside-out; this is true for me) or external value (living from the outside-in; more concerned about what others think, want and need). Going mainly for external values leaves us open to disappointments. We may fail to achieve them; or, if we do, others may not appreciate what we have done and may even laugh or criticize it; Often, once the external value is achieved, we realize it wasn't worth the effort.

I had an experience that highlights this point when I was testing for my black belt in TaeKwonDo. I had to travel over 300 miles to arrive at the testing site. If I passed, I would be able to stay the weekend and participate in the special annual black belt camp. If I failed, I would have to drive back alone in the middle of the night. I had practiced long and hard for the testing and was the only red belt in a room full of black belts who were judging my performance. I did the best I could do, and I didn't make any gross errors. Then standing in front of these sixth degree masters the head one said, "No one passed you."

No one? Not one? I had failed and felt miserable. But, driving back those 300 miles by myself that night was a powerful experience because I learned a lot about why I was practicing the art of TaeKwonDo.

I had felt a resonation in my body when I began doing the movements of TaeKwonDo. I enjoyed the stretching of my muscles, the beauty of the forms, and the flow of movements I felt when I was "in sync." Yet, I failed. I would have to wait months to retest for my black belt. The outer value had failed me. I would have to find an inner value that would sustain me. The false self within me I heard screaming, "Screw this, forget this, I'm not doing this stupid karate crap anymore. I'm finished. This martial art bull is a total joke." There was another voice, an even more bitter and critical one, "You suck, you are such a lousy athlete. You call yourself a martial artist, hah! You've never done anything right, you're always @#$%* up!

You deserved what you got, failure - because you are a failure!"

If I was going to quell these voices within me I had to go deeper and find the roots of something that would sustain my continuing the practice of TaeKwonDo. I started with a question I ask many people when they feel they have fallen out of love with the person they married: "What initially attracted you to each other when you first met?" So, I asked myself what initially attracted me to TaeKwonDo. As I did, I began to discover that the martial arts practice had very little to do with achieving the next color belt, rather, for me, deep down it had to do with developing a greater harmony between my inner and outer self. It was as if I could touch an inner silent dance - expressive of a harmonic relationship between time and space. How could failing a black belt testing take that away? When I came to this insight I felt a warm rush come over my body and a large smile emerge on my face even though it was two in the morning and I had another 100 miles to drive. I learned to become thankful for my failure. It seared away a little more of my ego and put me in touch with my inmost sense of self. I remembered also the words from my dream after the hurricane, "I'm not punishing you, I'm polishing you." In fact, the days that followed allowed me a deeper connection with people because I had failed. My fellow TaeKwonDo students and others could identify with my failure much more than any success. Over the following years, I would "fail" a number of testings at higher and higher ranks. Each time the "failure" became easier to bear. I almost began to feel a sense of strange joy as I have become more graceful in my ability to walk into and through the failure all the while discovering and searing away deeper and more encrusted layers of the ego.

In actuality, perfection is really inhuman. The imperfect, the broken, and the injured are what is most immeasurably lovable. Children are so lovable because they embrace their imperfection and are so unselfconscious about their awkwardness and vulnerability. When they fall down, and go "boom," when they walk out of their room having dressed themselves haphazardly, mismatched colors and dragging their "ba, ba" - we resonate with such unselfconscious imperfection. It helps us reach into our own heart. In fact, not only is perfection inhuman, I have a physicist friend who says if it were not for imperfection we would not be here. This is how he put it, "You see the belief in present cosmology is that before the Big Bang there must have existed a state of perfect symmetry. In perfect symmetrical time and space nothing can happen, no event, nothing. In fact, perfectly symmetrical space is timeless. So something occurred to break the symmetry. Only in broken symmetry can events take place." The implications of that idea are far reaching. It allows us to embrace our brokenness much more fully. Without it we would not be who we are.

A useful way to look at the false self, or the ego, is to see it as that part of us that grows only through an increase in outer value. That which is attached to rank, status, and achievement is measured purely by outer means. This is extrinsic value. Extrinsic value is not necessarily bad, it is just not the whole story. In fact, it is crucial during the first half of life. It helps us achieve a sense of belonging, safety, and security in the world. By contrast, intrinsic value is that which is an end in itself. It is not able to be measured by any external benchmark, in fact, we might go so far as to say it is immeasurable. It arises simply from a feeling of "ah, this is feeding my soul," "this is me." It is similar to an amness experience. It might be the way you feel when your son or daughter gives you a hug and says "I love you." or an indescribable feeling you get from a sermon, a piece of music or from watching a poignant movie. We know it as a feeling quality. It doesn't have anything to do with quantity. It is quality. It is where quality lives and breathes. Although we can't put it in a box, measure it and weigh it, it is crucial to who we are and we all know it when we feel it. The ego is a child of society, the soul is a child of divinity. Therefore, the ego develops through social validation, the soul through relationships with Nature and Being at large. Sometimes, these feel like internal states, but in a very real way they are the context from which social relationships develop. The ego helps us maintain our sanity, the soul builds bridges to the Great Mystery we are all part of. The way to divine contentment is intrinsic value.

YEARNING, CREATING AND RITES OF PASSAGE

Everything that has happened to me since has hurt.[12]
~Herman Hesse

As we begin to live more and more from the outside in, we begin to identify ourselves with that which is external. Our own innocent amness where self and world are united in a wondrous shimmering mystery is seen as childish, immature, and even primitive. Now it appears more grown up to be concerned with "real" objects in the world "out there": what car we drive, what rock group we listen to, how much money we make, and how many degrees we have. This stage is necessary because we must begin to adapt to the culture that surrounds us. In many earlier cultures this was accomplished through sophisticated rights of passage that helped the individual dip into the main stream culture of the time, but did so without erasing the wonder, awe and mystery of the vital connection with one's first person experience of the world. It is crucial that we grow out of our self-centered childish qualities of entitlement, "the world revolves around me" perspectives. However, in our culture you have two choices - either, "grow up" and jettison all of your innocence "throwing the baby out with the bath water." Or, remain a child and never grow into a responsible adult. The task becomes, how does one shed one's childishness, while retaining one's childlike qualities and weaving them, even wedding them to our adult self?

Lacking such traditional rites of passage, unfortunately, we are stuck with sad substitutes. The contemporary poet, Luis Rodriguez, helps us understand the desperate attempts at trying to answer the same deep needs that we have always had.

> *Gangs are not alien powers. They begin as unstructured groupings, our children, who desire the same as any young person. Respect. A sense of belonging. Protection. The same thing that the YMCA, Little League or the Boys Scouts want. It wasn't any more than what I wanted as a child....What to do with those whom society cannot accommodate? Criminalize them. Outlaw*

*their actions and creations. Declare them the enemy,
then wage war. Emphasize the differences - the shade
of their skin, the accent in the speech or manner of
clothes. Like the scapegoat of the Bible, place society's
ills on them, then 'stone them' in absolution, it's convenient. It's logical. It doesn't work.*[13]

One 14-year-old, Mark, who came to see me, had almost died of alcohol poisoning. He had been sleeping over at his best friend's house whose parents were out of town. They were both at that age when they had just enough knowledge of the "world of experience" to be dangerous. Unfortunately, they had no adult guides to satisfy their desire for passage to adulthood - men versed in providing them enough danger to test them and enough sacredness to make the journey meaningful. They had seen their parents and older brothers drinking alcohol, but were legally not allowed to drink themselves for another seven years. To them and to many adolescents, alcohol symbolizes adulthood. It symbolizes passage. They opened the liquor cabinet and found many bottles of different kinds of liquor - scotch, gin, vodka, and tequila. In there "innocence" they decided to be "men" by taking a shot from each bottle. After one, they decided they did not "really" feel anything so they took another shot of each to make sure the passage to adulthood would be assured. What followed haunted them the rest of their lives.

Mark described that night as being a cross between heaven and absolute hell. Feeling the effects of the alcohol they began dancing, joking, and laughing hysterically. But then the nausea began. Both of them began to lose consciousness as their drunken frenzy turned into

101

a torturous dance of pain, vomiting, and convulsions. Fortunately, they soon passed out. When Mark woke there was vomit everywhere. His friend was hanging half way out the window. Mark couldn't even move. The friends parents found them in the morning. Mark's parents were called and they took him to the emergency room. The attending physician recommended counseling. That's how he came to see me.

Fortunately, this young man did not die, but every year many do. His story makes a prime example of how our culture botches up the need for rites of passage. Alcohol, drugs, and cigarettes, because they are taboo, serve as such strong symbols of adulthood to children and teenagers. The bar mitzvah and bat mitzvah are attempts at preserving a rite of passage in traditional Jewish culture. Yet, the power and poignancy is often lost in modern versions. Like modern day Christian confirmations, they are aborted attempts at transformation; perfunctory social occasions with no true blood, sweat and tears that would mark a true rite of passage. One where the initiate would enter the cultural world of their elders through symbol, ritual and ceremony in this way tasting adulthood and beginning the long process of digesting and assimilating it without losing the vital roots of amness. If Mark and his friend had a culturally sanctioned vision quest available to them, high on a wilderness mountain top, prepared by fasting, and climaxed by an intoxication with the Holy Spirit, their drunken stumbling would have been instead an ecstatic dance of renewal and insight into their future roles as truly mature adults in the world. Hidden in the vice is always a distorted virtue.

Underneath their destructive behavior was an ancient perennial creative wisdom trying to be heard. Something in Mark was trying to die, while something else was trying to be born. I tell many a teenager locked in the grips of suicidal ideation that if they can find a way to kill themselves without doing bodily injury, they will begin to feel some of the freedom and transformation for which they are looking.

Mark and his friend still in their childhood state, experienced themselves painfully as being "not enough." As all of us do in such circumstances, they were then moved by a profound psychological need: Belonging. The thinking goes something like this, "If I am not enough, then maybe I can find something larger than myself, a group that will make me feel enough." This desire and the search for belonging become key during adolescence. As the umbilical cord continues to be severed from our parents and families, we seek out new connections of "enoughness." To see how powerful this psychological need is just consider the intense devotion we have to athletic teams. People painting vans the color of their favorite college teams and going to football games every weekend. The intense emotion of 60 thousand plus fans at sporting events, each cheering for "their" particular team. This fervor and intensity is seen in some people's fanatic devotion to a church, a gang, or any other social group, as well as in the proliferation of support groups. The feeling one may experience when hearing one's national anthem, or seeing one's national flag; such symbols stir us deeply because they offer through their promise of belonging a glimmer of maybe being enough.

Satisfying this need to belong is one of the main purposes behind rites of passage: to help the adolescent shed childhood securities and help bring him into the great, more inclusive world of belonging, not only to the group but more critically to Nature - to Life. Prior to the rite of passage, children belong to the tribe just by being their parent's offspring. But, following the rite of passage, they become full members in their own right! Since we do not have these rites today, we have dysfunctional, dangerous alternatives. The gangs Rodriquez talks about in our culture are created by the shadow side of this buried need. Without a rite of passage which addresses the inner civil war, the vacuum of the empty self, we live life as lack, as not enough.

Lacking such rites, we may have to go it alone. To do so, we may have to follow the way of the artist and rather than turning to dysfunctional groups that cannot truly initiate us, turn inward. This is the great moment Pablo Neruda took when he heard his inner self calling him to poetry and through it to a reconciliation between self and world and to an experience of reclaimed innocence.

> *And it was at that age...Poetry arrived*
> *in search of me. I don't know, I don't know where*
> *it came from, from winter or a river.*
> *I don't know how or when,*
> *no, they were not voices, they were not*
> *words, nor silence,*
> *but from a street I was summoned,*
> *from the branches of night,*
> *abruptly from the others,*
> *among violent fires*
> *or returning alone,*
> *there I was without a face*
> *and it touched me.*

I did not know what to say, my mouth
had no way
with names, my eyes were blind,
and something started in my soul,
fever or forgotten wings,
and I made my own way,
deciphering
that fire,
and I wrote the first faint line,
faint, without substance, pure
nonsense,
pure wisdom
of someone who knows nothing,
and suddenly I saw
the heavens
unfastened
and open,
planets,
palpitating pulsations,
shadow perforated,
riddled
with arrows, fire and flowers,
the winding night, the universe.
And I, infinitesimal being,
drunk with the great starry
void,
likeness, image of
mystery,
felt myself a pure part
of the abyss,
I wheeled with the stars,
my heart broke loose on the wind.[14]

Neruda is showing us the courage it takes to reclaim innocence. When he says, "I wrote the first faint line, faint, without substance, pure nonsense, pure wisdom," this is the moment of Tzu, of the twice born. Jumping into the nonsense, uncertainty and unpredictability of the self and blessing it as we express it. This is a powerful example of soul initiation through the creative process. Luis Rodriquez recalls a similar moment: "I didn't know how to write or paint, I had a great need to conceive and imagine, so compelling, so encompassing, I had to do it even when I knew my works would be subject to ridicule, would be called stupid and naive. I just couldn't stop." In the short film by Martin Scorcese in New York Stories, there is an artist played by Nick Nolte. His assistant is Rosanna Arquette and they have a turbulent love affair. She hangs on because he is a well respected artist, and she hungers for him to validate her and her own artistic work and tell her, "you're good." She ends up berating him one day, begging him to tell her if she is wasting her time or not. He goes into a rage and looks at her, eyes aflame and says, "It has nothing to do with being good, you do it because you have to, because you're compelled to, because if you don't you will go crazy, or die. That's what it is about!"

Even if we are not called to tap into the creative blessing of our own chaos, as these artists are, we can deliberately open ourselves to it and thereby help reconcile our social or extrinsic selves with what is deep within. When I have people write journals, my main directive is "no rules, write spontaneously, openly without editing or censoring, as it emerges, just let it out. Scribble, cuss, put in run-on sentences, write upside down, inside out, backwards, in circles, wherever you are drawn, go there. Doodle, scribble, salivate, whatever. The key is to keep writing." If they keep at it long enough the soul will awaken.

The surrealists called this "automatic writing." Their desire was to free the unconscious. Or, to paraphrase Plato, *you must go into your madness voluntarily so it doesn't come out involuntarily.* These are all ways of beginning to regain innocence and wholeness following the inevitable wounds and injures we all suffer. This is the process of *soul initiation.* There is a profound discovery here at the heart of the abyss; as painful as confrontations with non-being, desire and chaos are they lead to the awareness of the Other - that which is greater than us. In so doing, we are led to the inevitable conclusion that there is something innately good, freeing and alive in the darkness - creativity and spontaneity.

DESIRE AS LACK

As the process of desire unfolds we can watch its many manifestations. Desire in the West and East has traditionally been associated with lack. When we say we desire something, we usually mean we *need* it to feel whole. I often desire, for instance, a fresh baked croissant. I enjoy going to this little French bakery down the street from my office which bakes fresh croissants every morning. I walk into the store, smell the fresh croissants and feel a sense of desire within me to "have" a croissant. I now lack this croissant. I experience it as outside of me. As a result I desire it. My desire for a croissant hinges then upon my "wanting" it, and my not yet "possessing" or "having" it. I *lack* a croissant.

The Buddha, in his very insightful, meditative way, broke moment to moment experience down to such a degree as to come to a startling conclusion: suffering arises from desire. When we desire, we are in touch with our not having. We then go in search of fulfilling this desire as lack and usually are met with many obstacles. For instance, my desire for a house, a car, a beautiful woman sets me onto never ending quests for fulfilling my desire. But, each time *more is never enough*.[1] There is always a more beautiful woman, a bigger house, a faster car. This results in our obsessive chasing after "bigger" and "better" desires. Desire is the culprit. Desire as lack.

Of course we all have many desires arising from many needs from food, clothing and shelter to love, peace and joy. But, to the extent that we identify with these desires (I *must* have it. I can't be myself without it") and experience ourselves as lacking an "it," we set ourselves up for suffering - a lot of which is simply unnecessary. When I identify myself with my desire I then experience my self as lacking, as not enough. I am not rich enough, handsome enough, strong enough, and so on. We can trace virtually all forms of emotional difficulties down to this primordial sense of "not being enough." In depression one usually feels that one is not good enough, that one is somehow bad or guilty. In anxiety one feels oneself to be not solid enough which can result in panic attacks. When we have diarrhea brought on by anxiety, we are primordially living out this experience of not being solid enough. Everything runs right through us, literally. Obsessive-compulsive behavior is aimed at being cleaner, smarter, faster, more perfect. One in the grips of an obsession or compulsion never feels complete. If I check the lights one more time before I go to bed then I will feel safe. This one lacks safety, another lacks solidity, still another lacks a feeling of worth. We are not enough and we desire being enough.

This inevitably leads us to begin to desire being like, or even being other people! We imagine the movie star or multimillion dollar athlete to "be enough." If only I could be Mel Gibson or Emmit Smith, then I would be happy, I would feel complete. Adulation from hundreds of thousands of fans, millions of dollars, recognition, admiration, yes! Then I will be complete. Desire, desire, desire.

ONTOLOGICAL DESIRE

I am convinced, however, that all these desires are not the real thing - they are our ordinary human desire, but there is a more fundamental desire behind them and available to us: the ontological core of desire. We can move to desires that we very well mistrust "desires as lack," to an other level of understanding: the universe's desire to express itself. I am speaking of proliferation, the qualitative expansiveness behind *all-that-is*. This is the inmost core of all of our surface desires if we penetrate deep enough below the surface. It is Be-ing, the verb denoting the infinite creative presence that bathes us all. We observe it in the startling desire of the moon for the earth, and the sun for the planets. It is a sort of universal or divine love of the creative for the created. Dante's phrase, *"L'amore che muove il sole l'aetre stelle,"* The love that moves the sun and all the other stars. It is the blossoming of each of us into the world through our self-expression and creativity and circling back at the end into eternity as we do.

This universal desire, by definition, is always available to us, it is omnipresent, and we can tune into it as a way to help us overcome that feeling of being lacking which ordinary desire always gives us. Let's go back to my croissant. I am once again in the French bakery smelling these delicious fresh baked croissants. Only now, instead of saying to myself, "I must have one," I close my eyes and focus on enjoying the smell. Then, I imaginatively become the smell, creatively absorbing the croissant into my very being. Suddenly, the croissant is no longer outside of me, but part of me, in me, and I give thanks for the gift of be-holding the aroma, the delicate being of the croissant. Now this psychological maneuver may sound like so much airy-fairy, mumbo jumbo. I had to overcome some hard-headed inner resistance myself, once, when I first thought of doing it. But the more I let go of the assumption that I *needed* to consume, to *possess* the croissant materially and focused instead on the richness of the experience of acknowledging it, the more fully aware I became of the dance of the universe taking place within me. Naturally, the feeling "lack," of *having to have* the croissant began melting away. I began to move the croissant from being outside of me to its being within me and all without ever having eaten it!

This experience can be powerful for anyone, but for people with eating disorders, whose desire for food is especially symbolic of their sense of "not being enough"; it can be particularly helpful. The craving for food or the refusal of it becomes a tragic drama of self-worth, power, and control; an incessant tragedy of surface desires.

We can adapt the same technique for our usual frustrations desiring people. How many crimes such as rape are committed over relationships broken because of misunderstandings about such desire. Ordinary desire, based on lack, is inevitably a desire for power, control, and ultimately possession. When we feel empty and love fails us, the human animal settles for power. When we ordinarily desire another human being, a complex series of emotions unfolds. Take a simple example: You are walking down a street and see someone and feel a strong physical attraction. Your heart jumps, you do a double-take. You feel an emotional charge. At the same time, you feel empty because your partner at home may not seem as handsome, as beautiful, as desirable. You have a tinge of regret, a feeling of lack. If you were in a relationship with this magical other person you would be happy, feel fulfilled, you would finally, "be enough." You have projected an idea of wholeness, a wish for wholeness, onto this object of desire.

Our multimedia culture particularly feeds such illusions as these. Though as very small children we do not project in this way. Over years of being incessantly exposed to "what is desirable" through advertising on television, radio, newspapers, and magazines our image of who we should be, who our parents should be, what we should look like, how we should dress, how we should talk are manipulated so as to excite dissatisfactions, the sense of being lacking. Should, should, should. Cues for thinking, feeling, and doing are also taken from the outside in. If I walk, talk, or dress, a certain way I will *be enough*. As adolescents and adults we become more and more hypnotised into them believing that, "If I have someone who loves me who looks, dresses, talks, in that way, then I will be happy, never be depressed again, and I will finally be enough!" Again, this is all extrinsic values, ego values. They may help us "fit in" to some degree, but at what expense to our soul! For every increase in extrinsic value we pay out in soul loss.

Now, let us return to the example of looking at that gorgeous man or woman on the street. Desire-as-lack says, I need this person to be complete. If I could make love to this person, if I could marry this person. Could, could, could! As with the shoulds, I am not allowing myself just to enjoy the experience, like the croissant. Now imagine appreciating this person as one would appreciate a flower. Not to pick it, not to possess it, but to appreciate that the world has beauty, and I am part of the world, and, therefore, I too am beautiful. As with the croissant, enjoy the simple appreciation that arises, not trying to suppress it, not clinging to it and not acting it out. Not trying to hold onto the other person, or pursue them relentlessly, but simply letting the experience touch you without having to try and nail it down in time and space. When someone says, "take a picture it will last longer," to somebody who has been staring at them, they are fighting against this reality. The hope that a picture will fulfill the desire to hold on to another, or a moment denies the abiding truth of impermanence. But, when we can be-hold persons in all their beauty, we do not objectify them and we do not torture ourselves with the game of surface desire as lack. We then move towards a feeling quality akin to affection which seeks not to 'have', but rather simply appreciate. We can then embrace the moment in its joy without holding, grasping or imagining that we lack or need anything from this other being. You can go so far as fully imagining that you do not require anything from that other being. That you are as complete, as beautiful, as enough as you imagine that other person.

For the even more courageous, in particular if these others which you are envisioning and imagining is of the opposite sex, imagine you are them. Close your eyes, toss your hair back as they do, even if you don't have any, and imagine walking and holding yourself as they do. Imagine the full presence, "the enoughness," you imagine them having, being fully within you! An exercise I conduct often with individuals who are "infatuated" or "love sick" with someone who will not return their affection is this: I ask them to write down what it is that they are so attracted to in this other person they are obsessing about. When they have finished, we review what they have written down with this question in mind, "In what ways can I internalize those very qualities I imagine the other person having?" In essence, this attraction is a call not towards other-obsessing but to self-actualization. My apprehension of who I think this person is, calls me to actualize potential that lies fully within my own being. Whatever I love in the other is exactly the qualities in myself my soul is calling me to own and develop.

We make a mess out of so much romantic love today. We have close to a 70 percent divorce rate and rising, and 40 percent of all marriages on any given day in America are remarriages. At the root of the problem lies this truth: *romantic love is all too often misplaced spirituality.* In a materialistic society the only thing we allow ourselves to be lost in, to surrender to, is the rapture of romantic love for another flesh and blood person. Such urges only became fashionable some 800 years ago. The sparks were first struck by the troubadours of the 12th century, today in the 20th they have become a firestorm. So often, what we are attracted to in the other is exactly the qualities we need to actualize in ourselves. When we can withdraw the projection and use the energy of desire to take us back to our own spiritual growth, tremendous freedom and clarity in relationships become possible. As Ovid said, "Romantic love is a form of madness."

In such ways desire need no longer bring us a sense of lack, a vacuum. We discover, instead, the fullness and abundance of life, the flame of the spirit-that-moves-in-all-things. It initially emerges as the surface desires we all share: for food, shelter, warmth and love. But they are just expressions of something much more immeasurable, most often hidden, the desire of Being itself. This deep core of desire can be touched at any time in living our life. Amness is that fire: our first person experience of the world, our vital connection. Waking up in the moment and being blown away by the miracle of living. But, as we have more and more confrontations with not-me, we begin to disown more and more of who we are. To disown our fiery experience is to spend more and more time coveting that which we think others have and who others are. Without realizing what we are doing we begin to put out our fire. The only true fire.

Polishing And Naming

As we have seen, once we leave the shores of amness and begin to become aware of separation, the self emerges and imagines itself ship-wrecked and cut off from the vital source of Being. In Western Judeo-Christian creation mythology, we fall from grace, here understood as wounded innocence and leave the Garden of Eden, paradise, to the fall here understood as wounded innocence. The development of the self parallels this scenario as one continually confronts the mystery of becoming vacillating between the fall (injuries as one collects experiences) and redemption (re-uniting with oneness and amness); all the while trying to understand the grand drama of living. As the self develops through life we try to cope with further falls (injuries as one collects experiences) and understand what is happening to us. Two of our misguided attempts at understanding, however, can unnecessarily exacerbate these wounds: sin and naming.

We attribute our hurts to something we did "wrong" or some "flaw" in something that preceded us ("original sin"). But in a deeper sense nothing is "wrong," amness abides. And "sin" is not a fatal fault but a stairway to the stars. "Sin" in its original etymology did not mean some inherent evil but rather, "missing the mark." Big difference. When we "miss the mark," we have created an opportunity for learning. No one expects the beginner in archery to hit the bull's eye the first time. Every time we miss the mark is an opportunity to adjust and explore how we can improve. No mistakes, only lessons! No punishment, only polishing! Each time I failed a TaeKwonDo testing I was polishing my skill and grace as a martial artist. This is a key concept in the development of the self. Innocence is the knowledge of one's divine spark, one's sacred being that is inalienable. It is usually damaged when we attribute missing the mark to something fundamentally "wrong" with us. One is "bad," "no good," a "broken machine," a complete "#$%* up," "unredeemable," "trash," "garbage." Such naming destroys innocence and openness and an ability to learn from experience. Because a complete "@#$* up" is someone who cannot learn, "They don't just make mistakes by God, they ARE a mistake." The greatest gift we can give our children and each other is remembering that we can learn from "mistakes," and make "mistakes," without BEING a mistake.

Names that deny our fundamental capacity for connecting with Being can be so dangerous. We may accept them as our due for having lost our innocence in the process of growing. I remember a 5-year-old child I saw years ago who was the youngest of four boys. His parents brought him to see me because of continued behavioral problems. The name on the file was "James." Yet, as I interviewed the parents they continued to refer to the young boy as "Stinker". I asked them why. The mother responded, "Well, when he was just an infant for some reason he had a lot of gas and his grandmother used to call him Stinker. The name just stuck I guess." Trying to hide my disbelief I decided to interview "Stinker" before going any further. When I talked to this young man I asked him his name, he said without much forethought, "Stinker." Then I asked him if he liked his name. He looked up at me with his big brown eyes which began to fill with tears. He could not even say the word "no," he just shook his head from side to side, then dropped it looking at the ground once again.

I later had the parents come back in and I said, "The first therapeutic intervention I am recommending is simply calling your son by his God given name, James. I want you to tell all of his brothers and friends and family to call him James and to strike the name Stinker from your vocabulary. Come back in a month and let me know how things are going." Amazingly, it worked. His behavior improved dramatically. I never saw the family again, but I will never forget the power of naming since working with the case of "Stinker."

I have had similar experiences with clients who have had spouses who went by nicknames like "Tiny," "Junior,"or "Tubby." The wives would complain about their, "never growing up," "acting like a child," and "not taking any responsibility." I sent them home with the instructions to use their first names, and it always had some good effect. Unfortunately, every case does not change as dramatically as did "Stinker's," but if nothing else it usually opens a door for change.

PRUNING

Recall how we compared the self to the image of a tree. Taking the metaphor further we can see how "being before the I" is much like the seed of the tree. The acorn does not even look like the image of the future tree. It is prior to it, yet contains all the essential ingredients to be a large oak. Then with fertile soil, water and sunshine, the germination begins. Over time the germinating seed becomes a

117

shoot and eventually turns into the sapling; finally, a stage in the life of a tree that gives a hint of what is to come. The barest most fragile outlines of a trunk and limbs appear. The tree is beginning to unfold reveal and manifest itself.

The growth becomes more rapid, desire takes hold as it reaches ever upward. Then the wind blows the branches; lightning strikes; animals and insects nibble on the leaves, and the branches. The tree, so full of desire and potential begins to be pruned by life, reality, the elements, weather, and even people. Pruning, like the "not-me" experience, forces the tree to put energy into the trunk and into the roots, its foundation. In this way, a strengthening continues. The trunk widens and the roots deepen when the branches and leaves are pruned. A tree with unchecked growth may gain quickly in height, but its stability and durability are sacrificed.

Pruning, at first, feels like a death and at some level it is. But, a death that ultimately can lead to further growth, development, and strength. When we prune a tree, it is not simply that the tree now lacks a branch, rather it is that more energy and nourishment are funneled toward the trunk and roots of the tree. Therefore, the desire in the tree is not destroyed, but transformed. Its fire is stoked in the roots and trunk creating, overall, a healthier tree. Similarly, tragedy can polish our heart and prune our soul, ripening and deepening our rootedness in Being as a more robust self emerges. In this way tragedy and pain sear away the unhealthy layers of the ego, so a more luminous self can begin to shine through.

Pruning is also a useful image when working with relationships whose vitality has dried up. When people come to me and say their marriage is "dead," or "all the life" has gone out of the relationship, I ask them to imagine a tree. Is it that perhaps the case the tree only looks dead because it is winter? Perhaps the tree of the relationship in fact has some dead branches and leaves? Prune it back, care for it, water it, then let's see in the spring if life comes back. In this dynamic period of history, with its constant material progress and unchecked economic growth, we develop the illusion that relationships (and everything else!) should simply get better and better. Thankfully, there are and always will be teachers of impermanence. Few things are as organic as relationship, which actually follow remarkably the rhythms we find all around us, if we will just look and pay attention. In the seasons of relationship, one must learn to be a gardener and not a hunter. Thich Hach Nan the Vietnamese monk is fond of saying that when a man comes to him and says, "I am no longer in love with my wife, she has grown bitter and unhappy," he responds, "Your wife has seeds of happiness and unhappiness in her: which seeds have you been watering? Go home and try to water her seeds of happiness."

LETTING DESIRES DIE

When we are confronted by another's suicide a terrible darkness can cloud our sky. The question "why, why, why?!" haunts our mind. Many times the darkness so enshrouds others that the mysterious phenomenon of multiple suicides sweeps through a community.

The only way to understand this experience is to wade into the marsh, the bog where the dark spirit of suicide lies. We must look within our own darkness to understand how one can become lost in the despair that consumes a life in suicide. Within us there is a place that is hidden from the world. A closet perhaps where past wounds, failings, and mistakes are stored, accumulating dust and spider webs and sometimes germinating hideous feelings in the endless night that covers it. Without letting anyone enter this dark corner of our soul, we can easily heap increasing self-blame and self-hate upon ourselves, multiplying the hurt of the injuries and wounds. Our sense of worth is ever more compromised until we feel completely worthless, without value, a nothing.

It has been said that what hunger is to the body, depression is to the soul - spiritual hunger. More then anything else, suicide seems to be an acting out of the emptiness in all of us - the emptiness of a culture, the emptiness of dogmas that leaves someone utterly bereft of hope and refusing healing.

So often what is necessary, however, is not suicide but egocide: A giving up of the false self-identifications to which we are attached, and an embracing of that ego death which can lead back to a sense of our real being. Similarly, those of us who want to help the severely depressed, the sufferer on the verge of suicide, do well to contact our own amness. In the words of the Eastern sage of Taoism, Chuang Tzu, "The sages of old first got Tao for themselves, then got it for others."

Dealing with the suicidal feelings that plague many, we can find a powerful model for dealing with all our failed desires. Through our incessant confrontations with non-being, we can see it is essential to our becoming more and more conscious. The wounds we receive from the world then have a sacred quality. Our very soul is opened up and new questions begin to emerge about who we are, what we have been about and where are we going. The deaths of desire are always a call to our depths.

We all are vulnerable to wounds; illnesses, accidents, rape, abuse, loss of a job, a marriage, financial security, or sanity. We begin once again the dark night of the soul. We journey into pathos and touch anguish. Pain and despair threaten to crack or even explode the boundaries of who we thought ourselves and our lives to be. Good. This is when trans-formation (literally changing form) takes place.

When we are willing to relinquish our old myths and allow new stories, new myths to emerge in us, we are reborn. When we are not able to travel this path into pathos, grief becomes repressed and we repeat our same old story over and over. So often, many difficulties from depression to anxiety and even psychosis have their origination in such unlived pathos.

The wounding we suffer when our desires are disappointed amplifies our sensitivity and awareness. I often tell people that at such times they walk in a sacred state. We all have been touched by experiences like this when we do not eat, sleep or have no libido. Instead of seeing this as "pathology," we can see how it mirrors the journey one takes on a vision quest or during any form of spiritual retreat such as fasting. The challenge is moving from one's personal melodramatic tragedy to the grander pattern of sacred wounding and the inner development of a new story. To take advantage of them we must not simply medicate and cover up our grief; we must allow our small story of failure to become engaged in the greater universal pattern of rebirth. This is a natural process.

Stuart, after the break up of his marriage, found himself quite unconsciously drawing pictures repeatedly of medieval knights. He engaged himself in the drama of the mythic hero fighting the dragons, and when he consciously realized that, it helped him feel the greatness of his struggle. His local story connected with the pattern of a greater mythic tale and in so doing gave his life a context and meaning not before available.

There is deep suffering and soul-wrenching during our time, yet, it is exactly when we feel most destroyed we are about to grow. The Phoenix rises again. "The sacred wound is the critical act through which the mortal achieves divinity...So, too, must you breach that story that denies your full unfolding. You may deny and resist this truth with all the strength you can muster, but the woundings will continue, sometimes relentlessly, apparently meaninglessly, until you agree to wake up." (Jean Houston). There always is something trying to be born from the wound. Recall how it was when Moses and Jesus felt most alone, most abandoned, most wounded that the greatness, the divinity, the sacredness of their path, their life, their purpose was revealed. When in the grips of that grief, allow yourself to realize something is trying to be born through you. It is difficult, excruciating work, but it is possible and the sun will rise again.

The inner sanctuary of the self is often like a china shop full of our precious desires and their supposed realizations. When the shop is ravaged we do not want anyone else or any other redemptive relief or faith. But it is the breakage that allows time to create a stronger self, a broadening of consciousness and a more rooted ontological trust. Then, the healing ointment of forgiveness enters us and heals the betrayals we feel, whether by a person or a group or idea; Particularly when its someone with whom you have an intimate connection, a rich sharing of soul. Forgiveness then when it comes, is a potent force. Not only is the "betrayer" forgiven, so is life. Our heart stretches as we begin to notice how the "betrayer" moves us into the larger story of our lives. In this way, the betrayer and betrayed are carriers of divinity and sacredness to each other. It is no wonder that betrayal is at the heart of most spiritual traditions. To truly forgive, one must give oneself away. Even as one's heart breaks, it opens to vaster realms of Being, the reality of a love that transcends possession. A prayer that a client and I came up with who had experienced a deeply broken heart embraces this theme:

> *"God break open my heart, plant the seeds of love*
> *that flower, Lord Break open my heart and let me*
> *grow, My heart is broken and now I know how deep*
> *love goes, Lord Break my heart open and free me from*
> *my complicated way of loving, Lord in embracing this*
> *broken heart I am deeply free. Break me, purify me,*
> *renew me."*

Traditional psychotherapy takes almost an opposite approach, what I will call "wound denial." When someone feels wounded because of disappointed desire, it is more important to just stop the pain than find out what truth the broken desire is speaking. One might ask the patient, "What did you do wrong to incur this wound and how can you change your behavior to avoid it in the future?" The hidden assumption is that it is possible to live a wound-free life and failing to do so is to have made a mistake, or even to be a mistake. We must develop a way to bless our wounds, our darkness, our own personal abyss. In so doing we learn and our hearts grow as never before.

THE MYTH EXERCISE

Write down some of the illusions you have lived by. The painfully unrealistic expectations that have become etched deep down in your belly. Take your time. This is a powerful way to do some emotional house cleaning. You want to clear out enough "unreality" to the point that you can begin to live by the Samurai Warrior saying, *"Expect nothing, be ready for everything"*. Ah, now there is a powerful way to approach one's life journey! It is said that happiness is inversely proportional to the quantity of one's expectations. The more we expect, the less happiness we will have. I have found this to be so very true. Ultimately, what stands in the way of happiness is our inflated sense of entitlement.

To live with this burning ember one must become fearless. Not fearless in the usual sense of the word. Rather, being fearless in the most profound sense means *not fearing who one truly is*. We think of being fearless as being unafraid of the world around us. But to reach that state - an initial step is required - we must accept who we are and where we are.

124

Write down an answer to the question:

What is the name of the greatest illusion in my life?

Name your unrealistic illusions. The first of these are the ego illusions and identifying and naming them is a great step in psychospiritual development. Finally, after spontaneously writing without editing for as long as anything "comes out," Take the next step and answer the questions:

> *What would my life look like if I completely let go of*
> *that expectation?*
> *What would I have to give up?*
> *Would people still like me?*
> *Could I live with myself if I just never _____*
> *ever again?*

Again, do some spontaneous, unedited, uncensored writing until you have nothing left to write. You have begun the sacred quest of the soul's journey towards home. Leaving the shores of the known, limited, surface desires of your life and following a call from the core desires you know way down in your bones are crying to be heard.

PART III:

THE QUEST

"Soon the child's clear eye is clouded over by ideas
and opinions, preconceptions and abstractions.
Simple free BEING becomes encrusted with the burdensome
armor of the ego. Not until years later does
an instinct come that a vital sense of mystery has
been withdrawn. The sun glints through the pines,
and the heart is pierced in a moment of beauty and
strange pain, like a memory of paradise. After that
day...we become seekers."
~ Peter Matthiessen

CHAPTER 4:

THE QUEST
FOR CERTAINTY

Ah, what a dusty answer gets the soul
When hot for certainties in this our life!
~George Meredith

The quest for being starts from the assumption that we are not enough. We in some way lack what we need to be complete. Sometimes it is a lack of the basic building blocks of our lives; food, water and shelter. At other times we lack the fundamental emotional completeness we hunger for; love, acceptance and approval. We often times try to compensate for these through filling the emptiness with substitutes such as alcohol, drugs, junk food, clothes, cars, status, houses, friends, fame and fortune. The list goes on and on. The bottom line is that once cut off from our vital connection, we experience ourselves and our world as desperately not enough. Our own first person-experience of the world has become short circuited, inadequate and empty.

This sense of incompleteness is the starting gun for the quest for being. The incessant searching, seeking for wholeness and for feeling alive begins. What determines whether or not this searching is simply a "rat race" or a meaningful quest is the awareness of the seeker. The more unaware the person is of their divine discontent, the more likely they will simply gather more and more stuff. This truth is found on bumper stickers and T-shirts today, "The one who dies with the most toys wins; Buy Pepsi, get more stuff." There is nothing inherently wrong with stuff, however, when it becomes an obsession and the main purpose to one's life - then the amassing of more "stuff" begins to look like a caricature of an empty life; bigger houses, more expensive food, faster cars, more, more and more. Unfortunately, more is never enough. Because more food, sex, drugs, shelter, transportation and information will never fill the spiritual black hole within. "More" will never heal the wound or restore the vital roots of Being.

The more conscious one is, the more one has reflected on the question of "meaning" in one's life, the more one can move from the unconscious "rat race" that has no meaning, that has no winning, that will simply turn us around and around in the maze of materialism, to a quest for vision, purpose and clarity. In so doing, one can begin to restore the vital connection while also reaching forward to find a way to feed not simply our body, but our soul, the essential core and root of our being.

In the largest sense, we have all been "seekers" since the moments when our easy childhood experiences of amness became more fugitive. Our desires are, at bottom, blind seeking. If we allow ourselves to wake up to the futilities of this "blindness" we become "seekers" in a more conscious sense. We can become aware of the fact that all along, underneath the endless surface desires lies a more profound need. Of course, most of us still are unsure what this need is. Often after giving up on "things" we seek "certainties." We talk to ourselves something like this, "If I could just be certain, absolutely certain what is true and what is false, what is real and what is not, then I can control my desires. I need a black and white world with no grey, no ambiguity." This is at least a step towards consciousness. We, in seeking certainties, are more aware that we are seeking, yet this quest for control which so many of us fight day in and day out also has it's difficulties, as Janet found out:

> *The world around me felt so chaotic, nothing was certain. I was 23 years old on the outside, but inside I felt 3. I wasn't ready to make adult decisions, I was overwhelmed with my feelings. They made no logical sense. I didn't feel I could trust my emotions, they led into areas that felt unpredictable, uncertain, scary and just insane. So I clung to anything that sounded black and white, decisive, irrefutable. I tried to break the world down into manageable chunks of data. I felt control of my eating and cleaning. As long as I could eat only certain things and I could keep my house spotless, then I felt some sense of peace. The unpredictable wild aspects of life I just shut out of my life and mind. Unfortunately, the more I tried to shut them away, the more they would knock at my door.*

As Janet discovered, trying to measure and perceive what was true and false from the position of certainty was not so easy.

CERTAINTY AND REALITY

So far as the laws of mathematics

refer to reality, they are not certain.
And so far as they are certain,
they do not refer to reality.
                    ~Einstein

The word certain comes from the vulgar Latin *certanus,* or the Latin *certus* meaning "determined" and "fixed." Webster's dictionary defines *certain* as that which is "settled, sure, and considered inevitable; further that which is not to be doubted or questioned, is never failing, but always controlled, unerring, and positive." There is an immense human need for that which is unerring and unfailing. All over the world people ache for something or someone that will **never** let them down. Moreover, the great march of Western Civilization, with all the material benefits a quest for mental certainties has achieved, makes us particularly apt to keep marching even when we loose the very roots of our own divinity.

When I work with children in my practice, however, I do not see an inborn desire for certainty. Rather, there is an abiding wonder and a reverence for their moment to moment first person experience of the world. This is a birthright we all came into the world with, the ability to make something out of nothing. Children remind us of this in the sheer delight they derive from scribbling on a blank page of paper or making up a story. What I mean by *reverence* arises from the core of reverie that lies at its heart. *Reverie* comes from the word *rever* meaning "to wander," a "dreamy imagining or fanciful musing." A visionary state that is almost like daydreaming. Children immerse themselves in reverie quite naturally. In fact, we might go so far as to say that infants live in a constant state of reverie when they are immersed in amness. Their ontological foundation, and ours, is one of curiosity, discovery, and most important, play. Watching children playing, one discovers a rhythm and cadence to their behavior, as if they had mesmerized themselves. Silence and wonder live in that experience.

Early on, however, we all begin to learn that "certainty" is a valuable commodity in school and society. The ability to clarify what is "true" and what is "false" becomes crucial to our educational survival. Columbus "discovered" America not in 1493 or 1491, but 1492. If we are not certain of the answer, we quickly learn the consequence of getting something "wrong." We fail. I vividly recall coloring a tree in elementary school with purple leaves. The teacher said, "That's not right, leaves are **not** purple, they are *green!*" I remember jumping outside of my own experience of spontaneous creativity and joy and looking at myself from my teacher's perspective and suddenly feeling embarrassed, ashamed and guilty in being "wrong." We have all had experiences like this one. The culture we are taught follows more the words of Samuel Johnson, "He is no wise man who will quit a certainty for an uncertainty," then the words of Einstein at the beginning of this section.

As I grew older I realized I should have said it was a purple plum tree blossoming with vivid lavender flowers in spring time. Unfortunately, I had not yet learned how to stand in my own experience and feel grounded in it. Obviously, it is important for us to learn what others see. Teacher's are suppose to help "educate" children to reality, just as a psychologist must "ground" a patient with hallucinations in a psychiatric ward to "what is real" rather than "what is false." Tragically, in the process the vital connection to one's first person experience is lost. All too often the baby *(the vital connection)* is thrown out with the bath water (unconscious, asocial behavior and relating). How different the experience would have been if the teacher had said, "Michael, what a beautiful, colorful tree. It looks like plum blossoms in full bloom. Now how about drawing me a tree like the one on the playground with green leaves. Could you do that for me?" In this way one validates the unique vision and creativity of individuals while allowing them an opportunity to learn how to live in the more day-to-day world as well.

This approach is crucial to working effectively with those who may be having what are usually called "hallucinations." Being aware that such people are trying to express their authentic experience of the world - no matter how different or bizarre it may seem to me - I begin by validating their hallucination or delusion. I know that, in a very real way they are articulating in their own language as a way back to their *vital connection.* Once we are able to accept and validate a person's experience of the world, then we can begin to distinguish how much of the rest of the world they are able to perceive. Sometimes, if we patiently explore the other's world, we find ourselves learning some powerful lessons that shake our certainties about what is real and not real. Oftentimes what we call "craziness" is nothing more than invalidated experience. When confronted by the unknown, in an experience we are not familiar with, we feel uncertain, unpredictable and unreal. As a result we fear it, because it gets in the way of our quest for a certain, predictable, black and white world we have come to depend on and trust.

It is understandable that we may fear another's reality. It might crack the protective shell of the certainties we have sought to navigate our own experience of the world. But, we are ill-advised to deny the endless mysteries that surround us every moment of every day. To really open ourselves to the vast uncharted experience around us, to realize that perhaps nothing is certain, is the moment we really begin to meet life.

How precious will be the therapist on the psychiatric ward who could then approach the "crazy" one in this way: "What remarkable, intricate and beautiful visions you have. They are the spark of something vitally important dwelling inside you seeking expression. I honor them. I look forward to exploring them in detail with you soon. In the meantime, I am infinitely curious about what might these visions have to say about putting on some clothes and getting something to eat?"

I have a collegue who described the way he works with those with psychotic experience in a letter to a colleague about to work for the first time with "schizophrenic" patients. When he uses the term "primary process" he is referring to the seemingly meaningless language spoken by those immersed in psychotic experience. This primary language is distinct from our everyday, socially verifiable language, like the one I am using in writing this book:

Primary process language is like any "foreign" language. You won't do well trying to learn it from a book or tape. Just immerse yourself in it for that couple of hours a week. This is an act of faith, because once you find yourself thinking and speaking in primary process language, you have abandoned (VOLUNTARILY and out of "love") Ego defenses almost completely. You are responsible to help people who have no boundaries, limited and fragmented defensive structures, to learn that they have two languages and that you will teach them yours while they teach you theirs. There is no such thing as meaningless content; there is only stuff that we are not astute enough to understand. Just as you do with a dream (which is also in symbolic language images), feel free to ask for clarification. Don't expect people to translate; they can't. Like a dream, they will give you more images in an attempt to help you over where you are stuck. Play and humor are healing. The more fun everyone has, the better all of you will be able to deal with the pain and despair. Remain humble. Accept that you don't know anything. Repeat over and over that you are the student, they the teachers....Be in awe of that.[1]

Sadly, I have often found that many parents, teachers and therapists assume encouraging the creative uniqueness of a child's or client's world might lead to an ungrounded individual. There is an underlying cultural distrust at work here. My own experience, both personally and professionally, has been just the opposite. When we have our uniqueness and eccentricity accepted and even blessed, we become better grounded. In fact, much of what we call "craziness" - an inability to function well in the social world - falls away. It is as if the vital roots of our own first person experience of the world settle into real soil with some sunshine and water thrown in for good measure. When the soul has been fed, people are often more willing to put energy and time into day-to-day activities. The mistake we so often make is to wait to feed the soul until it is too late. Our culture has usually seen feeding the soul as the last priority. Feed the body first, the mind second and sometime in the far distant future we will attend to the heart and soul. We wonder why we live meaningless empty lives. The blessing is when the heart and soul are fed, when we have a true answer to our spiritual hunger; we can toil day and night in body and mind with joy in our hearts. The most beautiful example of this is a mother whose work of drudgery is transformed into divine work when she see's the smile of her children as the only payment she needs. If we could be inspired by God's smile in such a way, we could change the world.

Over the years I became excellent at drawing and coloring green trees. So good in fact, I became "certain" I knew how to draw a tree. My classmates and I had all become accustomed to drawing a symbol of a tree and no real tree in particular. We have all seen this kind of tree. A straight brown line for a trunk and then a green circle on top for the leaves and branches. At a very young age, we begin replacing any particular experience of a tree with the symbol of a tree. We do the same with words as we do with drawing. We lump all beings with trunk, branches and leaves into treeness. We then stop looking, really looking, at the incredibly unique beauty of each living tree. I had begun to do that when I had an experience with quite a different kind of art teacher.

On a fresh, crisp spring morning in Connecticut she took me outside and sat me in front of this huge spreading oak tree. She pointed at it and softly said, "Look, really look at this tree Michael. Look at the branches. See how every branch is different, unique, special. Now look at the leaves, look at all the different colors, shapes and sizes. Do you see a green lollipop?" With a tingle in my spine, I shook my head from side to side, thinking, "Nope, no green lollipop anywhere." Her entrancing voice sounded as if she was revealing to me one of the fathomless mysteries of the universe. And so she was. I could feel her love: love for art, for nature, for that oak tree and every leaf on it and perhaps, more importantly, her love for me and the potential within me to create and learn to love the world as she did. I smiled, she smiled back and said, "Now I want you to draw this tree. Feel it as you draw. Feel every branch, every leaf as it moves and simply just as it is. Follow every little unique twisting, turning line. Draw everything you see." Now those were words that fed my soul. We know when our soul is being fed by the pure joy we feel. I found that "pure joy" in her words and in her very presence. Fortunately, I was still young enough to believe I could draw in the way she talked. I sat down and began to draw with excitement. As I did, I found myself talking to this tree as I had to my old friend, "the maple" at my house. As we talked, I found my hands and fingers busily and joyfully creating with my new friend.

This teacher had invited me into the mystery of life, instead of creating a ready-made conformity that would make me retreat from my own experience, my own *vital connection* with the world. She did so much more than teach me how to draw, she taught me how to see, feel and be. Here is the key question; can we in our day to day lives invite each other and ourselves into the tangible "mystery of life" while still making a living, paying bills and raising children? Of course we can. It takes the kind of love and attention my art teacher had, the kind that lies within each and every one of us. More importantly, it requires seeing every tree as if for the first time. We have to give up our certainties about "how" trees and people are suppose to "look." We have to constantly be open to the "new" and give up the convenient flatness of "certainties."

Of course, some certainty is necessary and good. It is a matter of degree. The green lollipop I had become *certain* was a tree. I had reduced all trees to green lollipops. Certainty reduces the world to a manageable size. However, when the certainty begins to flatten out the world, reducing an indispensable depth and richness it is time to open our eyes again to uniqueness. By reducing the natural complexity that exists in the world, we can take the very life out of our existence that we initially only sought to manage better. Certainty, when it reduces too much, kills the essential mystery that underlies a passionate, full and meaningful life.

RELIGION AND SCIENCE

Obviously, in the beginnings of humanity the quest for certainty and predictability of some kind made absolute sense serving extremely functional purposes. Will we find shelter tonight before the storm comes? Will I see a bear or lion today that could kill me? Will there be food to eat tomorrow? Will we make it through the winter? Will I get sick and die? The great advancement of Western civilization has been working successfully to ease many of these uncertainties, soothing the fears of chaos lurking around the corner, eradicating the ravages of unpredictability. Leading the way have been the great institutions of religion and science.

Religion and science remain the two strongest influences in most of our lives today. It is not surprising then that they have led the search for certainty in our culture. Religion, many scholars concede, grew out of the deep human need for us to explain the unexplainable. With explanation, most believe, comes certainty. It was believed that if we prayed to a supernatural Being, that Being or God, would help us deal with the uncertainty of where we would find our next meal, where we would find shelter and most importantly what happens to us when we die.

Science in our own modern day culture has served a similar purpose, far superior to religion, helping us know where our next meal is coming from, how to have better shelter, and how to travel from place to place. It falls short of religion in addressing the "biggest" uncertainty of all: Death with a capital D. Though science has made inroads into our extending life by a few decades, it has not brought peace to our souls. We may succeed in delaying the end, but never can escape it. Nor has science changed that critical aspect of living - our incessant confrontations with non-being, all the little deaths before the big one.

Our inmost mystery and fear is the reality of death. The final reality of non-being, the fact that at some point in the future, we and all those we love, will cease to be. Death. Say the word "death" to yourself right now. Death. Make it resonate in your mouth making it palpable. It remains one of the most taboo words in our lives today. Sex is far from taboo anymore. Violence is not hidden. We see plenty of people being shot and killed on television. But killing is not the process of dying. It is the slow process of natural dying - the nursing homes filled with people experiencing what should be the most profound last stages of life. As a culture, we have not come to terms with mortality and contingency. Perhaps that is not surprising for a country that has never run out of natural resources. America was built on the feeling of infinite expansion, growth and potential. We worship youth like few cultures ever have. Even the ancient Greeks, who praised the luminescence of youth, were terribly aware of its brevity and held wisdom that only came with age in high regard. Perhaps we may even go so far as to say that old age is also taboo in our culture, as if it is something to be ashamed of that one has wrinkles and "looks old." The signs of age, such as losing hair or going grey, are things to talk about behind someone's back. Almost as if there is something hideously wrong with them. Because belief in unchecked, linear progress, our most widely accepted myth, even our religion, tells us death is to be avoided at all cost. It is seen as an embarrassment, rather than embraced as our salvation.

We gain psychic distance by reducing death to numbers, by simply reporting statistics. Yet, one statistic that might wake us up to reality is that within the next 100 years over 5 billion people will die. In a hundred years almost everyone walking the earth now will be dead. Where do they die. Where is all of this death taking place? It is tragic that few of us will ever be with someone while he or she takes the last breath. We run from it. Science and medicine hide it from us in the sterile rooms of hospitals, coding patients unmercifully as if death is a great evil to fight, as opposed to our ultimate goal, possibility and blessing.

The confrontation with non-being is at the root of incredible suffering in our lives. Death is the ultimate end-point. But, in creeps non-being, in more subtle ways; the economy going under and losing everything I own, losing my home, my favorite pet dying, losing my wallet, losing my marriage, losing my identity, losing my faith, losing my job, losing my child to drugs, losing my sense of meaning and purpose, losing my looks, losing my hair, losing my youth.

The quest for certainty in religion has to do with having answers to all such challenges. Tell me what to do to have a good life, to live a long time, and go to heaven. I will do it, just tell me what to do. We look outside of ourselves in this way to search for certainty and predictability. Religion, under the scrutiny of reason, began to lose its effectiveness as a guarantee of certainty while science became more reliable in helping us maneuver through the world. In a short 150 years science has performed miracles. It has cured illnesses, helped us predict the weather, provided affordable and reliable shelter, and shown us how to grow more food, more reliably, not to mention how to go from place to place faster and more securely. In short, above all other human endeavors, it seemed to have provided us with certainty.

But now even this has been discovered to be an illusion, non-Being again and with a vengeance, for at the very roots of science uncertainty reigns supreme:

> *One day I learned that science was not true. I do not recall the day but I recall the moment. The God of the twentieth century was no longer God. There was a mistake and everyone in science seemed to make it. They said that all things were true or false. They were not always sure which things were true and which were false. But they were sure all the things were either true or false. They could say whether grass is green or whether atoms vibrate or whether the number of lakes in Maine is an even or an odd number. The truth of these claims had the same truth as claims about math or logic. They were true all or none, white or black, 1 or 0.*
>
> *In fact, they were matters of degree. All facts were matters of degree. The facts were always fuzzy or vague or inexact to some degree. Only math was black and white and it was just an artificial system of rules and symbols. Science treated the gray or fuzzy facts as if they were the black-white facts of math. Yet no one had put forth a single fact about the world that was 100% true or 100% false. They just said they all were.*
>
> *That was the mistake and with it came a new level of doubt. Scientists could err at the level of logic and math. And they could maintain that error with all the pomp and intolerance of a religious cult.[8]*

When I first read these paragraphs from Bart Kosko's *Fuzzy Thinking: The new science of fuzzy logic,* I had one of those wonderful, "yes!" experiences. The words gave voice to ideas I had not been able to put into words, *and* he had the scientific authority to give them credibility. Over and over again as a chemistry and math major when I started college, I had felt this lack in science, this pretension, which finally led me away from the natural sciences. Of course, it took a virtual psychotic episode for me to breakthrough this period of my life. The Christian God I grew up with was killed by science for me, then the God of science that I put my faith and love in, died as well. I was set a drift in a chaotic storm with two great currents fighting over my soul, certainty, logic on one side and my emotions and mystery on the other. I felt crucified by the vortex that the two created within my chest. What was I to do. I became suicidal during this time in my life. I remember one whole night sitting on a bridge thinking how easy it would be to end my life. Just one step and I could plunge to my death. What I needed was an egocide, a certaincide, not suicide. I would have to one by one face the death of all the intricately built up expectations I had accumulated about what was true and false, black and white. I had to give up the easy solution of borrowing what my parents, teachers or lovers said was real and find out for myself by slowly paying intimate attention to what was in my own first person experience of the world. Although I felt great fear, I also felt freedom as I withdrew from my chemistry and math courses, uncertain of the future, uncertain of the present, uncertain of everything. The ground itself opened up beneath me, like a yawning abyss.

When we finally admit to ourselves nothing is true 100 percent of the time, it is like a pin hole in an air tight airplane compartment, everything gets sucked right out. Whether this happens to the physics major who has worshiped science, or the devout religious follower who has always thought the bible was 100 percent true all of the time. This awareness initially results in an existential crisis, but inevitably gives rise to something much more real: The emotionally, psychologically and spiritually robust quest begins when the quest for certainty is abandoned. It is a widely accepted psychological truth that fanaticism and fundamentalism are always signals of an unconscious uncertainty that has not yet reached conscious aware-ness. Moreover, when we remain caught in the illusion of black and white certainty, horrendous things can happen. It is only a matter of time until it becomes the justification for the old code of an eye for an eye, and as Gandhi use to say, "If you follow the old code of justice - an eye for an eye and a tooth for a tooth - you end up with a blind and toothless world". However, when we abandon search for black and white certainty, we can embark on the next stage of our psychospiritual journey; the quest for meaning, one which can bring us to the shores of a more loving world.

Loving, Mystery and Imagination

It is not surprising there exists such a precarious relationship between certainty and mystery in our world today. We might say that certainty relates to the realm of logic and mystery to the world of imagination. In our contemporary culture, for the most part, certainty and logic have been the supreme gods and mystery and imagination have been seen as unfortunate stepchildren, only to be tolerated as primitive childlike attempts at explanation when certainty and logic fail. The assumption underlying this modern conflict remains the belief (a myth) that one day, certainty and logic will eradicate and replace everything we relegate to mystery and imagination today. They are always subordinate to certainty and logic. This was not always the case.

One source of the subordinate role mystery and imagination play today relates to our confusing reason with intelligence. The origin of the word intelligence is illustrative. Intelligence comes from the Latin *intellectus,* in Greek it was expressed by *"nous,"* that which is directly and immediately knowable, apprehended and understood. This was in contrast to *ratio,* the Greek word for reason, which was always subordinate to *intellectus.* Reason was the tool, the shovel of *intellectus,* which is itself more akin to intuition. Moreover, intellectus as a mode of knowing was often likened to loving. In fact, in many cultures the verb to love, or loving, or to make love is the same as to know. When we say, "Oh, you know them in the biblical sense," we are invoking the ancient understanding that to truly know someone, or something, one must feel love for that person or thing. To be intimate (in-it-together, literally) is to understand, that is, to "stand-under" and deeply know, in the intuitive *intellectus* way.

Where *ratio* is the process of analysis/differentiation, *intellectus* is the process of synthesis/integration. *Ratio* proceeds logically and analytically, *intellectus* proceeds intuitively and analogically. We could go so far as to say that in the end the imagination *intellectus* is not so much in the mind, as the mind is unceasingly being bathed in the field of imagination and *intellectus.* Fortunately, intuition is just now

145

rediscovered (un-covered) as the powerful mode of knowing that it is.

I often imagine that my art teacher's invitation into the mysteries of life was not so much by a "drawing exercise," as attending to the sheer miracle and uniqueness of the moment, the tree. She was teaching me the art of beholding. To behold one has to have a well developed *intellectus,* a *nous,* a loving that opens not only my mind, but the heart and soul as well. Ultimately she was tutoring me in how to see, hear and feel the numinous in the tree; the unrepeatable, magical suchness of that particular moment. To open myself to the numinous in that special oak, I had to abandon my preconceptions, my assumptions, my quest for certainty and to sit there and see a tree, this tree, as if for the first time. To be like the bird who knows no two trees are alike, but rather, explores the soul of not only each tree, but each branch, each twig, each leaf as worlds unto themselves.

This is where we begin to behold the beauty of each particular being in our lives. When we let go of our certainty of who we assume this person, tree or experience is we then allow ourselves be touched by that which always overflows our simple definitions. In this way we let go of our expectations and assumptions that all too often cloud what is most precious. In so doing, we open ourselves once again to the true experience, the sheer breathless quality of existence. It is this "breathless quality" that has so much to do with loving. What takes our "breath" away is that which is beyond our grasp. When we can admit how much we do not know we have a chance at feeling how vast the world really is.

THE QUEST FOR REALITY

We fill our lives so much with our quest for becoming something - something that looks solid, something grounded, something real. The paradox is that we become so concerned with how we appear from the outside and what others think of us that we begin to forge a mask for the world to see, all the time feeling more and more alienated from the inside.

I recall going through a great phase of assuming I knew what the world was about. I slowly dismissed the unknown and the uncertain to the realm of the non-existent. I prided myself on having "grown up" and "grown out" of childish perceptions of the world. But as a psychotherapist who uses play and art as vehicles for working with children, I very quickly found what I had lost was my ability to behold the miracle of existence. The infinite qualities, textures and subtleties that exist all around us in every moment. The four and five year old children I saw lived in this enchantment, this 'beholding" every moment. For all of my learning, degrees and professed certainties, I was not "plugged in" to the same world as they were. I remembered vague glimmers of it, how exciting it would be to just "play" with my friends. The absolute joy in tossing a ball back and forth, the awe and laughter in playing hide and seek, or peek-a-boo. This way of being in the world becomes alien to most grown adults. Once again I had thrown the baby out with the bath water. What I had thrown away was precisely what I needed most - to remain connected to the world around me in a vital way. This profound sense of connection with the world comes from being able to let go of one's assumptions, preconceptions and categories of what the world is about.

We have already seen how we are taught very early that our experience, our world, is not enough. That our childlike world of imagination where the family car can turn into a Star Cruiser fighting the Legions of Darkness is completely illusory. Believing in spirits, dreams, and other worlds is immature, naive at best, crazy at worst. Yet, our natural state is to know that dreams have virtually equal status to the waking world. Moreover, to the infant and small child, the day world of waking conscious is as "dreamy" in all of its wonder, wildness and terrible beauty as the night world of dreaming consciousness. Unfortunately, in our culture we are taught that it is "not real" as if we definitively know what is real or not. How ironic now that our premier science of modern physics has discovered "reality" is much more strange and "unreal" then even children could have ever imagined. One day our arrogance about the status of the material world will seem as naive as believing the world was flat and the sun revolved around us. Let us not be so quick to assume we "know" much of anything.

I know a Native American healer who revealed to me what it would mean to truly live from our first person experience of the world. For him, the newspaper was pure fiction. If he did not experience something first hand it was not part of his reality. His dreams and visions were much more "real" to him than say, New York City, which he had never visited. This may be a radical idea, but perhaps it serves as a needed counter-balance to our obsession with what is happening on the other side of the world, while we ignore our own dreams, even though they may in the end have infinitely more importance and value. In fact, perhaps listening to our own dreams may turn out to be the best way to help those people on the other side of the world.

For most of our lives we have learned to identify "the real" with the repeatable. The "modern" scientific method is based upon this belief, that what is repeatable is what is certain and therefore true. This confusion ("to fuse with") poses a serious problem. Since life is always changing, nothing is truly repeated. The river of experience flows ever onward. No two bends in the river are exactly alike, nor two trees, nor even two rocks. As we are ever flowing on in our river of personal experience, so too is the river of the ever turning, ever changing and shifting world. Truly, we never step into the same river twice, live in the same body twice, come home to the same family twice, or see the same world twice. The room you are in now is changing this very moment. Subatomically the walls are breathing, the chair, bed or floor you are on is a flowing quantum streaming of electromagnetic energy.

Watch a cat. Cats never walk into the same room twice. They may have been there a hundred, no a thousand times, and they are awake, aware, looking at the myriad of cascading, flowing images, sounds, smells and movements. This is what we have to recover and gain by giving up the quest for certainty and embracing the quest for meaning. This is where we find a different kind of truth; where we may just learn that the foundational experiences of our lives lie in those unrepeatable, never to be seen again moments. This is not about scientific truth, but a truth of a different order altogether.

CERTAINTY EXERCISE

Make a list of those things in your life that you would like to be
more certain about. The ones you find yourself worrying and obsessing about the most. Now ask yourself if you can really live with not
knowing if they ever will turn out the way you wish? In fact, imagine the worst case scenario. What if the very worst thing happened
in each one of those cases. Now ask yourself, not *if* you could live
through it, but *how* you would live through it and make the best of
it. Then, most importantly, what meaning does my life have without
those certainties, what meaning would emerge from this worst case
scenario. How would I then answer the question of "who am I,"
"where am I going," and "who am I becoming." This level of letting
go is terribly difficult. It reminds us of the depth of suffering in the
world. When our precious plans and everything we work for can in
one mighty twist of fate be turned upside down and inside out. The
loss of a loved one, financial ruin, crippling illness - these desperate
times remind us of the incredible potency of life that continues on.
You will touch something more essential in yourself.

CHAPTER 5:

THE VISION QUEST

I understand the large heart of heros...
this I swallow, it tastes good, I like it well,
it becomes mine...
~Walt Whitman

I grew up listening to the tales of the Iliad and the Odyssey. My father who was raised in Florence, Italy, felt these classic mythic tales of heroism, tragedy and drama were good bedtime stories. I would listen as I drifted off to sleep, not knowing where the stories ended and my dreams began. Later, in my undergraduate studies, I realized how those tales of old helped draw me into the spell of the quest for the Holy Grail. I was not fully conscious of how these stories affected me, but they did. Somehow, deep in my bones, the hero's journey spoke to me. Whether an Odysseus journeying towards Ithaca or the Knights of the Round Table slaying dragons, the image itself of life as an incredible adventure flowed through my veins. The desire to meet life fully and completely, engaging in something that really mattered became etched way down in my soul. It is simply part of who I am. I have tried fighting it to no avail. Life became much more simple for me when I surrendered to it. We all have this hunger. The need to make meaning out of our lives, perhaps is the greatest and most ancient call that we all follow. Thoreau said it beautifully when he proclaimed, "I do not want to die without having lived."

These are great sentiments, strong feelings that are rooted in the very human need to transcend our mortality and impermanence. We long desperately to not be forgotten, to allow this ever so fragile spark of life within us to mean something. This immeasurable and inmost yearning lies at the root of the mythic hero's journey.

The quest for the Holy Grail is a vivid tale that symbolizes the universal and individual need for a quest for truth, meaning and purpose. Unfortunately, we usually imagine that we ourselves are not worthy enough to be heroic. We lack the courage, the stamina or talent. As a result, we will content ourselves with staying on the sidelines and let someone else do the "questing." I have found one of the most powerful ways to "quest for meaning" is to write a poem. This one came to me as I began to come out of a dark night of the soul:

THE RAPIDS OF MY LIFE

Glancing down,
I saw
shimmering through
the rapids of my life,
something hidden.

In a moment
I knew
what I did not want
to know.

It was time,
time to dive in,
go deep,
over my head
into the stream
of living.

*During times
like these,
there are those parts
of us who want to
stay dry
at all costs,
on the shore,
or in the boat...*

*Yet, there,
in the swift moving
water,
lay glimmering
my salvation,
and I knew it.*

*In leaping,
my faith grew...
like a small bird
who takes flight,
for the first time...*

*I felt the water
around me,
the rush
of being immersed...*

*Diving in,
deep,
over my head,
towards the
radiance
that was calling me...*

*My hands
reaching out,
suddenly,
in contact with
earth, gravel,
smooth river rock,
and something more...*

*My eyes adjust
the cool water,*

clean and crystal clear,
and there...there,
was a golden glow,
iridesent on the
river bed,

Gold.
What a
thousand civilizations
have lived and died for,
lying here,
In my own life.

Light in the dark,
shining from below,
I cradled it,
and knew...

Within the rapids
of my life,
lay hidden

treasure...

This poem is about how we must go down into the rapids of our life to explore and discover the Source of our experience. Thie gold is the pearl of great price, symbolic of a spiritual calling that requires some sacrifice on our part to achieve. We must be willing to get wet, to get dirty, to get wild if we want to taste the water ourselves, the water of life - to drink of the elixir that lies within the Holy Grail, to find the gold hidden beneath the rapids.

Going into the well is gut-wrenching work. These are times when we have uncontrollable crying spells. We do not eat, we do not sleep. It is as if all the colors of the world have faded and all the water that used to quench our thirst has evaporated. We trudge forward just to make it through the day. As we forge ahead something begins to break free. Simon, a young man I worked with, described his going into the well vividly. He had a lover whom he tragically lost. He felt that his muse, his reason for being, his best friend had simply been yanked away from him suddenly and without warning. He fell headlong into the well of grief:

> *It was as if the ground swallowed me whole. Every-*
> *thing felt alien, strange, different, unreal, most impor-*
> *tantly myself. I had no desire or drive, I couldn't sleep,*
> *I couldn't eat...I felt abandoned and alone. I knew a*
> *part of me was dying...It hurt so much I just wished*
> *all of me would die to stop the pain. Everything*
> *around me reminded me of her. No one could appease*
> *the wound I felt deep within my soul...At night I was*
> *completely and totally in darkness. Everything that*
> *happened to me just hurt from that day forward. There*
> *were times I would miss her so badly I would fall to*
> *the ground and deep howling sounds would come from*
> *my mouth...sounds that didn't even sound human, sobs*
> *that were primal, animal like. She understood me*
> *like no other, she adored me and comforted me like no*
> *other, she knew my hurts, my pains, and she loved me*
> *completely and deeply. With her I felt fully known and*
> *deeply loved.*

As the weeks and months went by Simon began regaining some ground. He described feeling completely disinterested to other women, no matter how physically beautiful. It was meaning he had lost. The meaning that had held his world together had suddenly vanished. Before, she was the center of his life, his universe, his purpose for being alive. Now he had to re-discover meaning, a new meaning in his life, centered in his own experience. Then he had a dream:

> *I dreamed I was paddling a canoe on a river. I was all
> alone, but somehow I felt very connected to the moun-
> tains, trees and wildlife all around me. I was paddling
> upstream, it was hard and difficult. Finally, the cur-
> rent slowed and I found myself in a large open circular
> body of water...It occurred to me that this must be the
> source of the river....A huge underwater spring where
> I could see down to the bottom so clearly....the paddle
> upstream had made me incredibly thirsty...so I bent
> down and began drinking the water with my hands.
> It was cool, sweet and refreshing. I could feel the cool
> mountain breeze caressing the leaves of the trees and
> the light from the sun set something within the spring
> ablaze. I leaned down and was drawn to the sparkling
> at the bottom of the spring. I didn't particularly want
> to go down into this water, but my heart said I must
> go. So I dove into the water, and swam down, farther
> and farther until I put my hands on the glistening...
> As I did I discovered they were pure, beautiful chunks
> of gold. When I brought them to the surface I felt
> overjoyed...tears came to my eyes...the gold glistened in
> the sunlight, with the droplets of water just sparkling.*

At the time of this dream Simon had not read David Whyte's poem. After we had explored the dream using his own associations and amplifications, I shared the poem with him. The synchronicity became both moving and empowering for him. The poem helped open up our working with the dream and led to his penetrating the meaning of "the gold" in a healing way. Simon began to see the gold in the dream as love that is not destroyed by the fiery pain of grief, but rather purified by it. I shared with him how gold is used as an amulet for wounded people throughout the world, the ultimate symbol of immortality and incorruptibility, for it never rusts. For Simon, the gold became a symbol of a more comprehensive and mature spiritualization and illumination of what love meant in his life. The gold helped him move from romantic love for this single individual, to Love with a capital "L". This golden Love he realized in no way depended on the external woman he had a relationship with. In this way Simon moved from feeling abandoned by her to cherishing the past relationship as helping him grow. Needless to say, this was a "big dream" for Simon and led to much healing for him, to put it in his words:

> *I came to realize my journey up the river, to the spring, and diving in the water and going deeper than I had gone was about my grieving over my loss of Julie; the gold was about a love that does not die, does not tarnish, but lasts and endures. I realized the love we shared went on, but I had to be willing to go into the river, the spring of grief, of emotion to retrieve the gold of our love that would transcend even the physical loss of her. It was then that I began to experience Love in a whole new way. She was the touchstone for my finding an inner experience of Divine Love.*

STAGES UPON THE JOURNEY

> *The standard path of the mythological adventure of the hero is a magnification of the formula represented in the rites of passage: separation-initiation-return: which might be named the nuclear unit of the monomyth.*[3]
> ~Joseph Campbell

Joseph Campbell, the great mythologist, helped distill the essential aspects of what he called "the mono-myth." His key insight involved seeing the hidden pattern beneath the worlds many myths, what he called the; "Hero with the Thousand Faces". He identified three main stages of the hero's journey. Campbell usually talks about the hero with the masculine pronoun; however, for our purposes I will be talking in terms of us and we. We have all had microcosmic heroic quests. This is not just an experience that occurred in ancient or medieval times, it is constantly being undertaken now in everyone's life. So I encourage you to let your imagination conjure up images and times when you have felt similar feelings as we discuss the path of the hero's quest.

The first stage is *separation* or *departure*. As the mythic hero we initially find ourselves contented in our common everyday life whether in a hut or a castle. Then something or someone appears luring us away, or calling us to adventure. We know instinctively that to respond means we must leave our known world behind.

The second stage is the *threshold*. The threshold is reached when, after our initial leaving the known world behind us, we encounter a shadow presence, usually a guard preventing our movement forward in our quest. Through intuition, creativity and courage we find some way to defeat, trick or out-maneuver this dark guard, and in so doing may enter the "realm of the dark" to fight dragons, be slain by an opponent, descend into death with dismemberment or even crucifixion. Once we heroically move beyond the threshold, we then encounter "a world of unfamiliar yet strangely intimate forces."

These forces may threaten, test, or help us on our sacred journey. Ultimately, there will be a supreme ordeal before we can gain our reward. The final triumph may be union in a sacred marriage *(Herios Gamos)*, a blessing from a father-creator, our own divinization or the stealing of boon that we came to gain, such as Prometheus' fire. All these rewards symbolize the expansion of Being, in what Campbell termed, "illumination, transfiguration, and freedom."

The final stage is the *return* or *incorporation*. After being blessed by the underworld powers, the resurrected hero must now leave the "kingdom of dread," and return to the world and restore the village with the gift of his expanded self (being), sometimes symbolized by a sacred elixir or other magical emblem. As Campbell summarizes:

> *A hero ventures forth from the world of common day into a region of supernatural wonder: fabulous forces are there encountered and a decisive victory is won: the hero comes back from this mysterious adventure with the power to bestow boons on his fellow man.*[4]

The hero's journey describes the archetype of our quest for meaning. Today, so many of our cultural heroes do not measure up to Campbell's description. Ask most children or even many adults who their heroes are, and they will more often then not pick someone adored in the media for mere money, good looks or athletic ability. Rarely, are such people those who have crossed the borders of the known world to emerge embodying more transcendent values.

The word hero, however, comes from a Greek root heros, ("to watch over or protect,") denoting more than simple celebrity. The hero was a protector and guardian of cultural values. In fact, the hero is one who symbolically infused new blood (value, passion, vitality) into a culture. As psychological archetype in Jung's sense; however, the hero lives in all of us as an image that pulses and breathes in our inner life. Most of us consciously feel there is no room for being heroic in our own lives. To "swallow" it and "make it mine" as Walt Whitman says, is for other people, not for me. Ah, but there is the miracle. Today, more then ever, the chance to confront one's own dragons, to travel into one's own dark wood is truly possible. It requires the inner journey that awaits all of us at every moment of our lives. It involves as much grandeur, suspense, and need for courage as any story of medieval knight's. To travel to the unknown parts of yourself, that is something not even Michael Jordan in his Nike Airs can do for you. At the same time, that journey is precisely what gives you more importance than a Michael Jordan, for you are the only one breathing with your lungs and living your life. You alone are the author of the novel of your life, the composer of the symphony of your unfolding story, the center of your universe...your first-person experience of the world. Native culture knew this. Native cultures could have forged you in the fire of this truth as soon as you were old enough and sent you forth to find the hero within. There is a name that resounds through all cultures and times for the initiation you would take at the threshold of adulthood, one that would parallel the heroics of no less than a Prometheus stealing fire from the gods: *vision quest.*

The Vision Quest

The sun was filtering through the clouds lighting up the mountains ahead of me as I drew near my destination. I couldn't see another human being in any direction. I had been backpacking on my own for close to a week, preparing for what seemed like my whole life for the coming days. A vision quest.

The phrase *vision quest* captured my imagination from the first time I heard it. A quest for vision. A quest for purpose. A quest for direction. I intuitively felt I had been on a vision quest my whole life, but now I had journeyed to the heart of the back country in Alberta, Canada, with no idea of what was in store for me.

Boys and girls undertook the traditional vision quests as the main rite of passage to mark their transition from childhood to adulthood. Arnold Von Gennep's book, *The Rite of Passage*, identified three typical phases: *Severance, Threshold,* and *Incorporation*. Obviously, these parallel the stages of the hero's journey according to Campbell: *Separation, Threshold, and Return.* Yet, the vision quest was not just a story told about heroes in the past whom we had no chance of ever talking to or meeting. Rather, the vision quest was a ritual that offered the initiate a chance to "swallow...the large heart of heroes."

One undertook a vision quest as a snake attempts to shed its skin. News goes through the village that the person undertaking the quest is going to die. In fact, the confrontation with death in the wilderness, one's own mortality, is the hallmark of the vision quest. This is the severance phase. Severing one's relationship with family and friends and ultimately one's own life. The vision quest both serves as a powerful vehicle for severing the umbilical cord we discussed in chapter 2 and bringing about a confronting of non-being (death) in a healthy way. The movement from severance, threshold, and to incorporation symbolically recapitulates our most natural progression - being born. The world we know we are leaving was our womb; our severance was the journey through the birth canal and crossing the threshold was our moment of birth. Incorporating what we were into our new world of adulthood is like the infant's bringing his womb-grown being into a new wondrous and wild world. The pattern of the rite also parallels the birth of consciousness into a social reality. In fact, we have here the core pattern of our day-to-day, moment-to-moment process of living. The great teacher of impermanence - The Great Holy Mystery - we might say, uses this ever-present vehicle to teach us. The constant transformations that we need to live over and over involves this severance, threshold, incorporation - it is the pattern we everyday mortals use on our spiraling paths of self-discovery and most importantly of soulful living. In our dance of being, we incessantly get to the point of asking ourselves, what in this moment am I being asked to separate from, let go of, sever. Where or what is the threshold, and then, what am I being asked to in-corporate, ingest, digest. This is a never ending, spiraling process, fundamental to all organic growth.

Attempting to submit myself to this pattern in embracing my own vision quest, I had spent months tying up loose ends with friends and family and also discussing with many people why I was undertaking this seemingly bizarre journey through grizzlies, mountain lions and the harsh elements, culminating in four days and three nights without food or water.

We recalled how throughout history going into the wilderness, alone without food, has been a universal way of obtaining Vision, emotional maturity, spiritual insight and the cultivating of one's inner voice or inner wisdom. Jesus went into the wilderness for 40 days and 40 nights while fasting in his struggles. Moses climbed his mountain in solitude to meet his God at the burning bush. In fact, every great prophet of spiritual intensity has undergone this solitary period of reflection, to then bring back its fruits to the community.

The severance permits the second stage of walking across the threshold, the actual ordeal of the passage itself. It is the birthing of self in the wilderness. It involves pushing oneself beyond one's normal way of being in the world; walking through the purifying fires of hell in an effort to polish one's soul. In this stage of confronting non-being, death, and contingency, we can rely on the template we have inside from the actual movement we have taken through the birth canal itself. When we force ourselves (or when we are forced) out of our habitual way of being-in-the-world, we are confronted with the new, the unexpected, the uncertain. On the vision quest, the uncertain and unpredictable events encountered are understood as inherently meaningful, bearing synchronicity, serendipity and most importantly, vision. All these are the fruit of the quest.

Incorporation is the process of harvesting the meaningful fruit of our symbolic confrontation with our own death. It involves the arduous act of translating the intense experiences and visions obtained during the quest into one's day-to-day life in society. This process or task can take days, months, even years. Jesus and Moses both had to come back to share what they had learned in the depths of their solitude. Their vision quests informed the rest of their lives and countless generations since. We can see here the inmost truth that relationship and communion increase directly in proportion to the depths one is able to reach in solitude. For, as one begins to tap what is most deeply personal within one's soul, one also begins to access what is most universal.

Who should undertake a vision quest? Clearly, tradition tells us that you don't have to be a monk, prophet or founder of a religion in order to undergo a vision quest. It is for anyone who hears the call. When should one undertake a vision quest? The most opportune times are usually during a turning point in one's life or when dealing with a crisis. Major life transitions such as divorce, death of a loved one, change of career, or finding out you have a terminal illness are all powerful moments. A vision quest turns the emergency into what it truly is, a spiritual emergence.

As has already been said, most indigenous cultures don't have the adolescent storm and stress or the dislocations of mid-life that plague western "civilized" culture. The crucible of such a rite of passage as the vision quest served to contain and; therefore, help transform these intense emotions into the birth of a new self, forged with a new name and new vision, as opposed to falling prey to addiction, despair, and even suicide. All of these destructive modes of being can be thought of as failure to enter the mythic/symbolic realm of death. Instead the person literally tries to kill the old self, without understanding rebirth and regeneration. The vision quest is a powerful and appropriate metaphor for one's whole life journey, the answer to the questions raised in chapters 2 and 3. It's most important feature is that life is not strictly about "dying" to the old. During the adolescent vision quest one makes a fearless inventory of one's childhood and retains those essential aspects of it that ground one's being in the world, for example, its profoundly personal mythic dimensions. Our imaginary friends need not be dismissed, but rather grown to become inner guides with whom we can dialogue. Many indigenous people believe that you would not make it to adulthood without a guardian spirit to watch over you. So when you enter adulthood it's time to make a more mature relationship with this "guardian." Teachers and elders who have touched us are still to be respected and honored. The moments of transcendence we experienced in childhood are likewise honored during the vision quest so we can retain those fundamental experiences of our soul's connection to *all-that-is*. In this way, we can grow into our wider functioning in society without sacrificing our vital awareness of amness. By making that childhood connection more conscious in the vision quest, we know the great arena of the natural world in a new more responsible way, one that allows us to take responsibility for our role in conserving it. In this process we throw out only the bath water of childhood (our self-centered egoism, self-importance, arrogance, unrealistic expectations, irresponsibility, impulsiveness) while retaining and nurturing our baby (genuine spontaneity, amness, vital connection to all-that-is, wonder, awe and knowledge of the imaginal realm of dreams and reverie). We shed the childishness while retaining the childlike.

It was past midnight, moonless black, when I prepared my altar on the first night. Questions, worries, and anxieties began to fill my mind. What if I got really sick? No emergency room up here. What if I started to have problems with hypothermia, dehydration, or stomach cramps? Then grizzlies, mountain lions and bobcats wandered through my imagination. I began working myself into full-blown panic.

I heard a rustling of leaves in the woods, not 10 yards away. My heart jumped. I looked in the direction of the noise trying to make out an image. Ever so slowly, I heard the noise move through the darkness towards me. It must be an animal of some kind. Friend or foe, grizzly or some psychotic killer hiding out in the back country? I froze starring at the image. It continued to approach, seemingly showing no fear. I sensed a gentleness, an openness, perhaps a friend. I closed my eyes and tried opening my heart. This figure in the night made its way through the dark apparently to reveal itself to me, coming ever closer crossing right in from of me, and ever so mysteriously passing away to the other side back into the woods. A doe. An almost pure white doe. Her beauty and grace touched me. My eyes welled up. Such a gentleness in the midst of my fears. From that moment on I knew all would be well.

One of the most powerful aspects of the vision quest is one's confrontation with nature. A burning ember that I brought back with me was the new understanding of the Native American phrase, "All is sacred." Nature and natural come from the same root word, **natura,** meaning literally, "to be born." In tribal cultures throughout the world, the natural world is seen to be continuous with the human world. It is not anthropocentric, that is, human-centered. Rather, human beings are considered part and parcel of all beings. Plant beings, rock beings, feathered beings are just as sacred as human beings. "All-is-sacred." To quote Chief Seattle, "man did not weave the web of life, he is but a strand within it."

As we trace the roots of Western culture, we can also find this truth deeply embedded in our own cultural heritage. The word animal, comes from *anima*, literally Latin for soul. Anima referred to the miracle of animation. The animating principal brought forth the qualities of color, form, movement. Today, modern physics and quantum theory reveals clearly that even what we used to believe was inanimate matter, at the subatomic level *is* animate, that is, moving, pulsing, fluxing and flowing!

NO WORD FOR WEED

Admit, assume, because, believe, could, doubt, end,
expect, faith, forget, forgive, guilt, how, it, mercy, pest,
promise, should, sorry, storm, them, us, waste, we,
weed, neither these words nor the conceptions for which
they stand (appeared in Native American language)...
they are the white man's's import to the New World, the
newcomer's contribution to the vocabulary of the man
he called Indian.[5]
~*Ruth Beebe Hill*

Before European culture encountered the Native American one, there was no word for weed. Now think about this for a moment. No word for weed. All plants were seen as sacred. They all had intrinsic value. One plant might be bitter, but it might have medicinal qualities. Or one might be poisonous, but what a fine coating for arrows for hunting it would make. What we usually think of as weeds are the most robust, tenacious plant beings around! What grows in the most desolate regions of the earth, the highest mountains, the arid desert? What is the first thing to grow after a forest fire? Weeds. Unfortunately, with the advent of agrarian society and cultured plant growth, we began "weeding out" the "good" plants, from the "bad." We have been busy doing this ever since, not only with plants, but with people. Much of psychology and the traditional medical model of psychiatric diagnosis is about finding out who are weeds and who are not. Instead of finding someone's intrinsic value and what may be special or different about them; we tend to categorize and divide them into groups of dysfunction based upon some "measure" of normality. As if "normal" is best or even for that matter that it exists.

We know how diversity is crucial for sustainability in an eco-system. Our prehistoric ancestors ate as many as 1500 different wild varieties of plants. Today, North Americans depend on roughly 30 cultivated plants for 95 percent of our nutrition. Of those 30, just four make up 70 percent of all farmland and our staple diets. Likewise, we have little tolerance for people outside of a narrow range of what we consider normal.

ALL-MY-RELATIONS

In Lakota Sioux the words, *mitakuye oyasin, (All-My-Relations)* is spoken at the beginning and end of most ceremonies and is spoken out of praise and a reverence for every being on Earth, from plant, to animal, to the smallest bug and mound of dirt. This is a deeply felt and immensely sacred phrase used in many native cultures and particularly in the American. In prayer and ceremonies, "All-My-Relations" refers to more than one's biological or even cultural family. All-My-Relations is a prayer to all-that-is. It is at once a solemn and joyful affirmation of our connectedness to Being with a big B, and all our relatives therein. The trees, the rocks and the birds are siblings. All-My-Relations refers to our essential connectedness to all-that-is, often spoken of as the Spirit-that-moves-in-all-things. Even in the prevailing Judeo-Christian understanding of the world there is the belief that God the creator, created all things. If He is the father of all, then all his creatures are related - siblings in the cosmos. Many great Christian theologians have called God the creative Ground of life, which means He is infinitely more than any single life process. Therefore, God is ceaselessly working creatively through all beings often called the Holy Spirit. Regardless the name, Holy Spirit or Spirit-that-moves-in-all-things, what both are referring to is our essential interrelatedness, not only between people, but also between the sky, the earth, the animals, trees, and our dreams. All-My-Relations when spoken with meaning and weight has the potential to change the world. Perhaps one day it will.

There was a practical side to honoring the Spirit-that-moves-in-all-things and All-My-Relations, for it allowed our native ancestors to communicate with everything. There is an old Shamanic saying, "If you love anything enough, it will talk back to you." What is meant here is that everything speaks the language of the heart. Knowing this, Native American healers talk to all beings - the feathered people, the rock people, the tree people, etc. This helped them live in harmony with the natural world.

LOVING THE QUESTIONS

The vision quest itself, at the root, has to do with answering the fundamental questions about our life and our place within *All-That-Is* and *All-My-Relations*. The word "question," derives from the word "quest." Therefore, on the vision quest, you come face to face with the root questions of your life: Why am I here? Who are my people? What am I here to learn? What am I here to teach? Where am I going? How do I feel about death?

These are not easy questions to answer and usually they arouse anxiety. That's good. This anxiety has a positive purpose in that it spurs us on. It's like the warning lights on a car dash board. The red light goes on when the oil is low alerting us to not ignore it, but rather to PAY ATTENTION, BE AWARE, ATTEND TO THIS!

I had a middle aged woman that I was working with who had trouble sleeping. I asked her to use her imagination to imagine the part of her that would not let her sleep. She imagined a figure of an old teacher telling her with wide eyes, "I want you to wake up, you must wake up! Wake up!" When I asked her what "wake up" meant to her she replied:

> *It was hard to admit to myself, but once I heard those words as a question, I realized all to painfully what the voice was saying, I had to wake up to the fact that I was living in a loveless marriage. I was scared to death to make the changes I needed to. I was also aware that my spiritual life was lacking and that this call was to become more aware and awake concerning the life I was leading and where I was going.*

The symptom, the anxiety that was appearing in the form of her insomnia had something to tell her. If she had just taken sleeping pills she would have missed the message. By accepting her anxiety and then going on to actually explore it, attempting to interact with it and learn from it, growth occurred. Many times underneath inexplicable anxiety there lies very real painful and fearful work to do. The anxiety is a harbinger. If we could embrace it, we would hasten our growth. In avoiding it and numbing it we get lost in a whirlpool or eddy instead of continuing to flow down the river of our life toward home.

If we don't go down into the big questions, the hole of our emptiness, we eventually run dry. Seeking for predictability, certainty and control of our basic needs is not enough. During vision quests an individual seeks to heal any personal soul loss, to make a particular life-transition and even to help heal the soul loss of the tribe or community. Most of us, most of the time avoid the big questions assuming they can not be answered. Rilke gives some practical advice on this:

> *I want to beg you, as much as I can, dear sir, to be*
> *patient toward all that is unsolved in your heart and*
> *to try to love the questions themselves like locked*
> *rooms and like books that are written in a very foreign*
> *tongue.... Live the questions now. Perhaps you will*
> *then gradually, without noticing it, live along some*
> *distant day into the answer.* [6]

The vision quest brings the big questions to the surface by not allowing us to avoid them through the vast array of addictions modern society offers. Any dependencies your body has or any ways you've been mistreating your body will quickly come to the surface during fasting. In particular sugar, nicotine, alcohol, and any other drugs will all result in someone having a much more difficult experience fasting.

The most important intent of the fast is for you to become more aware of the core of your being as it relates to the bodily manifestations of your personality. The relationship between body and soul is a vital but delicate harmony. Imbalance in one aspect causes imbalance elsewhere. When one begins to fast one is allowing something more fundamental than digestion to sustain your being. It is exactly this experience of having some deeper process within you take over that helps clear the cloudiness of your day-to-day life. One gets a clearer distinction between one's needs and wants and a hint of who in essence one truly is. The Buddha used to say that as long as he could do three things he would always be all right: fasting, praying, and waiting. Starting from the fasting experience, the vision quest sheers you down to what's most vital and essential in one's very being. In so doing one's fears of needing and being attached to so many of the physical, material "things" in the world begin to recede. One becomes more aware of how truly little one needs to simply be. One can then replace attachment and addiction with connection and compassion. In this process, one learns better that more is never enough, and truly, less is more.

On the last day of the vision quest. I was making preparations for my journey back into civilization. I began to have anxieties about how to incorporate all I had experienced; how to say goodbye to my brothers and sisters; how to stay true to myself and not let demands of the life I knew awaited me overshadow my renewed spirit. I had prayed to see my soul sister, the white doe, one more time. I had not seen her since that first night. I knelt down, kissed the grass, gave thanks to the earth, trees, air, and the Creator for providing safe passage. I looked up and there she was. Now, my whole being shook with elation. I wept.

In her gentle presence I knew all would be well. Come what may, life would flow on, as fiercely gentle as the river and the wind. My task was to let go and let it carry me where it may, each day closer to home.

At midnight on the last day of my vision quest. It was time to hike back and begin my transition back into civilization with a sweat lodge ceremony. I slowly made my way back to camp where a roaring bonfire greeted me with a circle of elders. I silently walked around the fire for what seemed like hours. My body felt like it was floating, as if its boundaries were merging with the midnight mountain air. As I entered the sweat lodge I felt on the verge of death. Nothing to sweat and yet, sweating away. I began to have the sensation that I was melting again as the door closed and the now-familiar smell of sage and cedar filled this steamy earthen womb. No light, except the glowing of the rocks from within the pit fashioned out of dirt. I saw light flicker and felt spiraling flows of energy up my spine. I died many times in the next two hours. I found myself vividly re-living the moments leading up to my childhood surgeries. There was a tension building between holding on and letting go. The unbearable heat began to affect my dehydrated body. I remember calling to the creator and saying, "I can't do it anymore. It's over. Take me now." I let go. And as I did I felt something in me give way. A subtle rocking and spiraling motion began to take over my body. My eyes closed and I remember sounds coming out of my mouth, like unrecognizable voices from some distant past, sounds of the earth itself undulating through me. It was more than a mystical experience. I left and Amness returned. I was Indian, Italian, American, plant, animal, tree, earth, branches, drum, rhythm, glowing ember, fire, smoke, heat, steam...and earth.

Ever so slowly in a dreamlike state with my awareness of time and space greatly altered, I slowly came back to what we usually call reality. The sweat lodge had formally broke my fast, my quest and my ego. Inch by inch, I crawled on my hands and knees toward the opening. Steam billowed out into the cool night air like some otherworldly presence. Then, following the smoke, I emerged and the steam poured off my body. The stars dazzled in the night sky. They were everywhere, bright in the crisp mountain air. Then there were hugs all around. At the same ceremony there was a baptism for a new baby who was given a new name. I, too, felt like a new born infant. Every sensation was intensified. The cool ground on my feet, the sweetness of the air as I breathed. The sounds of the wind through the branches of the trees. Then they handed me a buffalo horn hollowed out. It was the horn that provided the water for the lodge. It was filled with cool water. They handed it to me with both hands. I received it with both hands. I had almost forgotten my thirst. But seeing the water, knowing that it would soon enter me, become part of me, made me sense the depths of my thirst. The longing I had for water over the last days returned as did tears to my eyes. I began to weep. I paused for a moment looking at the cup, feeling the cool horn in my hands. I closed my eyes and lifted the cup to smell the water. I put the horn up to my cheek to feel the sensation. At that moment the mystery of all the world was contained in that single buffalo horn of water. God himself lay in that simple cup of water. As I breathed in and ever so slowly drank the first full cup of water I had in days, I felt every drop of it inching its way down my throat and into every cell of my body blessing my whole being as it did. I was alive. More importantly, I was glad and thankful for being alive. That water was like liquid joy and I cried as I knelt on the ground and thanked the Being of all beings for nourishing my soul, for having mercy on my body. I felt a sense of gratefulness I've seldom known.

Since then, I try to practice that gratefulness every day by starting every morning with a glass of water in silent prayer and meditation. I have a sip to each direction - East, South, West, North, above and below. I pause and remember the miracle contained in every drop of water.

THE BACKYARD VISION QUEST

So does one have to journey to a native tribe in the middle of nowhere to enact a vision quest? There is so much talk today of traveling to exotic places across the world that the person without the resources to mount an expedition to the Himalayas may feel spiritually travel-challenged. Going far on earth is not of the essence of the vision quest. The vision quest is an ancient rite of passage for engendering a moving confrontation with soul. It is fundamentally an inner journey.

Jeff Salz, an editor for **Escape** magazine tells of an adventurous ice climb he had just completed, the first ascent of a major summit in the Cordillera Urubamba of Peru. "We were descending in a bit of a blow. At about 17,000 feet the verglas separated from the rock. My

twin ice hammers slipped like sharp knives through a very thin pea-
nut brittle. Falling. Air. Space. Adrenaline. Fear. At last, the sudden
stop. The belay, threaded through a single ice screw, came snug on
my chest harness. I dangled, bruised but unbloodied, bobbing over
5,000 feet of blue ice."

When Jeff recovered and headed farther down the mountain after
the climb, he passed a pair of "scruffy, soot-blackened Quechua kids."
They asked him in amazement, "De donde vienen? (Where have you
come from). He answered, "De arriba de las montanas." They said,
"Porque? No hay nada arriba." (Why? There is nothing up there.)

At that moment Jeff's idea of adventure changed forever. "There is
nothing up there. There is only a fleeting moment of ecstasy... That
pint-sized philosopher had given me a gift, a reminder of one of life's
ultimate truths...It's the courage to keep moving forward from one
challenge to the next, that keeps us going. Because the adventure is
really inside. "

Perhaps the greatest challenge of all is the ability to keep the elements of true adventure alive and well within us: mystery, awe and
wonder, even in the most day-to- day, ordinary and mundane work.
Jeff Salz knows better:

> *Genuine adventure of Himalayan magnitude peer at*
> *me from places I never expected. I'm discovering that*
> *the premises I need to vacate are not geographical but*
> *psychological. Habits to be jettisoned, depths of honesty*
> *in relationships to be plumbed, heights of creativity*
> *clamoring to be scaled. And, interestingly enough, these*
> *adventures affect others, not just the adventurers, in*

*positive ways. My suggestion: let's not wait for those
two weeks a year to live lives charged with a touch of
daring-do. Let's bring the spirit we take with us on the
adventure trail back home. When we're on the road,
we seek out the unknown, the unfamiliar, the risky.
But at home, we often shy away from the same things
at all costs, staying in our comfort zones instead of
risking - a new career, a change in relationships. It's
ironic that the home front fears come from the same
specter of the unknown as the adrenaline rush we find
exciting when we're traveling...The greatest adventures
dare us to explore life beyond the familiar mountains
of metaphor. Dare us to speak the truths of our lives
to friends, families, colleagues. Dare us to take creative
risks at work and transform our leisure time, perhaps
making our physical and spiritual health a higher
priority then entertainment...It is an oft-overlooked but
undeniable fact that when we begin to edge our daily
lives more and more in the direction of our highest
dreams, every waking hour becomes an opportunity for
adventure. From where we stand each day, our own
individual higher-than-Everest challenge is clearly visible in surprisingly familiar places. If only we care to
look.*[7]

I read this passage to clients often. It appears to be very helpful in
providing a sense of the strength and daring that we can exercise in
even the most ordinary of times. Our quest is ongoing and we have
lost the spirit of adventure that can be found even in emptying the
dishwasher, struggling to find a kind word for a spouse you are angry
with or daring to tell the boss how you really feel. There is greatness
in these seemingly mundane occurrences, if we have eyes to see.

HERO VISUALIZATION

Sometimes it is difficult to become aware and ingest our own heroic qualities. An easy way to begin is to connect with those whom we have felt have been heroic in our own lives. So for this visualization I would like you to allow yourself to come up with at least three individuals who have been "heroes" in your life. Your heroes may be historical figures, relatives, ancestors and they may also be animals. The qualities these figures possesses in someway resonate with your own heroic potential. Close your eyes and imagine these heroes with you now. Introduce yourself, declare that you would like to talk with them in this imaginal realm to dialogue with them and become acquainted, so as to ask for their help in guiding you. Much as you met the illusions of your life in previous visualizations, now it is time to meet the heroes of your life. What are their names? What do they look like? What words of wisdom do they have for you? What can they tell you about where to go next in your life? Perhaps they can offer some concrete suggestions on how to deal with a present problem. Breathe life into their images. If you are worried about, "just making it up," give yourself permission to "make it up," Help the logical, strategic mind get out of the way, and let your imagination flow as it did when you were a child. The more your heroes live with you, in you and inspire you, the more you will begin to embrace your own heroic potential. Write about this experience and repeat it two more times during the next week creating the habit of on-going dialogue with your inner symbols of heroic potential.

CHAPTER 6:

THE PARADOXICAL QUEST

Man is an embodied paradox, a bundle of
contradictions.
~Charles Caleb Colton

As a sophomore in college I had begun to grow weary of my desperate search for certainty, predictability and stability as a chemistry and math major. I decided I needed a break. My parents agreed I could go to Mexico for two months to do an independent study project which would give me college credit. I would have a Mexican traveling companion, Ricardo, a dear friend and amateur anthropologist and we would travel into the central plateau region of Mexico in search of the birth place of Quetzalcoatl.

QUETZALCOATL

Quetzalcoatl. The name conjures up ancient Mexico. Some firmly believe he still is a god in present day Mexico. His name literally means "precious feathered *(quetzalli)* snake *(coatl)*." It is believed he was initially conceived of as an earth and water god. He was also the god of the morning and evening star (Venus), and his temple took center stage in the ceremonial life of the Aztecs. He was also associated with Ehecatl, the wind god. The temple of Quetzalcoatl at Tenochtitlan, the Aztec capital, was round in shape which was believed to please the wind because there were no sharp obstacles to stand in its way. Two major myths associated with him include how he went to the underworld to gather bones of the ancient dead. He then anointed them with his own blood giving birth to the present day human inhabitants of the earth. The feathered serpent also was known to have been expelled by the god of the night sky, Tezcatlipoca, and Quetzalcoatl wandered all the way to the coast of the "divine water" the Gulf of Mexico and immolated himself on a fiery pyre emerging as the planet Venus and known as "burning water."

One day my friend and I were walking in Chapaltapec Park and we came upon an astonishing fountain. Its outline was formed in the image of Quetzalcoatl. At the far end the head and tail came together. This plumed serpent was devouring himself, eating his own tail. This image was so immense and vital amidst the tumbling water and misting spray that I felt as though shaken awake and starred gaping at it. To the present day, all I need do is close my eyes and that fountain comes to life in my mind's eye, breathing in the present moment. The ancient image stirred something buried within that I felt at once I understood, yet for which I had no words. Since that day I have become clear that here was revealed the spiraling, circular nature of all things, and I had been hypnotized by a glimpse of the eternal dancing cycles of existence. Einstein himself said, if you look far enough into the universe you will eventually see the back of your own head. Incredible! This ancient god was living out one of the greatest insights of our twentieth century science.

Looking back, I can see how this plumed serpent filled my imagination as I began what I would only understand later to be my first vision quest - this foray into the central plateau of Mexico. Remember, I was raised on logic and reason. I thought my life's calling was to be a neurosurgeon. To be always exacting, precise, and analytic. Now this naive pre-med student had fallen in love with a plumed serpent - a love somehow connected with the radical science Einstein understood. I felt a pull, a calling, a longing towards this image of a precious feathered god that I could not explain. I had to find out more.

"Ouroboros" is the symbolic name for Quetzacoatl. The medieval gnostics had a similar image, usually depicted as a dragon, snake or serpent formed in a circle, eating its own tail, often with the caption *en to pan* (Latin for "The One, the All"). The plumed serpent image of the god Quetzalcoatl provides an added dimension of significance. It symbolizes the great marriage between the chthonic, mysterious earthy principle (the snake) *married* to the celestial world of form and spirit (the bird). The dragon in many cultures is often also a "plumed" serpent - a snake with wings. The body is often represented as half bright (day and light) and half black (night and darkness) similar to Yin-Yang symbology.

Quetzacoatl was working on me internally, although I did not realize the power of it until returning to the states. Three months after my encounter with Mexico and the plumed serpent, my world turned upside down. I gave up the pursuit of being a surgeon; changed my major, had a torrid romance, told my parents to "fuck off" for the first time in my life and proceeded to have a psychotic break down/break through. Quetzacoatl had awakened something buried within that was now coming to life.

THE PARADOX OF PARADISE

If the place I want to arrive at could only be reached by a ladder, I would give up trying to arrive at it. For the place I really have to reach is where I must already be. What is reachable by a ladder doesn't interest me.
~*Wittgenstein*

Up until my Mexican sojourn, I conceived much of my life as a heroic quest. Linear. I was very busy climbing the ladder; I went from 1st grade to 2nd, 15 years of age to 16 years of age, freshman to sophomore, minimum wage to more than minimum wage, so on and so on. My life had been a steady progression. I was scaling a mountain that I had come to believe would fill me with happiness, completeness, and fulfillment. I had now begun to find out just how inaccurate my expectations learned from Western, civilized, Judeo-Christian, scientific culture were. I had been touched by the inmost wisdom of Quetzalcoatl, the circular, spiraling serpent in search for its own tail, devouring as it is devoured.

From the time we are children we are taught verbally, visually, and spiritually that heaven and God are "up there." To be successful on earth, we must also ascend, achieve, move upward and climb the ladder of success. We even use the term "grow up." Why do we never hear the parallel expression "grow down," as the trees which only grow up to the extent they can grow down, letting their roots spread deeply into the soil. I suspected Quetzacoatl knew something about "growing down" and it appeared that I had a lot of "growing down" to do.

Paradox, comes from *doxa* meaning "opinion," and *para* meaning "beyond." A paradox is beyond opinion. Whereas orthodox (from *ortho*, meaning "straight") means "right opinion," or the one and only opinion. Paradox breaks this straight chain. It cracks open the hard egg shell of appearances to reveal the liquid formlessness just beneath the surface of things. A physicist will tell you there is no such thing as a straight line although we spend most of our time creating straightness. In nature straight lines don't exist. Cultures that have emphasized the roundness of the world help us come back to harmony with the perpetually curving, convoluting nature of reality, like our fingerprints.

Van Gogh was fond of saying, "Reality is round," and so it is. The sphere's of planets, the earth, the moon, the sun and the billions and billions of stars rotate perpetually a great cosmic round of dancing. The universe on a grand scale is curved, curving, circling and spiraling around and around. Then why have we as a culture become so obsessed with linearity, the straight line of progress? We live in boxes in our culture while creating a geometry based on the straight line, when the straight line is an illusion.

Then why were there ever straight lines? Straightness certainly has its purpose. It helps us go from place to place in as short a time as possible. It provides a sense of exactness, clarity. Straight lines divide. Straight lines create angles. To the degree that they help - wonderful, but to the degree that we confuse them with the great reality of curvature, roundness, and branching into unique infinite patterns, they can blind us to the truth of who we really are. Our vital connection to amness is not promoted by straightness. Straightness smacks of perfection. The word perfect comes from *per-* (Latin for "through") and *facere* ("to make or do"); *perficere,* means to finish. Perfection as finished does not exist. For something to exist, by definition it can never be finished, yet while something exists in time - it is forever changing. Therefore the world, the universe is never finished, it is forever undergoing transmutation, transformation. Perfectionism in this way is a form of deadness.

We gain great strength and emotional maturity by embracing paradox. It is a wellspring of deeper meaning that we fervently need in our lives today. Paradox is not the same as contradiction. When we contradict, we have two meanings crashing into each other, in essence destroying any meaning. As Robert Johnson the Jungian analyst observes, "Contradiction is barren and destructive, yet paradox is creative. It is a powerful embracing of reality...while contradiction is static and unproductive, paradox makes room for grace and mystery...every human experience can be expressed in terms of paradox. The electric plug in the wall has two prongs, access to positive and negative electrical charge. From this opposition comes the usefulness of the electric current. Day is comprehensible only in contrast to night. Masculinity has relevance only in contrast to femininity." We must avoid thinking we can live without paradox, for paradox denied brings opposition and contradiction. Destruction soon follows as we find ourselves crucified on the apparent dichotomies of life. The key is to honor both sides of our experience. This is the beginning of true understanding, "To suffer one's confusion is the first step in healing. Then the pain of contradiction is transformed into the mystery of paradox." In this way, "the capacity for paradox is the measure of spiritual strength and the surest sign of maturity."[8]

Unfortunately, we spend most of our lives avoiding paradox at all costs, primarily because it damages the ego terribly. It reminds us of our insignificance, the impotence of our rational, reasonable, analyzing that comforts us so. This pain is so hard to suffer that we would rather settle for the easy answers, the easy solutions, the black and white world of simply this or that...God forbid, this AND that. In an effort to combat this prejudice against paradox a small sign hangs over my office door , "Paradox Spoken Here" :

> *The realm of paradox, where we are able to entertain simultaneously two contradictory notions and give them equal dignity. Then, and only then, is there the possibility of grace, the spiritual experience of contradictions brought into a coherent whole - giving us a unity greater than either one of them...To heal, to bond, to join, to bridge, to put back together again - these are our sacred faculties.[9]*

Lost on the waves of time we find our hopes and dreams. One day we realize all we have worked so hard to achieve is but a puff of air.

We die on the side of reality that hides from us the secret joys of suffering. To have all of our most precious plans, projects and ambitions thwarted, called to a halt by a twist of fate, a sudden shift in worldly circumstance, when all that we thought we knew comes crashing down around us...then what? After new allegiances, new promises, new commitments do we begin to slowly realize the stark contingency of it all - the awesome impermanence of it all....that awareness begins to dawn in the caverns of our soul and we begin to die a little, perhaps a lot, and we also begin to wake up to the flux, the flow...and there as we suffer the agonies, suffer the perpetual polishing of our soul, there we begin to sense a deeper truth, through the impermanence, not in spite of it...there is a glimpse at the in-between of existence...the twilight awareness with the ego and its precious projects burned to the ground once again....there, precisely there...the moment opens and a chill comes over the body....the eyes glaze over....and an inward look that gazes beyond the horizon of tomorrow....there resides the numinous, the ineffable, the wonder and awful mystery that finally we melt into and join this time without protest, ***consciously marrying our ultimate failure, which is our entrance to the divine itself...***

THE EVER WINDING ROAD

To all, artists and otherwise, who are out on the road somewhere wandering, with no destination anywhere in sight, almost forgetting why they ever set out in the first place, yet still unable to turn back, because they honestly believe that the shortest distance between two points just may not be a straight line.

~Andre Gregory

When we appreciate the importance of paradox and let go of the naive notion that our lives should proceed along a straight line, we open ourselves to see our lives more like a forest rich with variety, change, and branches going every which way. Not only do we need to let go of our narrow view of people and the universe being well-oiled machines, so do we need to begin to let go of our preciously held assumptions about a linear development of evolution, time and progress. Especially, within the development of the self. So often people come to me and talk about how "@#$*% up" they are, how "evil," "imperfect," and "crazy" they are. The self-hate becomes a tyrant dictating a ban on mercy. However, when individuals are able to realize they are still on a path, even an adventure, life becomes more bearable and exciting. Yes, they have taken diversions, mean-derings, hopelessly "wrong" turns; yet, they are still on the journey of self-discovery. In fact, when they realize that by definition their quest is a paradoxical one, they feel much better and can take heart and own their life in noble and inspiring ways. Stephen Foster who introduced the way of the vision quest to modern Western readers talks about how he himself was able to keep struggling against formi-dable demons when he was able to view even his most "@#$%* up" times as part of his journey:

> *All the time I have been climbing the mountain," he thought with awe. He saw his struggles from a new perspective. He had not been stagnant, dead on the water, a failure to himself and others. He had been climbing a particularly difficult stretch. He had come up Inconsolable Canyon to Despair Gulch. Then he*

*attempted Wrong Way Ridge and got caught in Alcohol
Sink. But he had not succumbed to the muck of Self-
Pity Swamp, nor did he expire on Anger Mesa. He
kept climbing toward Heartbreak Ridge. See? He was
still climbing! He was not lost!* [10]

This perspective, this way of seeing and understanding our life journeys is the essential antidote to despair. For from being "@#$% ups" we can take heart in the nobility of climbing a sacred mountain. The only way to see this mountain is with the eyes of the heart, which Foster learned in the most unique way:

*This mountain was made of many things...his body
and its soul. It was his wife, his family, his home, the
everyday routines, his work. It was the rattlesnakes,
the hummingbirds, the earthworms, the trees, the flowers, and the stray cats. It was concrete, steel, electricity,
TV, gasoline, computers, fast food restaurants, peniten-
tiaries, ghettos, corporations, nuclear bombs, toxic waste,
and fried ice cream. It was will, faith, love, hope.* [11]

If our very selves and the foundation of what we call mind and consciousness is at its most basic sense paradoxical, how much more merciful will we be with others and ourselves in the lives we lead? When we pay close attention to nature, we discover the beauty of the twisting and turning of everything. We are made in the same way as wild nature, take the convolutions of the brain, the intestines, the dendrites of the neurons - traced in the very structure of our being is the mirror of the branching phenomena of trees and roots. Yes, the earth has grown us in her image. These spiraling curving branches, like rivers etched in our very bodies, tell us something essential about our life paths. Our lives are more like rivers than ladders; more like circles than lines. At times if our thought and behavior appears wandering, tangential and nomadic this may be telling us something more profound about who, why and what we are. More importantly, it may open us up to the life we are living in the moment, in the very heart of our Being-in-the-world appreciating this paradoxical experience called reality, called life. We can then move from viewing ourselves as a city, machine or computer and open the way towards the river of who we are. In this way our lives are more like rivers, than machines:

> *Rivers hardly ever run in a straight line. Rivers are willing to take ten thousand meanders and enjoy every one and grow from everyone. When rivers leave a meander they are always bigger than when they entered it. When rivers meet an obstacle, they do not try to run over it- they merely go around, but they always get to the other side. Rivers accept things as they are. They conform to the shape they find the world in, yet nothing changes things more than rivers. Rivers move even mountains into the sea. Rivers hardly ever are in a hurry, yet is there anything more likely to reach the point it sets out for than a river?* [12]
> ~James Dillet Freeman

WANDERING, QUESTING AND CREATIVITY

Stories go in circles. They don't go in straight lines. So it helps if you listen in circles, because there are stories

PART III: THE QUEST

*inside stories and stories between stories, and finding
your way through them is as easy and as hard as finding your way home. And part of the finding is getting
lost. If you're lost, you really start to look around and
listen.* [13]

~Deena Metzger

As we wed the notion of paradox to our life quest, we bless the importance of wandering. Wandering is a luscious activity. An art that we have lost. Native culture knew the inherent sacred quality in wandering. The aborigine of Australia, arguably the most ancient surviving culture on earth, call their vision quests walkabouts. In Swahili, the word safari means journey. The original word had more to do with a sacred wandering and connecting with the natural world. The quest is intentional, the wander tangential. The quest has clear direction, the wander has no direction. The quest is linear, the wander circular. The men quested for prey on the hunt. The woman wandered to gather berries. The experience is as different as day and night. The male is linear in his quest for the buffalo. The female is circular as she gathers. The paradoxical quest allows us to appreciate both - a way to embrace the circle and the line. On a quest there is time for wandering, and wandering is most productive when in service of a purpose, a vision, a meaning.

Wandering wisdom is very practical, very grounded, even though at first glance it appears foolish or esoteric. The well beaten trail is the last place to find berries. The animals and other gatherers go there first and usually the precious fruit is scarce. It is the one who is willing to stray from the beaten path that will find nurturance. At an

191

Easter egg hunt, it is the child who knows how to wander off the trail that finds the most eggs. The child who is not stopped by the fear to enter the wild and finds the courage to explore in the tall grass or peak under the pricker bush; this is where the eggs of new life are to be found. In the Advanced Personality courses I teach, I wander a great deal in my lectures. At first the students can be very frustrated. But, as they allow themselves to wander along with me, there can be great pleasures and insights found. To wonder as we wander. I have found without a doubt that wandering increases wondering and wondering amplifies wandering.

It is difficult to allow ourselves to embrace paradox and wandering in our consumer oriented societies based on the religion of progress and the machine of production. They are negative and pejorative words in our culture. In a world where there are "how to" manuals about sex, feeling good, communicating and losing weight, we have come to fundamentally distrust our own experience and our own intuition about how we live our lives. This is particularly true with creativity. The flow of creativity so often is blocked by trying too hard or becoming hard, rigid and rule bound. What we really need to do is get out of the way, unleash the flow, trust our instincts and ultimately move.

We have seen how the Enlightenment bolstered reason and logic. It had benefits but ultimately at the expense of intuition and imagination. To regain the wisdom of intuition and imagination we must regain our creativity. This move towards creativity means to scribble outside the lines, go into unexplored territory and wander into places not designated on the map of our lives. To rekindle creativity, spontaneity, and mystery in our lives it is helpful to "go where the dragons are."

Perhaps this is why the gift of the mysterious is one of the most profound we can give to our children. In some way this is the deeper truth behind the images of Santa Claus, the Easter bunny, and the tooth fairy. They are our inadequate ways of expressing the mysterious at work in the world. When my daughter asked me if Santa Claus existed I found myself becoming very somber at first, feeling that she was about to leave an enchanted part of her life, never to return again. Then something came over me and I found myself thinking, "wait a minute, Santa Claus is very alive and well in my life. I can tell you what he looks like, what he sounds like, and what he likes. I know him as intimately as many of my best friends. Of course he exists." I tried to communicate this to my daughter in my own inadequate way trying to give expression to this deep feeling and conviction I had. "Yes, of course he exists. No, he is not flesh and blood like us. He is a made of spirit stuff. One can't see him, put him in a box, or measure him or in any way really get hold of him; but he's there alright! He's there!" She smiled and with her smile both our eyes welled up.

Wandering is crucial to the development of creativity. To generate possibilities is also to be what the existentialists call "authentic." One who is living authentically is open to their possibilities and is not determined by external forces. The one who is "inauthentic" is living "as if" they have no choice in their life, as if they are completely determined.

Paradox And Mystery

Life is a mystery to behold, not a problem to solve.
~Gabriel Marcel

When I first read these words by Gabriel Marcel, I felt that power-ful "yes!" feeling. I had felt that truth since I was a child, but had such a difficult time putting it into words. I had also known that as I began to look at myself, others, and the world around me as a problem to solve logically and analytically, I became alienated from the mystery, from amness, and from my vital connection to *all-that-is*.

Mystery and paradox have a powerful relationship. Paradoxes if we allow ourselves to sit with them, instead of figuring them out, will fill us with mystery. One of the purposes of a Zen Koan is to do just this - exhaust the logical, strategic, and problem solving mind until it lets go and the full, robust mystery of "all-that-is" can enter our awareness. "What is the sound of one hand clapping?" "Show me your original face - the one you had before your parents were born?" "When you do nothing, what can you do?" The words in Koans do not communicate an idea; but, rather plant the seeds of a wordless truth in the soil of one's very being. If one waters these seeds, they germinate. Some will eventually grow into oaks, others into maples and still others into incredible flora. A powerful description of the process one may go through in letting the seeds of a Koan grow is expressed by the great Japanese Master Hakuin, "If you take up one koan and investigate it unceasingly, your mind will die and your will, will be destroyed. It is as though a vast, empty abyss lay before you, with no place to set your hands and feet. You face death and your bosom feels as though it were on fire. Then suddenly you are one with the koan, and body and mind are cast off...This is known as seeing into one's nature."

In a very real way, entering into the world of a Zen Koan is an intellectual vision quest. One does indeed face death. The analytic mind in this way symbolizes the heroic self, with a mission - solve this Koan, make logical sense of it. As mind/ego suffers under the strain, it slowly but surely experiences its own limitations and ultimate defeat. As the mind/ego surrenders, it also begins to transcend the duality, instead of solving the paradox. This is a suspension of thought, a move into openness, beholding the grand dance inside the koan. One's whole being becomes involved in the meditation and finally opens to the paradox, soaring, "beyond opinion" into a unitary experience of oneness. Marcel's invocation, "life is not a problem to solve, but a mystery to behold," urges us to see the world in such a way to make our awareness large enough for paradoxes to move and dance about. Then comes a much greater understanding of mystery than we are used to in our every-day lives.

Another example of living within paradox is the Daimyo warrior class of feudal Japan. They referred to their spiritual path as the dual way of the sword and the brush. Warriors were to embody both fierceness and sensitivity, a fierce gentleness. In this bloody time in Japanese history these fierce samurai whose motto was *"Expect nothing: Be ready for everything,"* would regularly put down the sword and pick up their brush, or enter the tea ceremony where exquisite courtesy blended into meditation and the outside world of death and destruction, for a precious hour, was kept at bay. Thus their path blessed the paradox of war and peace, fierceness and compassion, destruction and creativity.

In this period of our culture, the word mystery usually refers only to a detective story. The "whodunit" is a playground for the strategic mind and much energy goes into problem solving. Mystery with a capital "M" takes us to another level: the awareness of not - knowing at a fundamental level. If one really wakes up, right now, in the moment and takes a deep breath, one can begin to tap into the experience of being alive, without words, without concepts, without thinking, tasting the mystery of all-that-is. This is the original meaning of the word from the Greek **Mystos** - meaning to keep silent. That is, Mystery has to do with that which exceeds all words and gives rise to all words, what the Native Americans call, The Great Mystery.

Unfortunately, our modern culture has an innate fear of impenetrable mystery. We know it is packed full of illogical, the unknown, the unpredictable and the uncertain. It is no wonder that we have such a mistrust of it and have tried so hard to conquer it. Mystery novels could even be seen in our culture as an attempt to over and over again solve the mystery by reducing it to simply a puzzle. Each piece eventually will be put in its proper place. Then when the puzzle has been solved we can sigh in relief. Once again logic, reason and rationality have served us well against our fearful opponent Mystery. But, what if such mystery is not our enemy, but, rather our Mother?

Much of our fear of mystery has a great deal to do with our fear of death, which leads us to the next misunderstanding of what mystery is in our culture. The first major misconception is that mystery is a puzzle to be solved (science), the second is that it is evil (fundamentalism). The mysterious all too often is associated with the sinister. It is understandable that we have this innate fear stretching back to being fearful in the night. Our ancestors lived out their existence during the day while the nighttime was a time to be feared because of the mystery of the dark, the night, of dreams and ultimately of the greatest sleep of all, death. They feared losing their way, dying in the cold, and being eaten alive. The break of day must have felt each morning like a rebirth. In our own day, the light of reason and logic promises safety even in the dark. Yet, as Jung used to say, the brighter the light, the darker the shadow. After 400 years of an enlightenment, we have a heck of a shadow that has been cast by modern culture. Yet, by admitting and exploring our shadow much gold can be mined.

I often ask others to tell me about a time when the mysterious sense in all things filled them with awe and wonder as opposed to fearfulness. Unfortunately, most refer to times long ago in their childhood, usually prepubescent experiences. My own life has seen a complete inversion of my approach to mystery and the unknown, like Quetzacoatl eating his own tail: Embracing mystery as a child, fighting it as a youth, and now re-embracing the darkness in adulthood. The passage retraces the move towards acceptance, the move towards beholding. The strategic mind, our ego, needed to fight an incessant bloody battle with the mysterious and the unknown for most of our lives which result in neurotic paranoias, phobias, generalized anxiety, even a sense of despair at times. The strategic mind always falls hopeless in the face of deep dark mystery.

The Lakota word, "Wakan," helps us understand the ontological nature of mystery. Wakan means mystery, medicine and holiness and is used by the Lakota to designate all that is sacred. "Wakan Takan" is usually translated as "Great Spirit." A more apt translation is actually "Great-Holy-Mystery." Wicasa-Wakan is not rightly rendered "medicine man" but more accurately is "One who knows the Great-Holy-Mystery." Like most indigenous cultures the Native Americans understood the crucial role Mystery plays. It at once keeps us humble all the while, invigorating, energizing and providing the life blood to our days. It is not something to fear and be done away with, but, rather the very phenomena that brings us sustenance, feeds our souls and provides profound meaning to our lives. A seed must be buried in the dark soil for it to grow. So too our lives must be planted in mystery. Its not a rational explanation but something much more vital - a sense of the grand canvas that our lives our lived upon, our humbleness and at the same time our magnificence - something that is best understood in silence.

GO WHERE THE DRAGONS ARE!

As a child I felt terribly sad because the whole known "earth" was discovered. I recall vividly looking at old maps of the world my father had in his study. They were full of mystery and intrigue. Ancient map makers had the most fascinating ways of describing the areas that were unexplored. When they ran out of the known world, they would sketch, draw or paint an elaborate dragon on the edge of the parchment. This dragon signified to the explorers of the time that this region was unknown. Many took this symbol of the dragon literally. In fact, stories abounded about dragon slayers. A dragon slayer truly meant *"one who is willing to go into the unknown."* Many explorers of centuries gone past would not venture into the dragon's world, the unknown. Many saw the dragons for what they were harbingers of the new undiscovered virgin world and a doorway to the mysterious. We ourselves each carry around our dragons and our maps that chart the known and the unknown. We desperately need guides, mentors and ourselves to venture into the dragons we carry around with us. We, too, are called to be dragon slayers. Every day there are dragons to slay and fears to overcome. Dragons, like our everyday fears, are symbolic of the unknown beyond the edge of consciousness.

Ultimately, the dragon is symbolic of any adversary with which we struggle. Within our own psyches this means the uncertain, unpredictability, and unknown shadow aspect of ourselves. The *hero's supreme test then is fighting the dragon* that threatens innocence (sickness, trauma, darkness, and ultimately Chaos). The paradox is again found in that the dragon is also guardian of the treasures that lie hidden in the temple sanctuary:

> *We have no reason to harbor any mistrust against our*
> *world, for it is not against us. If it has terrors, they*
> *are our terrors; if it has abysses, these abysses belong*
> *to us; if there are dangers, we must try to love them....*
> *How could we forget those ancient myths that stand*
> *at the beginning of all races, the myths about dragons*

that at the last moment are transformed into princesses?
Perhaps all the dragons of our lives are princesses who
are only waiting to see us act, just once, with beauty and
courage. Perhaps everything that frightens us is, in its
deepest essence, something helpless that wants our love.[14]

In these few lines Rilke gives us a glimpse into the core of our paradoxical quest. We must undertake this quest in the end to confront ourselves and to ultimately see that the dragons we encounter are lost parts of ourselves waiting to be discovered, needing our help. One client of mine put it this way:

Finally, I began to learn to kiss the ugliness, the dragons that had I felt been pursuing me my own life. Then I gradually began to become curious about them. When I learned to kiss them what miracles took place, the frog became a prince. I never understood those silly fairy tales until I actually kissed the dragons in my own life.

The dragon and the frog have much in common. They are reptilian, they walk in two worlds - the water (unconscious) and earth (conscious). The flying fire-breathing dragon even unites two more - the air and fire. If we are able to have the courage to face our own darkness, our own paradoxical nature, we may become what Blake called the "dragon-man." For Blake, the dragon-man makes the infinite visible in the marriage of heaven and earth, the marriage of energy and form.

As I age, I am realizing how similar we really are to old Christopher Columbus who lived his own paradoxical quest. He didn't know where he was going when he started. He didn't know where he was when he got there, and he didn't know where he had been when he returned! The blessing in this, of course, is that there is plenty of territory that remains unexplored - maps with dragons on them. Every one who comes in my office has a map with dragons on them. We all have maps with Dragons on them. If a therapist really wants to enter the adventure of therapy and of life, he or she must be willing to be an old world explorer and tread into the region of the dragon. It is the hero's challenge that rings true as much today as ever, "go where the dragons are!"

As we have taken another turn on the spiral of growth, now we can understand more fully the end of Rilke's quote, "how could we forget those ancient myths that stand at the beginning of all races, the myths about dragons that at the last moment are transformed into princesses? Perhaps all the dragons in our lives are princesses who are only waiting to see us act, just once, with beauty and courage. ***Perhaps everything that frightens us is, in its deepest essence, something helpless that wants our love.***"

THE "GREAT MONSTER" VISUALIZATION

The paradoxical quest allows us to explore the other side of the hero exercise. This perhaps is the greatest challenge of all psychospiritual growth: first identifying and then assimilating the great monsters of our life. This is the great work of individuation, owning our own shadow. But, first before we learn to "kiss the dragons," we must identify them. So in this visualization you begin by answering the question as completely and honestly as you can, "what are the great monsters of my life?" Allow yourself to answer this question either literally or symbolically. That is you can "make up," using the window of imagination, a world with knights and dragons if you like. Ultimately you will still be projecting your own world into this imaginary one. It will be chock full of meaning, regardless.

After you have fully identified the "great monsters of your life," then ask yourself, "What are three ways in which I can begin to kiss (assimilate) these monsters, befriend them, even learn to love them?" This is not for the faint of heart. If it feels too much for you, wait until you do feel ready. This is also a powerful exercise to do with a therapist. Ultimately, doing this work is perhaps the single most important kind of work for all of us culturally to be doing because it helps us own our shadow instead of projecting it onto others. This is the hard, real growth work of true individuation. If you have no answers now, simply sit with the question over time. The important point is that true inner peace will only come as you slowly but surely digest these monsters and allow them to become allies instead of enemies.

PART IV:

THE DANCE

"Grandmother... Thank you for bringing me this far...I know now
that the fruit of the Journey is at hand. Share with me once again
your vision."

"It is very simple
Everyone knows the word,
but few live the experience,
Oneness...
Each is a petal on the flower of Creation,
dancing perpetually the rhythm of Being.
The flowering and fruit of the Quest is the Dance...
Tell her, my dear Grandson, tell her about...the Dance."

CHAPTER 7:

THE QUEST BECOMES THE DANCE

*At the still point
of the turning world.
Neither flesh nor fleshless;
Neither from nor towards;
at the still point, there
the dance is...*

~*T.S. Eliot*

The lights suddenly go out and darkness abruptly quiets the auditorium where I have come, 9-years-old, with my parents to hear my first live jazz. I have no idea what to expect. Wide-eyed I see the black velvet curtains slowly open. Then a light from behind me picks out five musicians and a drum's steady beat fills the auditorium and me with it.

I can still remember the tiniest details - the swell of the auditorium, exactly where we sat and the glistening pearl drum set from which that wizard captivated me with his earnest, yet joyous rhythm. His arms flew and his syncopating beat quickened my spine and made my heart jump. No, it leaped - in a triple-twisting, double back flip. My back began to pulse and it was as though something ancient in me was waking up, coming to life. *The music* was *alive!* I was *alive!*

And, savoring the moment, I wanted nothing more than to play the drums like that.

I now know what awakened in me was a conscious awareness of the beating of life itself, "rhythm," in both a local and a larger sense. It was also the discovery of the organic nature of improvisational music, moving, changing, pulsating. In all of our bodies the rhythmic gyrations of the cosmos are alive and well; unfortunately, they lie dormant, untapped by our waking conscious minds most of our lives. Yet, here was this adolescent drummer touching something vital in the inchoative memory of the very cells of my body waking me up. That is the power of rhythm.

At the time, however, I knew only that drumming captured my imagination and offered a path towards being more alive. I loved that feeling. So, I went home that night and announced my decision to become a drummer. It didn't go over too well: we were a quiet family. With time; however, my determination overcame my parents hesitancy, and I worked every night on my practice pad waiting for the day to play a real drum. Time went by and I eventually received my own "pearl white" set of drums that I adored. I dreamed about them at night, caressed them during the day and played them whenever I could. I had found Rhythm and I was addicted.

RHYTHM

Rhythm. The word suggests more than sound, it says, "Dance!" The drum brings us to our feet. We resonate with a moving center, our heart, that is always beating out its own unnoticed rhythm.

Throughout our whole life, bump-pump, bump-pump, we live this invisible beating dance and when we are old enough the drum like its echo calls us to express it. The word "rhythm" rolls off the tongue, its sound hinting at the feeling it evokes. The word comes from the Latin *rhythmus:* meaning measured motion and derives also from the Old German *rhein,* literally to flow as in a river. Therefore, rhythm refers to a regularly recurring quality, usually presented as a beat or accent and creating a sense of flowing motion. So, there are at least two basic qualities of rhythm.

Musically we are most familiar with the idea of rhythm as the patterned recurrence of strong and weak beats, alternating heavily and lightly accented. The particular form and pattern of such rhythm give rise to tempo, timing, and cadence which underlie a composition. Broadly speaking, rhythm creates the element of time in music. If we wed this notion to Plato's statement, "time is the moving image of eternity"; we see that rhythm can also serve as a window on timelessness.

The second quality of rhythm echoes the immense beating of all organic movements - the cascading waterfalls or wind caressing the branches of a tree. This vital aspect of rhythm predated the first human drum ever being played. It is the rhythmic landscape of our entire lives that sets in relief our day to day lives as part of a cosmic dance. We are talking about this more organic and general form of rhythm when we speak of the rhythm of someone's speech or the rhythm of a poem. Like the living flow of the cosmos, it creates patterns in the timeless dance of Being, not only in the birth and dying of stars but even in our artistic attempts to apprehend reality: the moving flows in art, literature and, of course, music. Even our activities of day and night have their rhythm from cooking breakfast to taking a shower to writing a book.

A whole area of psychological research, "interactional synchrony," studies the many rhythms in human interactions, both work and play. Video tapings record people talking or children playing. When replayed in slow motion the tapes show rhythmic dances we all engage in usually just below the level of consciousness such as movements of hands or the gentle rocking back and forth on our legs.

Synchrony studies teach us that the merging of rhythms increases the flowing of our vital energy. When a regular pattern of inhalation and exhalation corresponds with a particular stride or stroke, an athlete's endurance increases. Like the dancer who sets up a regular, efficient rhythm and then is able to continue dancing for a much longer time. We are carried by and through rhythm. Writers discover, sooner or later, that developing a rhythm for taking breaks, stretching, brewing a cup of tea, not only increases the length of working sessions but also their joy. Rhythm helps us take otherwise difficult tasks and provides a cadence that helps us with endurance, creativity and enjoyment.

As a vital element in each of our lives, rhythm daily reveals our connection to the grander rhythms of nature. A woman's menstrual cycle connects her to the ocean's and the rhythms of the moon. No wonder many believe rhythm was among the first concepts that ever entered the human mind. How could it be otherwise? The rhythms of night and day, of spring, summer, fall and winter, ruled survival. But they also gave hints of our human place in the world. When we found our rhythms nesting in the greater ones, we discovered Amness again, this time not simply immersed and undifferentiated as the infant, but as an individual "I am" experience dancing within the field of "amness" - where our rhythm reflects and mirrors the vaster rhythms. There have certainly been individuals who have discovered and practiced this truth. But, as a culture at large, we have lost this ability to "link up" to the greater rhythms of nature and the cosmos. There are many reasons why we no longer feel connected in a vital way to these great rhythms. Let us explore one of these reasons - the rhythmic impoverishment of Western music.

THE DRUM

There is a stark difference between so called "primitive music" and the music that has prevailed during the last 2000 years of civilization. Until 30 years ago the drum virtually disappeared from the cultures of cities world wide. From Greco-Roman times up until the 1950s, the drum plays, at most, a very minor role. We hear the kettle drum in some later symphonic music and drums sounded on the battlefields, but otherwise, they are silent. This lack is surprising when we recall that drumming instruments were the first fashioned by humans and considered *sacred* in most primary cultures - even those with no apparent relationships between one another.

The first percussive bows, similar to hunting bows, appear fully 50,000 years ago followed by such other types as scrapers, rattles, and bone flutes 15,000 years later. Twenty to thirty thousand years ago percussion instruments were already used for sacred ritual. The so-called "dancing shaman" of *Les Trois Freres* in the limestone caverns of southwestern France is depicted wearing an animal skin and playing a musical bow or concussion stick, is only the best known example.

Even when the first agrarian societies emerge, their earliest towns (e.g. Catal Huyak, circa 4500 BC) have sacred places where the cylinder drum beat holy rhythms. Such percussive instruments were necessities: they connected daily life to the divine and nourished our ancestors with the soul foods of resonant meditation and shamanic journeying for 2500 generations. With the gradual triumph of mind, however, we have put *more and more* important value in our head held high above the earth. Music became elevated too, and lifted itself into the clouds. The sacred drum gradually became something primitive, too earthy, or even sinister:

> *They cause much unrest to pious old people of the earth, to the sick and weakly, the devout in the cloisters, those who have read, studied and prayed, and I verily believe that the devil must have had the devising and making of them, for there is no pleasure or anything good about them. If hammering and raising a din be music, then coopers and those who make barrels must be musicians.[1]*

Unfortunately, this simplistic and prejudiced perspective still persists. I conduct psychospiritual groups at my office guiding participants in exploring various forms of meditation, many of which involve drumming. Inevitably, I get jokes but also serious inquiries: "What are you doing DeMaria? Worshiping the devil, doing voodoo or something?" I won't dwell on the eyebrows raised by onlookers some mornings when I walk into my office, briefcase in one hand, drum in the other. How odd, such reactions seem when we know how our ancestors embraced drumming for the vital purposes of sacred ritual, healing, and rejuvenating themselves to survive. What I have found; however, is that underneath many people's initial distrust of the drum lies an affinity, even a desire to explore rhythm themselves evidenced by the fact that 70-80 percent of first time "meditators" given a choice between silent meditation and drumming, choose drumming.

The drum has served humankind well and it is time we gave it back a fitting respect. Native healers I have worked with say that no one "owns" a drum. Each is simply a guardian, a caretaker for the drum whose voice will usually outlast our own. Though our own heart beating will end one day, the eternal rhythmic heartbeat of creation persists.

When we accept the drum and give it its rightful place, we are poised to become connected with something primitive that exerts a peculiar force on us, stirring us passionately. "Primitive" not in the sense of "inferior", but, rather in its true meaning that is "primary" and basic to our very being, an innate wisdom that escapes logical explanation because it is the ground from which all knowledge emerges.

The drum reminds us, as few other experiences, of the vital connection, the ecstatic relationship between the rhythm of

our life and all life around us. It is during the darkest of times, hunger, despair and darkness that the drum, mysteriously feeling at home in the dark, fills us with hope, connection and a sense of place. We speak of circadian rhythms to describe the rhythms each one of us have emotionally, behaviorally and physiologically. Circadian literally means *circa,* "about" and *diem,* "day"; that is, about or around a day. So a circadian rhythm is the particular rhythm associated with one complete earth rotation and for us our regular metabolic, glandular and sleep rhythm which persists through one complete cycle of day and night. When interrupted by high speed travel through time zones, it is interrupted. Jet lag is a disruption of our circadian rhythm and has very real effects. These are crucial rhythms that we depend on for our sanity and survival. As a psychologist, one of the first true signs of distress in an individual is when their sleep and eating cycles are disrupted. Rhythm is not just about music but rests at the core of our very lives. To master life we must learn to respect and understand rhythm, our own and nature's. At the center of the concept of circadian rhythm is the understanding of the circle itself.

THE SACRED CIRCLE

In that same cavern of *Les Trois Frere,* where the petroglyphs were found, there were also footprints discovered. These prints left some 40,000 years ago trace a circle. The drum, like a magnet, draws us like so many iron filings into a circle. Put a drum and a human heart together and we find two things - dancing and a circle. This is the primary equation our ancestors discovered in the twilight of human consciousness. Between the wild cry and the first spoken word lies dancing in a circle. These circle dances emerged out of their day to day harsh lives, like a tree's concentric circles growing outward. These dances were not "conceived" as much as birthed. They embodied and danced their cosmology which to them was a balancing harmonizing with *all-that-is*.

Is it just a coincidence that most drums themselves are made in the shape of a circle? Whether these remains of circling feet on a prehistoric cave floor or the arrangement of prehistoric monoliths such as Stonehenge, the circle's endless rhythm appears throughout the ancient world in Africa, Europe and North America as a symbol uniting profane and sacred worlds. The early night watchers of the sky noticed the circular movement of the stars and the earliest gatherings of our ancestors were circles around a fire.

So the beat of any rhythm, like the drumbeat, is circular, a constant return to an implicit unity. In this sense, the circle is a form in space that matches the sound form in air of the drumming vital rhythm of life. In a way a circle is visual rhythm. The circle unites both the dance and rhythm of existence. The circle closes the Alpha and Omega of life where there is no beginning or end, just the endless rhythmic cycles. The analogies go on: we ourselves originate from a small round egg. Our planet is circular, while its endless circular path as it rotates around the great spherical sun gives us the rhythmic seasons of the year.

Our ancient ancestors were immersed in such rhythmic circling. They greeted and prayed to the sun, the great circle of fire in the sky that gave them everything they needed, every morning. The lunar circle came once a month at night and revealed how to see through the darkness of their lives. When they gathered, they sat in a sacred circle. Like the God Quetzacoatl, the ever present sacred circle symbolized an ancient world view which ought to call in to question our modern perspective of unchecked linear progression. In the words of Black Elk:

> *You have noticed that everything an Indian does is in a circle, and that is because the Power of the World always works in circles, and everything tries to be round...The Sky is round and I have heard that the earth is round like a ball and so are all the stars. The Wind, in its greatest power, whirls. Birds make their nests in circles...The sun comes forth and goes down again in a circle. The moon does the same, and both are round.*

> *Even the seasons form a great circle in their changing, and always come back again to where they were. The life of a man is a circle from childhood to childhood and so it is in everything where power moves. Our tipis were round like the nests of birds and these were always set in a circle...a nest of many nests where the Great Spirit meant for us to hatch our children.[2]*

I have conducted groups over the last few years where we are deliberately conscious of "sitting in circle." There, I teach a variety of meditative practices including drumming meditation. What I have seen in the people has been very powerful. Karen had this to say about the importance of circles:

*I am not sure I can put into words what it means to me
to "sit in circle." Whenever we "sit in circle" together
I feel very at peace, relaxed and tranquil. It's as if
something in me is being put back together. I feel more
balanced and grounded. It is where I come from my
hectic week, to not have to be anything, do anything or
go anywhere, but to just be...*

The mythic structure of the quest itself ultimately blesses a certain circular movement as it ultimately always ends with a "return." So we come to realize as we repeatedly go forth on our quests that we always return anew, each time completing another orbit in our lives. Is this perhaps the genuine meaning of Arthur's "Round Table"? Our questing then is a circling dance, echoing the eternal rhythms of Being, both with and beyond all time and space.

The Medicine Wheel

One can not explore circle symbology very far without encountering the cross. The cross-in-wheel is found throughout the world. One of the most startling and moving cross-in-wheel symbols is that of the medicine wheel of the tribes of North America. Many native people credit the medicine wheel with bringing millennia after millennia of war, competition and intertribal conflict to a peaceful resolution. In fact, much of our understanding of modern democracy arose from some of the astonishing intertribal councils such as the Iroquois that inspired Franklin and Jefferson with their ability to find a way to unite many opposing voices. The medicine wheel does this because of its deeply ecological foundations that unite practical and spiritual matters; the conflict that has been the cross all of us have had to bear. How do we find a harmonic balance between them.

The cross-in-wheel motif of the Medicine Wheel in its most basic form is a compass indicating the four directions. One oriented one-self based upon these directions. To understand the sacred quality of the four directions, it is important to remember that in indigenous tribal culture there were no road signs. Being able to know east from west, north from south many times could be a matter of life and death. It is not surprising then that they believed, and many still do, that there were spirits in each direction - there was a certain feel, atmosphere, character and quality to the spirits of each direction. These four directions were also seen to symbolize and relate to the four elements that composed *all-that-is*. Determining directions had a great deal to do with knowing the track of the sun, moon and stars. Therefore, when one wanted to find out what "time" of day it was, one looked at the sun, the shadows from the trees. One was not iso-lated from the natural world, but immersed in it for practical reasons which resonated with spiritual dimensions. So not only are there directions, but the wheel simultaneously harmonizes the rhythm of a day, a week, a month, a year and a life time. In the East is the spring, the place of beginnings. In the South, the fullness of the summer of one's life. In the West there is the place of autumn dying and in the North winter. In this way, East refers to the literal direction, as well as the time of day, the season of the year, and the stage of one's life.

Now, obviously depending on where one lived in the world some of the "quality" of the direction would change. That is why many tribes have different elements and colors that symbolize different directions. The important point here is the understanding of a wheel denoting the ever changing, rotating seasons of the year that rhythmically disappeared and returned embracing a cross symbolizing the individual quest of each human being, intimately connected in a sacred dance.

Here are the circles within circles that we live out everyday, every month, every year, and within every life. All linear progression is surrounded by and balanced within rhythmic cycles that are not only respected, but celebrated in dance. Jung had this insight in his understanding of the mandala:

> *There is no linear evolution; there is only a circumambulation of the self. Uniform development exists, at most, only at the beginning; later, everything points toward the center. This insight gave me stability, and gradually my inner peace returned. I knew that in finding the mandala as an expression of the self I had attained what was for me the ultimate.*[3]

Still after fifteen years of teaching Advanced Personality courses to graduate students in psychology, mainstream psychology has virtually no models that take into consideration this truth. Based on the mechanized paradigm of Newtonian physics as we have seen, our Western first world psychology (with a few very notable exceptions) typically ignores the organic cycles of human development.

One Western symbol, however, symbolically unifies the paradox of the linear, masculine quest and the circular, feminine dance in our spiritual development. Though the symbol has pagan roots, we know it as the "Celtic Cross": a cross with equal axes joined by a surrounding circle. To the ancient wisdom of the Celtic people this symbol represented the union of the heavenly and earthly forces. The crossed axes represented the forces of our spiritual expansion pushing out to the four directions. The circle symbolized the eternal unity of these apparent manifestations. In our terms, the cross represents linear aspects of questing, the circle denotes the dance within which they are contained. However, even in the Celtic Cross we can see how the circle is "subservient" to the cross.

A homelier Western symbol appears also in daily life. We think of it only as a delicious food, but it also echoes the medicine wheel and even has a place in the Christian religious calendar. I refer to the British custom of eating "hot crossed buns" on Good Friday. Probably descended from the cakes offered by Greeks to the goddesses Artemis, Hecate and the moon, the round cakes, symbolized the Full Moon, the feminine yonic circle and the cross represented the masculine/solar four quarters of the year, the two solstices and two equinoxes united in one form.

When we add rhythm and thus the wisdom of the circle into our understanding of the quest, we open up a more inclusive understanding of our life journey. Yes, it is a quest, *and,* it is a dance. The Plains Indians of North America knew this. For them the Vision Quest was primarily masculine and individual in nature. It was the way for one person to find their connection to the divine, their unique life vision. However, this individual quest had an intimate and integral relationship to the great Sundance which was primarily feminine in nature evoking the divine, vital connection to all our relations within the great circle of life. The Sundance animates the Medicine Wheel into a living, breathing, three-dimensional reality. In the middle of the Sundance grounds lies the sacred arbor. The dancers are pierced and attached to the arbor as we are all attached to the creator by an invisible umbilical cord. Many people are initially horrified when they find out the practice of the piercing Sundance. The process is an ancient one. The Sundancer is pierced usually with one or two incisions made on the chest through which an eagle's bone is inserted and then tied to the sacred tree (arbor) in the middle of the circular Sundance grounds. The dancer, after making an agreement with the Creator of how long he will dance while pierced, anywhere from 15 minutes to four days, without food or water, will then break free from this symbolic umbilical cord signifying the connection of all things leaving very noticeable scaring upon his body. However, much like the stigmata of Christ, the suffering is seen by these sacred practitioners of the Sundance as bringing one very close to God, the Creator. It is as if each dancer is bearing the cross of his people. Embraced by the great circle, he dances within, symbolizing his human community, the community of all nature of which he is a part, and the Great Mystery which is the all encompassing circle.

Our Western, primarily Christian understanding, is usually too based on linearity alone. For example, we forever wait for some "event" in the future that will then answer all of our prayers instead of heeding the wisdom of the circle and looking into the moment for truth. As Jesus himself said, "The Kingdom of God is Now."

This idea of interfusing quest *with* dance is nothing new though it may sound new to many of us. The Yoruba tribe of Africa see their dances as "journeys." Each time they are performed, they are improvised and so are always different thereby fusing an element of linear time, change and history with the eternal circling. For them *everything* is a journey and thus at once new and known, an adventure and a dance, dangerous and yet comforting:

> *The whole life span of man or a woman is a journey. That is our belief. Ajo l'aye (literally, "journey of life"). When you are going to start your life, you go through a journey. Even when you are coming to the life, you go through a journey. And if you want to develop on the life, it is a journey. So it is just journey, journey, journey all the while.*[4]

As with the Yoruba, so with most native people the world over, strict linear time does not exist in either the mind or life. The human soul is always coming into the world and then leaving the world in an unending cycle. Yet, since the fourth dimension (time) exists, too, nothing is ever repeated. As with each circling of the seasons, one's journey is neither simply cyclical, nor linear. It is both. When the circle and the line make love, when the quest becomes also a dance, then we find the symbol of symbols that evokes the timeless odyssey of the soul...the spiral.

The Sacred Spiral

Like the circle and the cross, the spiral has been an ancient model of the soul's journey since prehistoric times. Though found in many petroglyphs the world over, it is hauntingly absent from our daily understanding of life. The spiral is finding us again through a surprising means - science. Ceaselessly exploring the natural world, scientists have revealed the spiral everywhere; from the sub-atomic quantum world to the farthest reaches of the universe in the grand movement of the galaxies themselves. Billions of stars spiral around one another in to what we can with some accuracy call a cosmic dance. Between these great extremes are the spirals of hurricane and tornados, the awesome spirals of birds circling their prey, the water going down a drain, and perhaps most significantly, the double helix of DNA, the ultimate spiral encoding all life.

The irony remains that although science has helped us discover the importance of spirals, its very methods and aims, primarily quantitative, divorces us from the very "meaning" of the spiral. No matter how many spirals we see, we must go deeper to find its actual significance.

The spiral is ubiquitous. Look around and you will begin seeing it everywhere. Traditionally it was the doorway between the waking and dreaming worlds, the upper and lower natures of man. For most of us, we see this evoked in dream sequences in the movies that always start with the obligatory spiraling tunnel that always marks a gateway between the inner and outer worlds. These kaleidoscopic spiraling images can be extremely disorienting causing nauseous vertigo one minute and then bliss and ecstasy the next.

Ancient symbol of eternity, any spiral implies that it could go on forever, yet at every point it also represents endless change. If life were only a circle, we would dissolve into the same exact place from which we started. Though we do return, through death, to the great source of *all-that-is,* we do so changed. Amness is entirely different for the infant than it is for the elder.

Trying to answer the question, what is the meaning of a spiral, is like asking the meaning of music. Spirals are expressive patterns of meaning, much like music. A spiral encapsulates the waxing and waning of life. There is always a growing, a sense of going forward, waxing, developing, learning. Then, imperceptibly at first, as the direction shifts, we find the other side of the spiral bringing a sense of returning, retreating, waning, wasting and diminishing. This applies to our whole existence. We usually sense our lives as a linear line or path between birth and death. However, as we have seen over and over, is that this is the journey, this quest has cycles to it. There are many small deaths on the way to the great death. There are perpetual rhythmic rising and falling, triumphs and defeats in one lifetime.

Imagine being on isolated point on an actual wheel that is making a track in the earth. Now, the life of a linear point dreads the approaching end of one's life, like the moment it hits the ground. However, the point on the wheel after passing through that moment of hitting the ground, comes back around. The point feels like it is dying and being reborn all the while it is circling around and around. The end and the beginning are simply arbitrary points on the wheel.

DANCING

True ease in writing comes from art, not chance, As those move easiest who have learn'd to dance.
~*Alexander Pope*

The spiral of life reveals to us that our questing journeys must also be danced. The journey is not so much straight linear progression as it is a continual unfolding of circling what we love, what we are drawn to, what calls us forth. Remember, a flower unfolds in its blossoming in a circle. This was very true for Leslie, a professional woman approaching middle age who had spent most of her time being superwoman by both raising children and developing a career. When her marriage fell apart, she felt profoundly wounded. When she learned to let go of seeing her life as a race from here to there with no room for "mistakes" or "imperfections" she found great satisfaction in the day to day "dance" of her life:

I just simply struggled for so many years to try to "make" my life the way I thought it should be. Striving for success in terms of climbing the upward mobile ladder of contemporary American society to "make" something of myself. Not that doing so was wrong as much as it became so painfully obvious that with each failure, I came face to face with a gaping hole inside. I came to realize I was missing so many other parts of me. I was being run by some automatic pilot that kept

pushing me ever forward and upward, instead of re
-connecting with lost parts of myself. I realized ever
so slowly, that this quest for meaning that I had begun,
took me as much backwards as forwards. Sometimes
I would curse the process of getting to know myself, it
didn't "fit in" with my clean cut image of myself. I
had to confront and look at so many inner demons.
When I realized I wasn't climbing a ladder anymore.
That's it, when I realized that I wasn't in some kind of
bizarre race, that I could relax and begin to smell the
flowers, look at the sky, feel the grass growing beneath
my feet. When I found out that not only was that OK,
but perhaps, that is what might be most important for
me to do. Wow, that was a wake up call. I've learned
to dance again, the way I was as a child. Freely,
openly...even with the most hideous parts of myself, I
have begun ever so slowly to bless those dragons and find
out even they had gifts to bring and truths to tell.

Over time she began to walk into the wounded part of herself and in so doing retraced her path and thereby began to retrieve parts of herself that had been locked away. She realized forward questing had to be balanced with a re-claiming, a re-turning of lost parts of herself. She came to know that doing so was not a failure, a simple regression but rather a progression as well. A polishing of her soul. Formerly, she had learned to walk straight on her own. Now she could allow herself to dance and be danced by life. In a very real way she learned to follow a different rhythm then she was used to.

Dancing and questing have a kinship. In a way every quest is also a dance, and perhaps every dance is somehow a quest. Yet, there are differences. When we are on a quest, we are looking ahead, we have an end in sight; as Leslie said, climbing a ladder. But, when we are immersed in dance, we live the very rhythm of being. We become one with life's very heartbeat an end in ourselves. There is no place to go, we are already where we need to be. In dancing, we just let the rhythm unwind us. Questing expresses our becoming, dancing expresses our being. The anthropological literature on indigenous cultures teaches us how dancing and music-making are "Medicine" restoring us to ourselves. Often when a tribe's spirits are low from traveling great distance, or warriors become exhausted and hungry on a long hunt, they build a fire and begin to dance and sing in a circle. Then their "spirits" lift and they "feel" better. They say they are "inspirited" to continue on their journey. In so doing they are restoring the vital connection - plugging themselves back into creation and recharging their batteries.

Even today within the recesses of our own bodies we vaguely remember this ancient connection when we are in a "bad" mood and a particular rhythm begins playing on the radio and begins to enter our soul. Our "spirits" return. A smile comes over our face and we feel the sap of life begin to flow again. This is not just entertainment, it is medicine. I have heard teenagers reduced to sobbing when their parents take away "their music" as if they were taking away their very souls. Who has not also felt the body begin to move in an almost magical rhythm when the drum beats out its syncopated beat, almost as if the drum itself is calling the human body to move, dance and express itself.

Then there is the story of Karen Hartley on Christmas Day of 1997.

Finding herself stranded in the freezing mountain snow of the Utah wilderness, she knew it was either dance or die. She knew her only way to survive was to keep her brain occupied with playing music in her head, and dancing to it to keep warm. Intuitively, reverting to an ancient practice of ecstatic trance dancing she danced from dusk until dawn. Dancing, literally, saved her life.

I'm not sure whether traveling medieval knights gave themselves over to the dance, but we do know they often traveled with their own minstrels, when far away from home, who would minister in song when the knights became weary. Just so, all have used music and dance to connect with hidden springs within ourselves.

Dancing And Being Danced

O body swayed to music, O brightening glance, How can we know the dancer from the dance?

~W.B. Yeats

Drumbeats, circling, spiraling - dancing, dancing, dancing...if an aspect of our life's journey is dancing, Yeats has it right when he proclaims that our movements are necessarily part of a grander dance. If we are dancing in our lives, whose music do we hear, what song is it that we are dancing to, are we listening to the beating rhythm of our own hearts or somebody else's? Do we follow the rhythm of a different drummer? What is our particular rhythm and how does our dance fit with the great dance of the natural world, the cosmos itself? When we dance there is always a partner. Sometimes visible, sometimes invisible. Are we aware that opening ourselves to the beat brings with it an awareness of the *vital connection* we have always had with rhythm of the universe? In honoring our connection to rhythm, we are honoring the gift our mother gave us so long ago - our beating heart. The Cherokee's had a term "The Rainbow Bridge" which expresses the importance of working with the rhythms around us and entering our rhythms into the grander rhythms of the community and the cosmos.

People intuitively appreciate those who have learned to "dance" in such a way with whatever it is that they do. And we understand that the most awesome skill is expressed by those who "dance" at the heart of their very lives no matter what it is they're doing. This is the larger truth that Alexander Pope implied when he wrote: "True ease in writing comes from art, not chance, for those move easiest who have learned to dance."

Unfortunately, we still do not have much of a language of the dance, of the circle, and the spiral. Our language for the most part is rooted in the linear. Terms like "circular reasoning," "convoluted thoughts," are pejorative, and their manifestations are even considered psychiatric symptoms during a typical clinical assessment of "mental health." There are psychopolitics operative in our science and medical communities that are still artifacts of the Newtonian/ Cartesian mechanical model of the universe where clear and distinct ideas are given priority over the powerful faculty of imagining. Imagining (what I prefer to call imaging) is a faculty of knowing just like thinking; a way of apprehending the world; a verb; a way of interacting with each other and the world whose time has come. But if we just do not have the language, yet, to breathe, depth, pace, and pulse into the very body and blood of the wisdom of the spiral, we are on our way.

DANCING EXERCISE

Take a few minutes in quiet meditation breathing deeply and relaxing. Now, pick some music that is very moving to you. The idea is not to just pick some "dance" music but to find some music that literally moves you from a place deep inside. This may be sad music, glad music or any other kind of music. Now turn the lights down and allow yourself to move to the music. Start slow and gradually allow the music to truly move through you. It can help if you visualize the patterned sound entering every cell of your body, resonating with the very center of your being. The idea is to find your soul's spontaneous response to the music. It takes at least 7-10 minutes of this experience, until you feel yourself becoming less self-conscious and "lost" in the music. I recommend keeping up for twice that time, more if you desire. When you are through, write your spontaneous impressions, feelings, sensations about the experience. This is a form of a "music bath," that I recommend people take at least once a week. Such a music bath is to the soul, what a physical bath is to the body. Dance yourself to health. If you feel awkward doing this exercise just remember, *it is only those who don't hear the music who think the dancer's crazy!*

CHAPTER 8:

DANCING BETWEEN THE WORLDS

God respects me when I work,
but loves me when I sing.
~Rabindranth Tagore

I stared up at the crow's nest protruding 50 feet above the wooden deck. The hot Florida sun beat down through a translucent blue sky outlining like a halo the tall main mast of the pirate ship. I stood half petrified looking at the sight. We were in the Florida Keys, I was 13 years old. My family had taken a summer trip and we had detoured to visit this ship, restored to the finest detail. Ratlines up the masts led to a crow's nest which was topped by a white skull and cross bones on the flags menacing black background. As my brother Randy said, giving it the official kid approval; "Cool, just like in the movies."

My two brothers, Brian and Randy, always appeared fearless to me. If truth be told, their strength and daring in the face of every kind of danger intimidated me. No surprise then, when they scurried halfway up the ratlines and looked down to laugh at my timidity. My older brother Brian snickered, "Go ahead Michael, there's nothing to it." Then as usual Randy poured it on, "What's the matter Michelle, is it too scary for you?" Then they both chorused, "Mikie wo-o-o-n't do it, he wo-o-o-n't do anything, he's too-ooh-scare-ed!" Countless times this had happened; at the high dive at the pool; on the "Hell Ride" at the state fair; even at home climbing trees. Over and over again I froze in the face of their challenge, constantly avoiding crossing over the threshold to step into my fear.

That day something changed. Maybe it was the skull and crossbones, maybe it was the Florida heat, but something hidden and buried, though clawing to get out finally did. In that moment, I felt my heart pound like a thousand wild stallions and a part of me that always closed the gate on them for some reason conceded on that day. Before I knew it, the gate was thrown open and the stallions ran free. All of a sudden I felt a surge of energy spiral up my spine. I could hear my heart pulsating in my chest. My eyes glossed over. Images of pirates, gunpowder and canons filled my mind, my very flesh. In an instant I was not playing pirate, I became "pirate." A fearless pirate. I gave out a blood curdling yell that stunned my brothers, my parents and even a few tourists who were shocked by the family drama unfolding before them. Next thing I knew, I had jumped on the rattling and started running up it past my brothers, past the first cross mast, past the second, screaming all the way. My goal was the crow's nest and I felt an exhilaration and a surge of energy unlike anything I had ever felt before. It felt like I was climbing towards the sun itself. I had no fear. I had entered a place of transformation where I could become what I wanted and needed to be.

I jumped in the crow's nest and yelled "Ahoy! Mates ahoy! Land Ho!" Then out of my mouth came a song, spontaneous and loud. It had a lousy melody, made up on the spot, but it was *my* song, sung with *my* voice. My brothers just stared upward at me, their jaws dropping in disbelief. They themselves were too scared to go farther than half-way up the mast.

Something changed in me from that day forward. My relationship with my brothers also changed. I had come in contact with a different part of myself, "the-pirate-of-me." Something "other" than who I had thought myself to be had emerged. Had I willed the "pirate" out of me? Had I just imagined the "pirate" out of me? Had the "pirate" emerged spontaneously and independently from me? What does "making it up" really mean anyway? I have mulled over these questions for the better part of the last few decades. What I do know is I began dancing with the "pirate-of-me" and as I did, it had real and profound effects in my life.

Looking back I can understand that entering the world of a pirate was no accident. The pirate represented part of my shadow self, my double. Up until that moment, I had been the model good boy who always did what his parents told him. Or, at least most of the time. A pirate was the furthest thing from my day-to-day identity. Yet, it had energy, the energy of wild horses trapped within. My former persona of the "nice, quiet, do-as-you're-told, drink your milk, altar boy" gave way to something deeper in me. The poets of old would say, "Go to heaven for form, go to hell for energy." I liked that, it reminded me of the marriage I had to make between the altar-boy-of-me and the pirate-of-me. These were two worlds that I had to learn to dance with. Like the drum, the pirate spoke to me of something latent inside my soul that needed desperately to be expressed and honored. I have grappled with that pirate ever since. He has gone from being a dark stranger to a powerful companion. What I have learned, without a doubt, is that when I have been able to "hang out" with him and learn from him, he has been a welcome friend and teacher. When I have tried to tyrannically silence him, suppress him and throw him into some dark prison house he goes from being a helpful buccaneer to a very dark figure intent on revenge and "going wild." The key is our relationship to each other and how we ultimately "dance with" one another.

As a psychotherapist I have found many people discuss similar experiences where they find themselves connecting with other aspects of themselves that lead to a broader sense of self. As opposed to a simple linear development of one persona, they are confronted sometimes through creativity, sometimes through trauma with a whole different "other" within, not without. This is where the quest for our true self blossoms into the dance of our many selves.

THE ORCHESTRAL SELF

Listen to the voice inside you.
She is waiting to be found
Once you've heard that sound inside you,
You will always stand your ground
~Chloe Goodchild

Enter the orchestral self. The word orchestral originates from the Greek word *orcheisthai*, meaning to dance. In the primitive Greek theater, when there was still a sacred significance to the movement of the dancing chorus, the orchestra designated an actual place, a circular space where the dancing chorus performed. We have forgotten the mythic origins of this rich word in our Western heritage. Imagine for a moment going to the premiere of *Titanic,* with the sacredness of going to Easter mass at the Vatican. This would just give us a hint to the magnetic quality of the Greek theater. It was at once high story telling, sacred ritual and psychodrama all rolled into one. At the center of this was the *orcheisthai,* an actual living, breathing circular, spiraling space, a dwelling place where the sacred was given voice and movement. Originally, the *"orcheisthai"* was a dancing chorus, a group of players who described and commented upon the central action of a play with song, dance and recitation. There is little doubt that this original *"orcheisthai"* of the Greeks bore remnants of the sacred circle dances practiced by so many aboriginal cultures. A dancing, chanting circle, usually around a fire brought enchantment back to life. The circle dance was where indigenous people expressed interconnection and interdependence with the great web of life - all being players in an immense dance of life, death and rebirth. In fact, the Native American hoop dance, where dancers weave themselves in and out of each other is a symbolic mirroring and uniting with the act of the Great Mystery weaving the web of the universe. This was actually the basis of the great vision Black Elk had for not only his people, but for all people:

> *Then I was standing on the highest mountain of them*
> *all, around about beneath me was the whole hoop of*

232

*the world. And while I stood there I saw more than
I can tell and I understood more than I saw; for I was
seeing in the sacred manner of the shape of all things
in the spirit, and the shape of shapes as they must live
together like one being. And I saw that the sacred hoop
of my people was one of the many hoops that made
one circle, wide as daylight and as starlight, and in the
center grew one mighty flowering tree to shelter all the
children of one mother and one father. And I saw that
it was holy.[5]*

The Greek's "orchesthai" was the "hoop dance" of the Greeks - a dancing, singing witness to the eternal drama of living a life. The hero in the tragedy was cradled in the dancing space of the *orcheisthai*, the sacred hoop dance of our Western culture where one's individual life found a place within the many lives of the divine drama of all things. As our tribal ancestors the Greeks drama was not pure entertainment, but expressive of their cosmology, psychology and theology, all rolled into one which was not just taught but danced, sung and experienced.

It was only later in Roman times, that seats were placed in the Greek *orchesthai*. However, initially only the front part of this section was reserved for the musicians. Gradually the name of the place was transferred to those that used it. The "orchestra" in time came to mean the band of musicians when originally it meant those that danced and sang to the music. In addition, the orchestra of the ancient Greeks would be multiple voices singing the same song. Multiplicity in unity.

At the root of the orchestral self is the Gestalt insight that the whole is greater then the sum of its part. Gestalt is the German word for organic form. In this way a gestalt is an irreducible perceptual pattern. A classic example of a gestalt is a musical pattern that although it can be played in different keys, retains its essential structure. Whether I play "Mary had a little lamb" in the key of C or G, you will recognize it although I am using completely different notes. It is the relationships between the notes that count. The crucial point is that there is a meaningful emergence once all the parts are related, that is not present in the parts themselves. It is in their relationship to each other that meaning and form emerge.

Viewed in this way, we can view the orchestral self as not being a monarchy, a totalitarian state, or a monoculture. But rather, the orchestral self emerges as a meaningful montage where one's various voices are not put in any superior to inferior grading, there is no hierarchy - no "above" and "below." Like the notes in "Mary had a little lamb," E is not better then C, they are both essential to creating the melody. Likewise, the violins are as important as the flutes and percussion section within an orchestra. Just because the flutes have quantitatively half as much sheet music to play, the qualitative effect is just as important. This is where the original meaning of the term orchestral comes in very useful, that is, not only is there a musical quality at the heart of our understanding of ourselves, but that it implies a dancing chorus of voices. It is at once differentiation and integration, multiplicity and unity, much like our cross-in-wheel, as the ancient symbol of the self.

When we first start working with our many voices and images, they are seen as distinct worlds, ignoring and misunderstanding each other. The next step is allowing ourselves to be aware of these different voices. We do this by encouraging communication between these separate dimensions of ourselves. Some have called this process "dis-identification" in the service of psychosynthesis. Others have called it active imagination in the pursuit of individuation. Just by the shear fact of becoming aware of these other dimensions of ourselves, we are able to step back even if just for a moment. The psychological truth here is that whatever we become aware of in consciousness, we are by definition already greater than. This is a very comforting thought to most people as they embark on this hero's journey of self-discovery.

The way we become aware of our distinct voices usually proceeds as follows. Consider a particular feeling, attitude or trait you may have. Now, close your eyes and simply ask that part of you to clothe itself in an image. This may be a man, a woman, an animal, some abstract apparition, a monster, or literally anything imaginable in the universe. Once the image has appeared let yourself "hang out" with it. Dialogue with this part of you and let this image talk and express itself - literally allow it to "come to life." Give it a voice. As the conductor of your orchestral self, imagine how interesting it would be to find out what instruments exist in your orchestra. More importantly, what is in each musician's repertoire, that is, their particular stock of skills, songs, roles and plays. What range and depth of emotions they bring and what particular gifts or weaknesses do they have? Are they a candidate for a solo or do they need a great deal of guidance and direction? Perhaps they have a lot of raw emotion but tend to be immature, self-centered, and have difficulty listening to the other players. In a word, what *qualities* do they bring forth? Now you may go on and even give this image or voice a name. It may be a personal name like "Karen," or an animal like "panther," or an archetypal name like, "The Magician."

Take some time to write the experience down including the feeling quality you experience during the exercise. For example, notice how your body felt and what sensations and insights developed. Most people report that just by exploring their emotions and feelings this way, they feel more relaxed. In this short exercise it is possible to contact a vivid, living voice/ imaginal player in our orchestral self with pulse, breadth and depth that is literally part and parcel of us.

In this way, the various voices within us, the different "roles" we play, are like musicians in a jazz combo or players in an improvisational play, or notes in a musical score that always exist in relationship to each other and the more communication that exists between the members, the more harmonic their interaction.

Joshua provides a good example of this truth. Joshua was a 30-year-old artist. He liked the idea of "orchestration," but he said very early on in our work together:

> I'll buy that I have to orchestrate, but my inner orchestra's more like a rock band. You see there has been the "lead guitarist" who has dominated the show for the last decade. He doesn't want any "touchy feely" stuff in the band, he only wants to play the music his way, hard and loud. So, he usually drowns out the bass player, and he ran off the keyboard player.

PART IV: THE DANCE

It was not surprising that Joshua had real difficulty in sustaining long-term relationships. He had over identified with the "lead guitarist" within and lost the ability to hear the melody, the softer sides of himself speaking. This played itself out in his relationships. But, until he became more merciful and aware of his inner "band" he would not be successful with the "relationships" in the interpersonal realm.

We began by giving him a chance to step back and "dis-identify" from the lead guitarist. It was such a dominant role in his life it was very hard for him. However, over time he was able to ask what was keeping the lead guitarist from really hearing the other "band members." The dialogue between his inner "lead guitarist" and the inner "keyboardist" who had left the band went like this:

LB: O.K. so why did you leave.
KB: Because you drowned me out. No one could ever hear me above all the racket you made.
LG: @#$% you! That racket is "real" music, not those airy fairy melodies you call music.*
KB: You see how you hurt me, you're just an @#$hole.
LG: You started it, calling my music "racket".
KB: Well, why did you call for me, I didn't think you missed me anyway?
LG: (after a pause) It's hard for me, it's hard for me to admit, I do need you, and I do miss you, I just get scared, scared of being hurt. I really do think everybody hates me most of the time.
KB: That's the first time I've heard that. All I ever heard was anger, hate and rage in your music. So are you saying you are scared of little old me?
LG: I wouldn't go that far, it's just that you're so open, I just don't see how you don't get hurt. That's what scares me your vulnerability.
KB: That's funny, I mean you scared of me; thanks, I mean, I can care about you and understand if you let me see your vulnerability.
LG: So, do you have new songs?

237

KB: Maybe.
LG: I really would like to hear. I'll just put my guitar down for awhile and let you play.
KB: Really?
LG: Really.

There is no way words can do justice to the encounter Joshua had within himself. This young man never had shown a tear before this inner exchange, yet this time tears rolled freely down his cheeks as he allowed himself to begin to love an exiled part of him.

In this way we can see the self as a kaleidoscope of possibility, a multidimensional playground. Every person that knows us sees a somewhat different perspective, a alternate profile of us and thus assembles us within their own province of meaning in a myriad of ways. It is always up to us, in our own perspective towards our own dazzling array of experiences, history and feelings to dialogue and get to know the inner intricate, subtle and beautiful relationships that are always going on in and around us - one moment flows one way and the next moment in another.

Initially, seeing ourselves in our true multiplicity can be decentering, destabilizing however, in our embracing of this uncertainty comes fresh insight, possibility and renewal. If we can, like the conductor of the orchestra, follow the intricate counterpoint of consonance and dissonance, moving between cacophony and harmony and keep practicing, listening and cultivating our many voices - then we have the opportunity to in a real way, re-construct, renovate and recreate ourselves in a vibrant fullness while being grounded in something tangible and real. In this way, we reach out towards our future, our becoming while remaining conscious and caring of our past, that is our being.

The beginning stages of recognizing one's multiplicity, the many voices that each one of our lives house, can feel chaotic. It is as if we are opening a door to the inner chamber of ourselves, and we are horrified and shocked when what we first hear is a cacophony of sound. In the first steps towards opening the flood gates of multiplicity there is a great clamor and all the voices within that have been repressed, silenced, exiled come rushing back. We fear desperately that we will become lost in a mire of contradictory voices. Yet, over time, the orchestral self harkens to a deeper wisdom then cacophony, that resides on the other side of polyphony, that is, harmony. The many voices can become a concert.

A scenario that has come to be very useful in my own "work" with the "pirate-of-me," goes something like this. The "pirate of me" had been a player in the orchestra of myself, but was later exiled from playing because of his unruly behavior. For some reason I had been given the notion that "my orchestra" should not have pirates playing in it. So, he was put in shackles and escorted to the dungeon. Every so often, however, when I was very tired, stressed or my guard was down, that is, my inner "guards" were sleeping on the job, the "pirate" of me escaped, ran to the orchestra room, picked out the kettle drums and started beating unmercifully. When the rest of the orchestra confronted him he said, "@#$% you! I'm not stopping, you've locked me up all those years and I'm not going back in come hell or high water. I'll make you pay for locking me away all those years." Now, when the dialogue gets to this point, we start wondering why we started this "soul retrieval" work of returning the exiled parts of us. We say, "Oh, my God, now I will become a stark raving lunatic!" However, truth is, life does pick up its tempo - the heart pounds and the adventure of self-discovery gets underway. To prevent the pirate from developing a complete take over of the orchestra - a mutiny of law and order, what is needed is the sustaining of the inner dialogue. This is "the work" of personal growth.

The conductor within starts the peace talks with this comment, "You're right, we did shackle you and throw you in the dungeon. We were scared of you for this very reason. You are impulsive, unpredictable, chaotic and down right terrifying. Yet, we were wrong to try to do away with you. I'll tell you what. Let's just spend some time getting to know each other. How about a deal. We promise not to throw you back in the dungeon if you promise to stop banging those drums. I'm sure we can find a place for you within the orchestra. You may not be able to run the whole show, but if you show a willingness to work together, I promise we can use you. In fact, we would love to add more rhythm to the orchestra. You might be just what we need to get out of this rut we have been in." It is this dynamic interplay of image and voice, multiplicity and unity, unity in diversity that allows the concert of the orchestral self to emerge.

There are usually two main difficulties people have in working with the orchestral self. These are universal not only at an intrapersonal level, but also at the interpersonal level. The first difficulty is when we are not able to access a particular sub-personality, voice or player in our inner orchestra. If the conductor within has no way to even know about this part of us, there is no way for a dialogue to occur. This is a severe limitation. This inability will be played out interpersonally as well. We all know this kind of person who refuses to hear and understand new perspectives, new people and new experiences. This rigidity is a reflection of how many voices within they are repressing and avoiding dialogue, sometimes consciously, other times not so consciously. If we desire greater harmony in our inner life and our outer world, we must be courageous enough to at the very least hold peace talks within to get to know the many different players in our inner orchestra.

The second danger, is the person who is over identified with one and only one player within their inner orchestral self. Joshua serves as a prime example. He is clearly over identified with the Lead Guitarist of himself. Although Joshua is able to at least hear the other players within he is just not able to put himself in their shoes; he sees himself only as the Lead Guitarist all of the time. It was a radically new experience to realize he could actually play the role of the keyboardist. Similarly for myself, I had known the existence of the "pirate-of-me" for some time before I could actually allow myself to experience from the inside out what it would be like to "be" him. So the goal becomes being able to move from identifying and dis-identifying, engaging and disengaging with these different perspectives, voices, ways of being-in-the-world that we all have access to whether we want to admit it or not. This is crucial not only for our own lives but for our whole world. Most wars and international conflicts, both old and new, are always reflections of the level of inner orchestration the people involved have achieved. How different our world would look if the "conquerors" of the new world, instead of projecting their own shadow onto the indigenous cultures and calling them "savages" and proclaiming their cosmology and art as "useless" could have dialogued and "danced with" their language, culture and life. It was an opportunity where the best in both worlds could have emerged. Instead a battle of shadows took place. So too work on our own harmony is also working on the good of all man kind. The words of Jesus ring true, "Before plucking the splinter from your neighbor's eye, take out the log in one's own."

SYNERGY AND JAZZ

Perhaps it is not too late...
and I must borrow every changing shape
To find expression....dance, dance
like a dancing bear.
            ~T.S. Eliot

I have found the term orchestration to be unique in psychological and philosophical literature in that it does not imply integrating the many "parts" of oneself into a homogenous whole - a melting pot where all difference dissolves. There is rather a synergy which allows for differentiation (each voice, each player in the orchestra remains distinct) and integration (all members playing the same song). In the orchestral self there is neither a gridlock of antagonism nor co-dependent fusion. This is the fundamental point. All the players in the orchestra are able to enter a dialogue and create a web of inter-relationships. Here quest and dance are both present. We seek the ever-new voice and each voice is seeking its own truth like a soloist in a jazz combo. Yet there is a dynamic interrelationship that must always exist, a dancing with and between each individual unique voice that requires a certain form, playing within a certain key and range, a sub-mission to a grander pattern. I had an native elder tell me about the Vision Quest with this caution, "Yes, the Vision Quest is a mission, you are on a mission from God, as the Blues Brothers say (this elder obviously goes to the movies and has a sense of humor); yet, my son no one goes on a mission without first asking per-mission and understanding their sub-mission. You must submit to the greater call of your people and of the Great Mystery." It is this submission that each individual voice in the orchestral self must learn. This echoes again the two dangers for each part of the orchestral self; our inability to access that part of us at all and becoming stuck in one and only one part of us. Synergy implies being able to identify and dis-identify, connect with and disengage from any one limited part of us.

Of course, prior to synergy, when the client initially walks into the "inner room" of the self, it is like members of an orchestra all playing a different song in a different key. All they hear at first is "noise." Over time, as each individual "voice" has had a chance to "speak," get to be known, understood and appreciated; they all become much more cooperative and begin to play the same song in the same key and at last, polyphony. The crucial point here is that they continue to be able to have their discreet voices, talents, gifts, yet they are inter-related, resonating with each other. In this way the creative tension between unity and multiplicity is maintained. Instead of reducing all voices to one, the voices create a harmonic resonance, the orchestral self. The *vital tension* between allows for the vital connection within.

As communication and awareness intensify, a more democratic and diverse orchestration occurs. In fact, since there is greater mobility between the various players, many people find they like the term *jazz self* to orchestral self simply because orchestration sometimes feels to rigid, like classical music.

In the *jazz self* we move into the realization of a pluraversal self. Instead of a universe, that is literally one version of reality; we begin to realize we are a pluriverse where multiple versions of reality co-exist, informing each other, bringing breadth and depth to our experience.

One of the observations then about the orchestral self is that each of us is both a single "I" *and* at the same time dozens of "I's" each of which is constantly and forever taking over briefly at different moments in time. In essence what we have been talking about is not a simple continuity of self-same identity, rather there is an oscillation, a vibration constantly from moment to moment. This oscillation, this orchestration of potentialities is non-linear and dynamic and runs forwards and backwards in time and space. The orchestral self is less a stream that always moves in one direction, then a kaleido-scopic web of interconnection, each finding its place in relationship to the other voices. Through these relationships we find an ecological

244

constellation we call the self.   I still find a great deal of resistance and even animosity from traditional mental health professionals towards this idea of "many selves" implicit in the orchestral self. For them, multiplicity still smacks of the pathological. During a staffing in a psychiatric hospital where I worked, I remember a heated discussion with the chief psychiatrist.   I was presenting the case of a young anorexic woman I had treated during her stay in the hospital. He was unhappy I had kept her in the hospital as long as I had and felt my understanding of the case was completely erroneous. I was discussing how she was caught in an internal civil war of debilitating self-hate, when he responded, authoritatively, "There is no such thing!". He went on, "Biologically self-hate makes no sense. There is just one person. You need more than one person for hate. Do you think she has multiple personalities."

He had made the error that much of traditional psychology and psychiatry makes, that is, forgetting that we are cultural not just biological. He was trained in the classic medical model that saw patients as an organism first and foremost that by definition was a self-consistent identity. The psychiatrists refusal to admit the young girls self-hate, helped her brush it under the rug. From a view of multiplicity, what became empowering to her was for her to begin to see part of her hated another part of her. Neither the hating part, nor the hated part were all of who she was. She was greater than both parts. In essence, we could then find out what each part had to say, had to reveal about who she was ultimately. Instead of me having an agenda, or life view that denied her experience, I simply let her

245

amplify both parts and gave them a chance to speak.

Our work together proceeded as follows, "Tell me about this part of you that hates you. Whose voice is it that says, I hate you? Do you recognize it as someone you have known? Is it male or female? Is it old or young? What does it want you to do differently? What would convince that part of you that you were worthy of mercy and love?" We then asked questions of the hated part of her, "How old is the part of you that is hated? How does that part of you feel? Is it male or female? Ask that part of you what it needs most right now?" The synergy began to develop, she widened her perspective of who she was, and thus, who she could be.

The concept of synergy is a helpful one in trying to describe what happens when one begins to explore the multiplicity of the orchestral self. The term was first used by the anthropologist Ruth Benedict in trying to describe communities of tribal culture where she observed high and low synergy. For Benedict and Margaret Mead understood a community to be of high synergy when there was co-operation between its members to insure mutual advantage for all involved. The low synergy community is one where advantage of one individual becomes a victory over another. We can therefore talk of low and high synergy within one's self. Are the different "parts" interacting for mutual advantage, or is "one" part of us constantly claiming victory over the other parts of us? Buckminster Fuller also used the word synergy. For him synergy was the dynamic energy that existed in a whole system where the behavior of any system always exceeded whatever could be predicted by examining any one part. In this way, when people have marveled at the amount of energy some people have had, a voraciously creative individual like Leonardo da Vinci, or William Shakespeare, we could say that they were drawing on vast reservoirs of synergy. In their own way the many "parts" of themselves worked together with virtually no snags or civil wars that usually drain most of our energy. The French psychoanalyst Felix Guattari also used the term transversality to describe the degree of openness that exists within any one group. The higher the transversality, the more each member of the group is able to express what they feel in the way they feel. He was describing groups of people yet, the term is very apt for exploring the orchestral self. Ultimately, our desire is to open up and develop a rich and high degree of transversality and synergy within the orchestral self.

The real power of the orchestral self is found when we begin to view ourselves each moment anew. Only in this way can we truly risk who we thought we were and perhaps venture outside our habitual ways of being and learn to relate to other people like and unlike ourselves. Then we can catch a glimpse of how amazing and far reaching the whole inter-contextual network, the field of being, truly is. We now can begin to see the outlines of amness emerge once again as we see that although profoundly distinct, we are all part and parcel of an entire fabric, a mosaic of being. This is perhaps the sacred elixir we have finally discovered on our quest. The infant knows oneness, amness, but remains undifferentiated without a sense of multiplicity and distinction. After passing through the stages of ego development and ego loss, we come to see the discreet moments of ourselves as distinct and differentiated, but united in a great field - distinct, individual and yet, profoundly related in *amness*. Like the colors in the peacock's tail, our many selves find a pattern, a form, that turns potential chaos into brilliant elegance, sublime beauty. It is here, in the dance of the orchestral self, where the agony of the quest blossoms and gives birth to the flowers and fruit of the dance. Without the work of the quest, the colors could just as well merge into a monoculture of brown mud. If we are able to widen the horizons of who we believe ourselves to be, the meaningful pattern emerges. This is the realm of soul. When we have become fully transparent to ourselves while all the while learning to genuinely love and bless the many voices within, we become fully known and deeply loved.

We can then let go of the single ideal, the rigid belief, or assumptions we thought defined us and allow a grander vision - one that includes and even favors multiple perspectives and is grounded in an extremely flexible approach to reality. How do we move from the overwhelming sense of initial cacophony to the wisdom of polyphonous harmony? The conductor within says, "First and foremost, walk into your fear; it is where the concert takes shape."

HARMONY

A few comments on harmony are necessary. In the last chapter we discussed rhythm being the soul. In the orchestral self we move from rhythm to melody to harmony. The origins of most harmony we hear is rooted in the chanting of medieval Christian monks. Early chant began as simply adorned prayer with certain vowel sounds given greater accent and given a particular fixed pitch. Over time chants were divided up into two or more vocal lines or parts that were identical except for being separated by a number of steps. This style of singing prayers or chants were called *organum*, the term that eventually became the root word of organ, an instrument that was capable of playing many different parts. It also became the root word for the organs of the body which when first observed were considered also like players in an orchestra - all distinct, separate, yet intricately and exquisitely working together for the good of the whole organism. Similarly, the monks whose voices though different, remained synchronized upon the same words and same tonal center. In fact, this was the original form of the Greek *orchestrai* again, many voices singing the same words. In Greece, these words and songs were danced. For the monks, who had left out the dance, they added different levels or layers of voices. In the thirteenth century, particularly in Notre Dame Cathedral in Paris, a number of composers wrote music in which certain voices moved out of sync, giving them independence to move across time for long periods before falling back into unison. It is almost as if, since the physical dance was repressed, the singers began to get up and move through sound. Truly, the first "jazz" monks!

To the medieval listener the sound of these monks was revolutionary. Chant had evolved into polyphony. That is, several independent lines were sung simultaneously. The effect is a song that is identical but sung several beats apart. This became what we know as a *canon*. The most common form of canon we all knew as children from singing "frere Jacques", or "Michael Row Your Boat Ashore",

in Rondo. Over time, polyphony broke completely free by grant-
ing each individual voice freedom of movement. Harmony drew
composer and listener into the world of depth, that is vertical sound.
Music in harmony expresses the relationship between sounds given at
the same time. For example, a chord is many notes played at once.
The harmonic resonance is the resulting sound from the relationship between notes played at the same time and their relationship
over time. In harmony we experience a vast array of overtones and
undertones that vibrate with each other giving rise to the auditory
sensation that most of us feel in our very bodies that we describe as
harmonic resonance. In harmony we are being bathed in a sonic
field. The exercise at the end of chapter 7 is an example of such a
"bath." Often I recommend taking a "music bath" at the minimum
of once a week. A "music bath" does the same for the soul as a water
bath does for the body. The music actually has this watery quality of
"washing" over us. It flows like a stream.

This relationship between notes known as harmony, hinges on the
concepts of consonance and dissonance. Consonance arises when
two or more notes played together, or in succession, provide the
listener with a sense of being at rest - we might even say amness,
the *vital connection*. Dissonance is usually defined by multiple sounds
creating a state of tension leaving the listener with the sensation of
yearning and longing, seeking resolution - the *vital tension*. It is this
very relationship between tension-resolution that is at the heart of
all music composition, orchestral harmony and life. What is even
of more interest is that our perception of which musical intervals

constitute consonance and thus harmony versus dissonance and thus cacophony, has been in a constant state of flux. It changes from one culture to another, from one historical epoch to another, and more recently, from one generation to another.

Generally speaking, the pattern over time from one musical era to another, has seen a constant movement towards expansion of the groups of chords considered consonant. It is as if chords of greater complexity begin to enter our musical lexicon over time. Physiologically and psychologically our ears are slowly able to find harmony in stranger and more exotic harmonic contexts. As our musical exposure and experience increases, so does our ability to find harmony in a grander musical field. Perhaps the greatest openness to the tonal landscape is expressed by Miles Davis when he says, "Do not fear mistakes. There are none." He would clarify by often saying in his raspy voice, "There are no wrong notes," that is, what truly matters is what comes before and after each note that gives it meaning. There is no wrong note in and of itself, again context and relationship. It is the relationship between one note and another that matters, not the note in and of itself. If one stays aware and vigilant enough, one can always make lemonade out of lemons, consonance out of dissonance. The metaphor applies to our lives. No one experience in and of itself is "wrong," it depends on what precedes and follows; how we weave the experience into the rest of our lives. It is not denying it, nor inflating it, but placing it into a greater context, a vaster rhythm.

What I like best about the musical metaphor of the self, is that it reminds us that the self is not an entity, not a product, a static object in space but something always and forever moving, developing, passing away, then emerging again, always in relationship. To combine what we have been saying with the preceding chapter on rhythm, we catch a glimpse of the vastness of the orchestral self. The soul is the rhythm, each melodic line is a sub-personality. When these voices are playing the same song in the same key, we have harmony; a true integrity forged from the orchestration of the self-soul resonant field.

THE ECOLOGICAL SELF

I have found over the years in my work that people are dealing with the multiple domains of the orchestral self and often times they are required to move beyond simple personification and sometimes even a more dynamic model than orchestration. The move has been to include the very organic understanding of seeing each person as a vast ecology, an inner geographical landscape and world. In this way, the orchestral self is an expansive, intrinsic ecology. (An ecology is defined by interdependence, recycling, partnership, flexibility, diversity, and, when all of these are working in harmonic resonance, sustainability.) This has occurred quite naturally as I found people spontaneously describing the many aspects of their experience, different sides of themselves not with a human image, but one of an animal or a geographic or abstract image. Sometimes they would come up with an archetypal image such as "the princess," however, increasingly, clients would speak of a "lion," a "wolf," or even an "oak tree." It was a profound validation when I began to learn that many cultures had discovered this process and had many methods for connecting with and communicating with these aspects of Self. Far from primitive, they reveal a depth of understanding of the multiplicity of the world, and the mirrored multiplicity of the psyche all existing in one grand field of Being. This perspective today is being explore by deep ecologists, eco-philosophers and a new breed of eco-psychologists.

The word ecology comes from the Greek *oikos*, meaning household. Therefore, one's inner ecology could be seen as studying our inner household. In reality, it is actually the relationships that exist within the inner household. The study of ecology grew out of organismic biology which was a reaction against the Newtonian mechanistic view of the universe which saw the world and human beings as machines. Two powerful terms we understand now that grew out of the eco-logical view is that of *community* and *network*. These communities are actually ecosystems. An ecosystem is a complex community hosting many smaller organisms each with a certain degree of autonomy that at the same time are integrated harmoniously into a functioning whole. Our Earth houses some 5 million species of plants, animals, and microorganisms. These beings interact and influence their envi-ronments forming vast ecosystems. These ecosystems are extremely varied, from the Arctic tundra to the South American rain forest. The amazing thing about an ecosystem is that if it is left undisturbed it will move towards balance and stability among the various plants and animals. These complex ecosystems are also remarkable in that they are able to compensate for changes caused by weather or intrusions by other animals. They are enormously diverse. We can contrast this to a monoculture of say a field of cotton. Having only one dominant species the cotton plant, this ecosystem is extremely fragile and susceptible to drought, insects, disease and overuse. Whereas, a forest can adapt and remain quite robust in the face of extreme weather changes that would destroy a nearby cotton field. The complexity and multicultural diversity of the forest gives it sustainability and stability.

In this way we can look at the orchestral self as being an eco-system in a very real sense. Most of traditional psychology, psychiatry and psychotherapy is still functioning within the mechanistic view of ourselves that want to reduce us to one simple "cotton field." Although it provides good produce, it is not very adaptable, sustainable or stable. The irony is the more we try to reduce ourselves to "just one thing and one thing only," the more fragile we become. In particular, in our age of specialization, people professionally and unfortunately personally try to strive more and more for one way of being. The orchestral self provides a way for us to begin and find a more natural diversity within the multiple cross currents of the self. In this way we can bless the multiplicity of the vast self, while nourishing our adaptability, flexibility and sustainability.

In the field of ecology, three fields of living systems are seen to exist - organisms, parts of organisms and communities of organisms. One of the keys to ecology is that there are no hierarchies in nature. The moss in an eco-system is as important as the eagle. We certainly may want to relate and identify more with the eagle, but the moss also has its place. The ecological perspective is at the heart of the orchestral self.

This emerging paradigm shift is only very slowly being recognized in our day to day lives and in our view of ourselves. Most of us, on a day-to-day basis, still live within the monocultural mechanistic view of ourselves. The orchestral self is ecological and blesses unity and multiplicity. That is, we can shift our attention from the forest to the trees. We also know the forest is not only made up of trees but of dirt, moss, mice, birds, wolves, and eagles. Throughout the natural world we find the incredible mosaic of nature which is actually multiple systems nesting within other systems of relationships. Ultimately, we realize there are no parts at all, but rather patterns within an ever flowing stream of relationships.

Inherent in the ecological view of the orchestral self is that we are *of* Nature, not apart. This is a perspective that has gained a great deal of attention over the last years in a movement called deep ecology. The term deep ecology was first used by the Norwegian philosopher Arne Naess some 20 years ago to describe the distinction between "shallow" and "deep" ecology. In Naess' definition, shallow ecology is anthropocentric seeing the human as the center and measure of all meaning. Humans are thought to be above and separate from nature where deep ecology sees humans as intrinsic parts of nature, not separate, and as only a strand in the web of life. Thus deep ecology is a spiritual awareness in the sense that human consciousness is a mode of nature herself of sensing its belonging, interconnectedness to *all-that-is*.

I found clients quite spontaneous when we would do visualizations of a particular "trait" or "feeling" clothed in an image. What would emerge could just as well be plant, animal, cloud, spiraling purple mist, as much as a person. As I became more comfortable allowing clients to reveal these different sides in whatever way spontaneously they emerged, the greater the benefit and the deeper the work would become.

As we have explored the various contours of the geography of the self, it goes without saying there is almost an infinite variety of ways to divide up and explore the many variations possible within the self. There are many popular forms of exploring this from exploring the different parts of the self from the stand point of the ego, id and superego to Jung's understanding of the anima, animus and shadow. Each are metaphors attempting to describe something that in essence is beyond description. A metaphor is a bridge, but only a bridge. There is a paradox of identity and difference at the heart of every metaphor. Each metaphor of the self, whether stream, train, or romantic only gives a hint at the vastness at the core of each and every one of us. Ultimately, there are infinite perspectives. Just as each reader of this text is a world unto him or herself, and will see it very differently, so too can we never "pin down" the self. It will always and forever exceed and over flow any definition.

If we maintain an ecological perspective we can see how there is a time to call on our fire: our passion, intensity and emotion. At other times our water: We must be like the river and flow through and around certain obstacles. At still other times our Air or Earth: We must be able to fly like the wind one moment and at other times be stable as the earth - grounded and firm. Shamanic work with animals is another way of exploring the infinite textures of personality of our "different" selves. If we truly are on our way to being oneself, seeing how the whole world mirrors the vastness of who we are, then it only stands to reason that the whole world is speaking to us.

How do we constellate/orchestrate these many different voices? Through the greatest synthesizer/orchestrator of them all - mercy, which is the art of loving in a true and authentic form. Many times a certain degree of mercy is important before we can even discover many of the other hidden voices which reside within us. If we are open enough and brave enough to walk into our fears of the unknown and venture forth, the fear will give way to a richness and depth unimaginable before. There exists meaning underlying the seeming chaos of competing different voices and images, as the rain forest that first appears to the alien eye to be a vast array of impenetrable uninhabitable chaos turns out to be a an exquisitely designed rich world within whose depths lie untold miracles.

We could spend a whole book on describing this process in detail, it also can take a life time to "get to know" all of the different dimensions within oneself. In fact, if we truly are part of *all-that-is*, and *all-that-is*, is mirrored within us; becoming oneself literally is an endless adventure. Yet, one more comment is essential. Who is the conductor ultimately in our lives? We have tried to touch on the sacred witness, the soul as this conductor. The most merciful aspect of our self. This mercy if it is to be genuine and as powerful as it needs to be, vitally connected to amness, it must ultimately be that part of us connected to the God. Plotinus, the wise philosopher of old saw the situation beautifully:

> *We always revolve about the One,*
> *but we do not always pay attention to it.*
> *Like a chorus singing harmoniously around its conduc-*
> *tor becomes discordant when it turns away from him,*
> *but sings beautifully when turned inward and fully*
> *attentive -*
> *we similarly revolve around the Oneness of God, but*
> *do not always look to him.*
> *Yet when we do, we find our home and resting place. Around*
> *him we dance the true dance;*
> *God-inspired and no longer dissonant.*[6]

THE INNER COUNCIL VISUALIZATION

Listen and attend with the ear of your heart.

~*Saint Benedict*

This visualization takes at its heart the above phrase. This is a powerful practice that can transform you, the longer you work with it. It is not to be done without a truly genuine intent. It is a synthesizing of everything we have explored up until now. We are joining in a sacred ritual that has existed from the very first stirring of humans living in community. We join our ancestors from the ancient cavern at *Les Trois Frier*. Start the visualization by becoming relaxed and receptive. Now imagine you are in a large clearing in the woods. It is night time with the stars a glow and a small sacred fire burning in front of you. Now send out a call to the four directions to ask for your inner council to convene around the fire. After some time, one or two people may show up, perhaps none, perhaps a whole group. There may be people who were very close to you who have died. It could be people you have admired. Simply notice who or what appears. This is the beginning of your inner council. Take your time and slowly allow yourself to identify these voices one by one. If you find yourself becoming overwhelmed, stop and just begin working on the first image that comes to mind. They may be people: men, women, children or they may be animals - they may be angelic, demonic and they may be trolls, fairies, ogres or jesters. You might see Jesus or Mary. Whatever you do, don't "mug" the voices at this circle. Begin by simply identifying who is there. This may take time, a great deal of time, so do not bite off more than you can chew. Simply notice, be curious who is there. This is not a circle of judgment. If you take a judgmental attitude you will probably find very few if anybody showing up at this gathering. This is a sacred circle where everyone has a voice, but no one is allowed to dominate or take complete control, it is a democratic circle. Slowly but surely you can begin to have the different voices heard and allow them to talk. Begin to hang out with these different voices, get to know them, what they want, what they need and what they fear. If they appear angry and seem fearful, remember anger comes from hurt, fear or frustration. Ask them what it is they fear, or where have they been wounded, or what are they frustrated about. For most of us, we need the help of someone versed in this area, ideally someone that has experience both in spiritual direction and depth psychology.

CHAPTER 9:

EVER FLOWING ON

The world is the river of God,
Flowing from him and flowing back to him.
~The Shvetashvatara Upanishad

There once lived a young boy. The boy's parents died while he was still an infant. He had a clubbed foot and was very ugly. Since the boy's parents had died, the tribe had experienced a drought in their village. As a result, many of the men and women felt he was cursed so they avoided him and no one would adopt him. Life became more harsh as the hunting and gathering became more and more scarce, for without rains the plants would not grow and without plants the animals would starve. So, too, now the people of the village were hungry and thirsty and there was nothing for them to drink or eat. The tribal elders held a council to decide what to do. After much talking they came to an agreement. There lived a witch in a cave atop the great mountain called Storm Maker. However, everyone feared making the perilous climb up the mountain to the cave where she lived, not to mention having to confront a woman said to have supernatural powers. It was said that the source of the spring water that used to flow into the village before the drought lie in the cave of the witch. Many had heard tales that those sick or ill could be cured by just a few drops of water from the source of the spring that lie deep within the mountain, tended by the old crone. But, who would go? They decided to send the boy. They congratulated themselves on such a stroke of genius, for they felt he was the source of all of their hardships anyway. The elders decided if the boy survived the ordeal to the witch, was able to bring back a cup of the magical spring water, he could come back to the village, if not it was then the Great Mystery's will that he should die. It was decided. The boy would be sent up the mountain the following day.

The day he ascended the peak of Storm Maker the boy felt weak, vulnerable and unloved and most of all thirsty. He had wondered why his parents had died, why he was deformed and now why the villagers were sending him away. He felt he was just not enough, deformed, ugly and of no use to anyone. Tears streamed down his face as he painstakingly climbed the mountain towards the dark mouth of the cave, barely visible from where he stood. He climbed the steep rocky slopes up beyond where no trees could grow. Finally, after a whole day of struggling, he approached the entrance to the cave trembling and exhausted.

At the entrance, much to his surprise, purple and white wild flowers grew in abundance surrounding the small plateau that surrounded the cavern's opening. There had not been rain in months, no flowers grew down in the village anymore, yet here on this rocky cliff they flourished. Amazed and intrigued, the flowers made him feel a little better even as his heart pounded and the tears streamed from his eyes.

He summoned all of his courage and boldly stepped inside. There grew a thick layer of moss covering the floor of the cave that cushioned

261

his feet that had become bruised and cut from the long climb. He saw spring water streaming down the sides of the rocky cavern, like tears from the mountain itself. It made him smile as if the mountain itself was crying with him. As he peered deep inside the cavern he could see a small fire in the distance. There were shadows dancing on the wall. At first he thought the dancing shadows were from the fire itself, yet as he drew nearer the fire he made out the outline of a human figure dancing around the fire, humming a strange and wonderful song. He approached the figure and began to make out the outlines of a very old woman, gnarled hands, hunched back, and long streaming grey hair. This sight shook him, for the silhouette appeared to be of a young lady. Slowly the dark figure lifted her eyes looking straight at him. Her eyes shown with a brilliant light. It shocked him, for although they were fierce eyes, they also were full of love - a look that somehow felt strangely familiar. A warmth and love pierced his heart in that moment. Immediately he was no longer afraid, in fact, in a way he felt like the whole space around him shifted, as if he was now in a dream, a warm and content feeling flowed through him. He felt more at home than he had ever felt in the village. He had heard the word sacred before, but never knew what it meant. In the presence of this old woman he felt a sacred space.

She stopped her dancing and humming and sat silently by the fire as she began to stir the ashes. He stood motionless. She lifted her head up from the fire, and their eyes met again in the quiet solitude of this inner chamber. All that could be heard was the crackling of the fire. He, as if called by some mysterious force, moved closer and sat down opposite her. He sat enraptured. She, after what appeared to be an eternity, looked up at the boy and studied his face. He, also, could not take his eyes off of her face full of wrinkles that somehow made her beautiful - deep ridge lines that looked more like river beds than wrinkles. He knew this woman had wisdom and compassion. He could not contain himself anymore. He had to ask her all the unanswerable questions that he had longed to ask. In her presence he wanted to speak the unspeakable, say the unsayable. He blurted out. Why am I here? Do you know where my parents are? Why did they die? Why was I born so ugly and deformed? Why has God and then my village forsaken me? Who am I? What is to become of me?

She sat quietly rocking, looking at the boy, then gazing at the fire humming a light song under her breath. He kept on, "You must tell me, I know you know the answers to these questions. You are the wisest person I have ever met, that I have ever come across. You surely know the answers. Please, Please, I beg of you. Speak to me."

With that pleading the old woman brought her wide opened eyes to his, while putting her finger to her mouth whispering, "Shhhhhhhhh.... Shhhhhh...." as if to quiet his racing mind. She then motioned to him to come to her opening her arms. Half of him felt terrified, the other half yearned to sit by her. He slowly moved towards her and sat down resting his head on her shoulder as she held and began to rock him.

He had never known this experience, never felt love like this that streamed through his body. She then hummed a magical song that did not seem to be of this world. A warmth and contentment spread throughout his body. Her song echoed softly in this dark cavern with the eerie light from the fire creating the feeling that the sound was coming from every direction of the cave. A feeling of contentment seeped into every cell of his body as all of his worries, anxieties and fears melted away. As he listened to the otherworldly music he almost forgot about his mission and fell into a dreamlike state.

After a long while he opened his eyes to see the old woman by the spring at the back end of the cave. He drew nearer and told her that he had come to ask permission for a cup of the water from the source of the spring. The old woman ignored him at first. Then she began taking different sized and colored jars and began filling them with the spring water that shimmered from the fire light. After a long period of silence the old witch spoke, "You are thirsty aren't you?" He replied, "Yes, oh, yes, thirsty." Then seemingly ignoring this plea she went on, "You are a river. Your suffering, abandonment and misfortune are so many rocks, twists and turns in the stream. They help the river that you are find its voice." The boy did not completely understand the words the woman spoke, but they intrigued him, he said, "All I know is I feel alone, scared and confused. There are too many different voices inside of me, all telling me different things, most of them opposite. How do I know which is really me?" The old woman busily went on pouring water into the different colored jugs, continuing, "Do you see these jugs of spring water?"

He was mesmerized by the fire light filling the cave and now realized the weeping on the sides of the cave came from this mysterious source of spring water. "Yes," answered the boy. "Do you see how the water appears to change color and shape depending on what jug

I pour it into?" Since each jug was a different color it did indeed look as if the water changed colors and it filled perfectly any vessel she poured it into, the water simply adopted the shape of the jar with grace. "Your confusion arises by confusing your essence, the water, with your circumstance of the moment, which is like the jug. You change colors depending on the situation you are in, what person you are with, what job you have in front of you. You become confused because you keep identifying yourself with the color in the jug as opposed to the water itself. Your essence, who you are before the jug, in the jug and after the jug is this ever flowing spring water. Although it seems for a moment that you are something solid, fixed and permanent. In the next moment you can be poured out of the present circumstances of your life and take on a completely different color and shape."

The boy began to understand the woman's words, yet he remained terribly thirsty, "Yes, I understand. Now, can I have a cup of that magical water to take back to my village so they will like me and allow me to stay?" She laughed to herself, amused by the boy's impatience, "No, one thing still is required." Even though she would not give him the water just yet, the boy began to see this old woman as anything but an evil witch; rather, she was a woman of wisdom, patience, and love. He couldn't put his finger on it, just what it was, but she had such a timeless quality about her. In fact, in that very moment he wasn't even sure he wanted to return to the village. She seemed to read his mind, "Would you like to stay here and learn the secrets of the spring?" In disbelief, he stammered the words, "Yes, more than anything." She looked at him intently, and continued, "If you do, you also realize you will never be at home, not completely, in the village. Because of your deformity, you have a humility about you that I trust. If you ever lose the humility, the water will dry up and cease to flow. For the water has a name, it is called, 'love.' It lies at the edge of darkness and light, joy and sorrow, night and day. Deep in this mountain cavern there is only twilight; always some light, some shadow; some weeping, some laughing, some seeking, some dancing. This is the secret of the spring. For this is the water of life and the water of death. Whoever drinks of it will surely have life and taste joy; but will also taste sorrow and death. Those who curse the sorrow and refuse to grieve will dry up and become like the desert where your people live. This much is true. You may have a cup of this water, but you have had the source all the time as your people have had. It is the spring of your own heart, the healing will come when you cry into this cup. Your tears are of the same source as this spring. This mountain is the heart of our creator, this spring as all springs, are the painful and joyful tears of creation. As the creator is birthing a child in every new breath, each new step requires pain and joy. Take this cup back to your people, teach them where the sacred spring lies, in the depths of their own heart. If it has ceased to flow it is because their heart has hardened, as they showed their hardness towards you. If there is no grief there is no love, if there is no love there is no life." As she spoke, tears welled up from the boy's eyes and fell gingerly into the cup. Her words touched him in a place inside he had not felt before. He knew in that moment his people would live, for even though he had not even touched his lips to the spring water within the cave his own tears began to quench the thirst he had carried within for so long. Finally, the old woman after placing her hands in the spring water touched his heart and his head while whispering in his ear, you have a new name and it is also the name of your people, *"Ever Flowing On...Ever Flowing On..."*

For the rest of his days the loving soft voice of the old woman was a constant companion, for whenever he closed his eyes from that day forward he heard the words like the gentle sound of a river coming back to him, *"Ever Flowing On...Ever Flowing On....Ever Flowing On...."*

The Rainbow Bridge

The soul would have no rainbow if the eyes had no tears.
~Native Minquass Saying

The Cherokee speak of the rainbow bridge which connects all things and all people. It is a beautiful image that speaks directly to discovering and honoring unity in diversity. The rainbow, like the peacock's tail, teaches us a wisdom we desperately need in our world today, that all colors, all people, all beliefs, can find a way to live together; unity in diversity. The old woman teaches the boy this with the different colored jars.

Like the light passing through the millions of droplets of water acting as prisms which create the stunning rainbow this is a powerful way for us to conceive of the relationship between our essence and the many different aspects that we are, individually and collectively. The old woman's teachings did not stop here. She goes further by revealing to us that like the rainbow, the beauty arises not in spite of the rainstorm, the deluge, the hurricane, but through it. Our grief over our loss, like the moisture in the air after the rain, provides the opening, the clearing, the opportunity for light and thus life to show its true colors. As the Minquass saying goes, "The soul would have no rainbow if the eyes had no tears."

Our world has left the wisdom of the heart far behind. The Cheyenne say, "Our first teacher is our own heart." Unfortunately, most of us abandon this teacher, like our culture has, for many false ones. Many native people feared the white man most because he viewed crying as a weakness. This is a danger in many contemporary people I work with in my practice, particularly men. The grief is so great, the village within them is such a desert, they either have no idea where to look for the water of life or they fear that if they open the gates there will be a deluge and flood of so much stored up tears they will be overwhelmed. For most of them the mountain they have to climb is the one of their own heart. Arnold had such a task in front of him. He began to realize what he needed through a dream:

> *I awoke in a cold sweat. There were masked men and women around me operating on my internal organs while I was awake. It was torturous as I watched them take out my heart and lungs and rearrange everything inside. They kept shaking their heads. They were taking me apart in a torturous gruesome way. Then they removed my heart, holding up for all to see*

*to examine it, again shaking their heads as if to say,
"what a shame". My heart appeared to be like a piece
of beef jerky, all dried out and shriveled up; without an
ounce of moisture. I awoke with a knot in my throat,
I couldn't swallow. I felt stark terror as the words went
over and over in my head, "my heart has died".*

Arnold was in his 40s and his children had recently left home. He found he and his wife had become strangers over the years. Their children were growing up. By the time the children left, they barely knew each other. His heart felt dead, numb. His children had filled his life up until then. They had provided the water of life to the desert of his marriage. Now he found himself in a job he felt no passion for and a marriage that was dry and arid. Instead of seeing the dream as pathological, we explored the dimensions of the meaning of the operation as a profound way of his deeper self not only signaling that his whole inner world needed to be reorganized and rearranged, but that his subterranean self was already engaged in the task. Of course, it would be painful and difficult to do such symbolic, emotional surgery. He accepted the challenge and began speaking his truth to his wife and to himself about how his inner life had become a desert, how his heart had dried up. For Arnold, "the water of life," became a powerful metaphor as he talked about how to moisten his heart and bring it back to life. He mentioned that in the dream his heart looked freeze dried like food you have on a camping trip that says on the package, "just add water." Slowly, but surely he found water. The first place he began to return was when he allowed himself to cry. He could only remember 3 times in his adult life he had ever cried. His grief would become his magic spring water.

Whenever we encounter the need for change, of letting go, often times we need to connect again with the "water of life." Water is the great transformer. Water is that which can melt and dissolve hardness, moisten dryness. For men in particular, if light is reason, too much of it can dry us out. Dryness comes from sterile, worn out old patterns that no longer work for people. It is found in our world of relating to ourselves or others. People often describe feeling as if a part of them is dying. Often times, the only and perhaps best way to re-connect with the water of life is through grief. It is as if we are traveling along a lonely dusty road, yet it is the tears which give us a hint that we are traveling the road to water. What precedes and accompanies a healing rain in nature? A dark sky. It is re-connecting with the sorrow in the depths of our souls that we can begin to find the source, the water at the center of our lives. These are not simply pretty metaphorical terms. We are nature and nature is us. Our bodies made of two-thirds water mirrors perfectly our earth which is also composed of two-thirds water. At the heart of the survival of our whole race, and for that matter, all living things depend on water for survival to one degree or another. Water is what has brought the earth to life. So too can it bring us back to life.

A few years ago there was a song with a line I could not get out of my head, "I miss you like the deserts miss the rain." We all have a desert of one sort or another within that thirsts for water. People will do crazy and destructive things to get that water back in their lives, usually missing the most direct route - through their own grief. Grief connects us with the *danse macabre,* the dance of death. For death puts us in touch with who we really are, searing away our illusions, our delusions, our grandiosity and at the very same time in its ability to humble, then, like the old woman, gives us a gift, ironically, the water of life.

THE WATER OF LIFE

Water is life. Water has been a powerful symbol throughout human history for deep spiritual nourishment. This is not surprising when we remind ourselves that since the beginning of time all creatures great and small, plant or animal, has depended on water for their journey through life. To the alchemists water was the *prima materia;* the primal material from which all life was born. The modern scientist would agree. Life arose from the great oceans of the world. Many native cultures refer to the great oceanic river that surrounds the world as, Grandmother, from whose womb all life emerges.

Our story reminds us at a mythic level this truth, but it also reveals more. It reveals that the source of the water of life is much like where we started amness. It is no surprise then that there is always a river flowing in Eden or in Paradise. There are few better metaphors for amness than water. Although it is constantly moving, it is infinitely adaptable. Without effort it simply takes on the form of any vessel containing it.

It is no wonder that the ancient sage Lao Tzu's favorite image of the Tao was that of water:

The highest good is like water
Water gives life to all without striving.
It flows in places men reject (the lowest) and so is like the Tao...
It can not be grasped...
Tao in the world is like a
river flowing home to the sea
The softest thing in the universe overcomes the hardest...
Why is the sea king of a hundred streams?
Because it lies below them....
That is how they are kings of the hundred rivers.
Under heaven nothing is more soft and yielding than water.
Yet for attacking the solid and strong,
nothing is better.[7]

Lao Tzu's successor Chaung-tzu felt the same way:

When water is still, it is like a mirror...And if water thus derives
lucidity from stillness, how much more the faculties of the mind?
...The fluidity of water is not the result of any effort on
the part of the water, but is its natural property.[8]

Water is a symbol of the perfect dance. If you spend anytime at all watching the flow of water you will soon realize aesthetically it never falters, never makes a mistake. Like clouds, the infinite shifts and changes all appear within a certain grace and beauty. This is one of the kinships also between music and water. They both move in waves. They both occupy whatever space is given to them. They both flow. Remember Miles Davis saying, "There is no such thing as a wrong note." He knew about the relationship between music and water. To many water is the blood of the earth itself:

Water is the blood of the Earth, and flows through
its muscles and veins....Therefore it is said that water
is something spiritual. Being accumulated in plants
and trees, their stems gain their orderly progression
from it, their flowers obtain their proper number, and
their fruits gain their proper measure....Man is water,
and when the producing elements of male and female
unite, liquid flows into forms...When water is pure, the
people's hearts are at ease...Hence the Sage, when he
rules the world, does not teach men one by one, or house
by house, but takes water as his key.[9]

The Taoists were first and foremost naturalists like the Shaman before them. They were incredibly astute observers of the natural world seeing an unbroken continuum between rock, plant, animal and human. It was the continual transformations that they found that led them to see water as a crucial unifying principle flowing through all the diverse multiplicity of creation. Allen Watts had a vision of this dancing of the universe:

As one grows older, it becomes ever more obvious that
things are without substance, for time seems to go by
more rapidly so that one becomes aware of the liquidity
of solids; people and things become like lights and rip-
ples on the surface of water. We can make fast-motion
films of the growth of plants and flowers in which they
seem to come and go like gestures of the earth. If we
could film civilizations and cities, mountains and stars,
in the same way, we would see them as frost crystals
forming and dissolving and as sparks on the back of
a fireplace. The faster the tempo, the more it would
appear that we were watching, not so much a succession
of things, as the movement and transformations of one

thing - as we see waves on the ocean or the movements of a dancer.[10]

Amness is the source. Then like snow flakes each of us become an "I am" distilled into a crystalized lifetime appearing with such beauty and grace. Then we melt into the river of our lives and continue our quest until we unite again with the ocean of amness.

THE SOUL AND THE CANOE

We may not be surprised then that the soul's journey through life is often represented by many Native Americans as paddling a canoe flowing down a river, ever towards home. It is the river of life. However, for each one of us living an individual, unique life, the particular river of our lives is one we have never been down. We have no idea what is around the corner. Yet, we flow on. Through twists and turns, ups and downs, wide calm sections, narrow rapids, we are flowing down this river.

During a lifetime we inhabit so many roles as we float down the river: husband, wife, son, daughter, father, mother, student, teacher, employee, Christian, Buddhist, American - the list goes on and on. It's surprising we can still fit in the canoe. We incessantly run into life circumstances that question our roles, our definitions our pat solutions to "who we really are." On a very practical level we have seen, throughout our lives, that we may be known by many names and play many roles. Some of the various names I have masqueraded as have been Mike, Michael, Mikie, Demo, Brant, Doctor, Mister, sir,

Father, Son, husband, and some not so flattering. These are so many different colored vessels that the old woman shows the boy - different colors of the rainbow bridge, different players in the orchestral self. But, ultimately, who is the water?

If the self is a river then I am less the noun Michael, and more the gerund, Michaeling. When I first told this to my client name Dan he laughed, saying, "So I'm to go home and have my wife call me 'Danning' tonight?" However, weeks later he told me how powerful thinking about himself this way had become and how it really "shook up" some very rigid ways he had looked at himself. He put it this way:

> *At first it sounded crazy, calling myself "Danning." My wife and I had a good laugh over it. Her Janning and me Danning along. The whole idea seemed preposterous, ridiculous. Perhaps, that was the power of it. I couldn't get the name out of my head. It made me smile. More importantly, I was able to begin to see the whole course of my life not as some chaotic mess, a failed climb up some mountain that I kept falling off. But, rather, this image of the river kept at me. It has really helped me be at peace with my past, my present, and giving me more trust in my future. It's helped me let go more. Not be as controlling.*

For those still resistant, I usually quote one of my favorite sayings by Dr. Seuss, "You're on your own. And you know what you know. And YOU are the guy who'll decide where to go. Don't stew. Just go right along. You'll start happening, too."[11] We begin to be who we are, become who we are *through* the process of living a life. Change happens, transformation occurs, and we are constantly moving, flowing, and becoming. So, yes, many times it feels like we are many different voices, but if we take the time to acquaint ourselves with the currents and crosscurrents of the self; we can help these voices begin to sing the same song, in the same key; while keeping their distinctness; unity in diversity, like the forest or for that matter the cosmos; but when we have the lens to see that not only is the cosmos like a oneness doing everything; so too are we a unity, expressing, flowing in wondrous multiplicity; the rainbow of the self. Of course, we are both being who we already are, all the time becoming who we may be.

Thus we see two fundamental elements of this emerging understanding of the self; multiplicity and fluidity. Although to our minds raised on a Newtonian view of the universe that has viewed people as well-oiled machines this appears new and radical, to our tribal ancestors these aspects of self were common everyday realities that they lived. In fact, many indigenous people so thoroughly practiced the multiplicity of the ecological self that they talk of dying many deaths in one life. Then after each "small death" one will often take on a different name usually composed of verbs, animals, and elements. It's not uncommon, for instance, that a shaman in certain cultures might have seven or eight different names over the course of one lifetime. For example, they might say, "Oh, that happened when I was 'Snake in the Grass', or you knew me when I was 'Running Bear.'" We all have an intuitive understanding of the power of these poetic names that provide glimpses into our vaster nature. The names have texture, breadth and depth. They lend both multiplicity and fluidity to the understanding of ourselves.

What else can the river image that the old woman provides the young boy teach us about ourselves? Two other major points come to mind. One, that no we do not have absolute freedom, infinite possibility that is so popularly touted today. We do not choose the river of our lives. We do not choose what is to be born through us any more than we choose who our children are going to be. We must listen carefully to the whispering of the river, have a clear sense of the currents and cross currents, the whirlpools and eddies. Sure, we can spend our lives struggling trying to paddle upstream, cursing our life, the river and constantly fighting against our true nature and our lives' natural flow. This is an important existential corrective to much of the New Age movement today. There is something real to be found in the world that we bump up against and must learn to co-create with. The river is not our creation, in fact, it would be more accurate to say we are a creation of the river. We do not create life as much as life creates, shapes and forms us. Life is co-created by all the creatures and beings in creation in a fabric of inter-being and interdependence.

At the same time, there is a second point. If we trust the river and listen carefully and reverently and co-create with it, we realize that within the limits of the river we do have endless possibility. That is, there are infinite options to how one might maneuver down the river. Do we paddle left or right, fast or slow? Do we go straight down the rapids or around them? Do we portage around the waterfall or dive head first over it? Do we stop for a while and enjoy the awesome beauty that exists all the way down the river? Do we give thanks for everyday on the river, for every rock, stone and turn that adds to its challenge and beauty? Not only must we learn where the river is in our own life, but the lesson of the river is learning to see how we ourselves continue to flow through life and death. As the old woman tells the young boy, "Don't over identify with the color of the jar the water is in, remember who you truly are, your essence is the clear water itself."

Frank Lloyd Wright the visionary architect knew about the complex relationship between our flowing and dancing with nature. He believed nature in her pristine state dances and flows with a harmony we can only hope to emulate, never control. Therefore, he believed our goal in architecture was to find a way to dance and flow with the rhythm and harmony we already find always and forever ongoing in the natural world. If we ignorantly try to control and stifle it, we bring harm to ourselves and our world. We have come a long way from the natives who would cry and apologize to Grandmother Earth whenever they tore at the surface of the soil to plant seed or disturb the natural setting. They would begin by asking permission. How different perhaps our housing and roadside developments would be if we had that sensitivity to the earth. If we had to ask permission and get on our knees and say prayers before the back hoes and steam shovels would begin tearing at the fragile flesh of the earth.

We have many examples of how we have tried to control arrogantly the natural world, ignoring the obvious more comprehensive rhythms we find around us, only to fall on our faces. The Army Corps of engineers learned this the hard way after they tried to tame the great

Mississippi. They literally tried to "straighten out" the Mississippi River because it was so "inefficient." There were people losing great profits because the commercial boat traffic had to make so many meanders instead of just going straight to the Gulf of Mexico. Skill at dancing, however, requires submission, a willingness to obey and learn what grander, more comprehensive organic patterns are present. Otherwise we go against the music, the essential rhythm around us and our attempts are clumsy, misdirected, and we usually end up falling over our own feet. They *created* massive flooding, by trying to *straighten* the great river. We learned the meanderings were elegantly designed by nature herself for the mighty Mississippi to flow as it does. We are finding with the help of chaos theory and working with non-linear dynamics that what in nature appears chaotic and convoluted has a very real reason for being there. We have a long way to go for psychology to catch up in this regard.

From a broader perspective, what appears as randomness has an underlying order and beauty that cannot be deduced from any linear logic. So the Army Corps of Engineers have since learned to "dance with" the river instead of simply trying to redirect it. Conscious engineering still takes place, but with an appreciation for the natural flows, harmonies and dance that pre-exists it. When we can extricate ourselves from the misunderstanding that the world is a machine for us to fix, we can avoid some of the perilous and tragic consequences we are only beginning to now realize are the result of ignoring the non-human dimensions of our existence in the great web of life, and realize that we are in the most basic and fundamental ways not different from nature, but quite the contrary intrinsically interconnected, part and parcel of her.

The human mind likes to attribute a sense of permanence to names, whether it be the name Michael DeMaria or the diagnostic category Schizophrenia. Our egos fear that great teacher of impermanence. Perhaps, the reasoning goes, if we can name everything we can control everything, know everything. In the process we have missed something so vital to our lives; the essential wisdom of the heart that only comes from the most profound kind of humility. This is one of the greatest teachings of the river. It finds its direction by following the lowest course. It can not move unless it moves downwards. What we referred to as the missing piece in so much modern psychology and education today, *the ability to grow down for every inch we grow up.* The more we see all the different aspects of ourselves, both light and dark, high and low, the more we become aware, like consciousness itself of the *"ever flowing on"* quality of existence. At its essence existence is this impermanence, this change, this ever flowing on. We ultimately are not God, but neither are we the Devil. I am ultimately not reducible to my role as "husband," "psychologist," "white male," "honest," or "deceitful," but the awareness itself of these particular moments of existence and becoming. We start to realize it is all simply flowing through us, moving through us. If we are truly honest with ourselves, we realize before long that anything and everything that we depend on, identify ourselves with and try to hold onto for security, sooner or later crumbles. The river flows on, and takes us with it whether we like it or not. This also means, yes, one day we will die. All the identities we worked so hard to forge will, like writing in the sand by the ocean shore, be washed away. The less we identify with any particular moment or role, the more we find the vast self that is aware of all roles and more importantly the felt experience of not playing any role. We once again touch the reservoir of *amness,* this time with the awareness of differentiation and an appreciation and even love and connection to all the various roles of our life.

To understand our lives from the perspective of the river has proven itself so very helpful in my day to day life and in the lives of those I work with. For all of us to realize that it is right, good and inevitable that the river keeps flowing, that in our perpetual letting go, we too are also flowing on; towards new vistas, new canyons, new terrain that we never imagined. We are not born to be static creatures, for in our very essence is the aesthetic beauty of the river itself. To begin every day by asking, "Where is the river flowing today?" is a profound psychospiritual practice in the art of being. For we ride the most ancient river of all, the river of our own breath, that ceaselessly flows on. Knowing this we can ride the waves of the moment, of the breath, the blood coursing through our bodies as we die so many times in one lifetime. In a way every expiration, breathing out, is a death, we expire. In every in breath, every inspiration, is a birth, a renewal of spirit. To practice this is to make this automatic rhythm conscious, becoming aware of the river of our lives which will in time allow us to face the ultimate and grand expiration transition at physical death, where we finally come face to face with who we truly are, and if we have truly prepared we will not shrink in fear, but celebrate the river flowing into the ocean.

Direction And The River

Is "ever flowing on" the same as "going with the flow"? No, it does have a direction. Although it may meander here and there, it continues towards a distant horizon with determination and persistence. As in life itself, one must have projects, goals, which continue to challenge you, pull you forward, like a gravity pull. If the challenge is too great there will be anxiety, if the challenge is not great enough there will be boredom. So flow occurs when the activity leads to further growth and discovery.

If we stay at the same level for too long, we will become bored or frustrated. As important as being in the moment, is having an eye on the horizon. If I am canoeing down the river I have to be vigilant both of where I am and where I am going. ***It is this dynamic relationship between past, present and future that is the river of life.*** Many eastern practices tend to focus far too exclusively on the present moment while the western practices often over emphasize the past and future. Rather the best of both practices incorporate a dynamic, sacred tension between one's being (present) and one's becoming (future). This is to live one's life in accordance with the river.

This blessing of our essential multiplicity shows an ancient wisdom that we have lost and that furthermore, provides a healthy and effective way of dealing with the contingency of our lives and impermanence of nature. At the same time, it allows us an opportunity for connecting with the greater patterns and flows of life, by realizing we, too, like the forest, are a vast ecology that must circle endlessly through ever-changing seasons with their ever-present lessons of living and dying.

Photons are mysterious, just like the self. Although they light up everything we see, including the rainbow, no scientist has ever been able to pin them down. With out photons you could not be reading these words, yet where "is" the light? They come out of nowhere and return to nowhere. They can not be stored, measured, weighed. Physicists have tried to pin them down in space and time, yet, it is as if they have no home in either. Light, the manifestation of the dance of photons, has no volume and no mass. Investigators into the nature of the soul said it did not exist because you could not locate it in space or time right after death. A body measured and weighed the same before and after death. Any good scientist knows that you cannot prove something does not exist. So the soul, like a photon of light, can not be located in space and time. It cannot be measured. Yet, it is every bit as real as the photon and also has a similar job of helping us see. Just like the amazing dance of electrochemical activity in the brain, the liminal shifts between a molecule, a thought and an action. Where does one end and the other begin? It is the ever flowing field of being.

Although photons can't be fixed, located, they light up all we see, all we feel, all we touch, they are completely out of reach. It has much to do with contradiction and paradox again. The way the self flows through time and space is much like a photon: there, yet not there, like the darting dancing of a flame; observable, objective, but fiercely out of reach to try to contain it, grab it, get hold of it, make it into some kind of a certain predictable something. To make it into a noun, a thing is to lose it. Yet it's still there and still lights our way.

OPENING AND CLEARING

*A person is neither a thing nor a process, but an
opening or clearing through which the Absolute can
manifest.*
~Martin Heidegger

The river of the self has brought us a long way and, yet, there is
farther to go. Heidegger's words to us are crucial here as we begin to
come to the end of our journey together, "A person is neither a thing
nor a process, but an opening or clearing." This is the same call that
John Muir is making to us in the following lines:

*I care to live only to entice
people to look at
nature's loveliness. My own special
self is nothing. [I want
to be] like a flake of glass through
which light passes.*[12]
~John Muir

Muir is talking about becoming this opening or clearing of which
Heidegger speaks. At this point in the journey, whether I am working
with people individually or in a group, they have traveled a very long
way when they have glimpsed themselves as a river and not as a rock; a
verb, not a noun; yet these are processes; the next step is to become an
opening, a clearing. This is where ever flowing becomes ever opening
- to open to what is in each moment.

Part IV: The Dance

One of the reasons I feel this is so difficult for the Western, contemporary mind is that opening feels like nothingness and emptiness. In a way it is. Nothingness as no-thing-ness; not being a thing. We have had a hard time in the West seeing emptiness as sacred. Therefore, we also shield ourselves against openness, transparency. We are more comfortable posturing behind opaque rules that are proliferating at an alarming rate in the very professions (like psychology) that should be leading the way towards transparency.

Music is such a powerful reminder of this. Music is so fiercely there, yet not there. One can not see it, put it in a box or measure it, yet it stirs our soul and moves us to get up and dance. Like light, music reveals the language of the heart which has always been transparent. It is no wonder that there has been such an ancient connection between music and the soul. Both are invisible, both whisper to us of the mystery and paradox of life and death. There is an African word for breath that also means dance. The Greek word for soul is psyche which also means breath as well as butterfly. There is an ancient connection between music, the soul and death. As the great composer of the Viola, Marin Marais said, "Each note should end dying...as if someone you love just vanished into the shadows...mysteriously fading from life, leaving tears in your eyes." The center of the self moves like a photon between a wave (fluidity) and a particle (stability), being and becoming and also like a photon is dimensionless/weightless and immaterial, an absence that makes presence possible; an opening, a clearing.

Many times, those I work with eventually are ready to enact a vision quest. With nothing to eat, no one to talk to, nothing to read, nothing but wide open space, the one immersed in the vision quest soon knows why the Sioux called it *hanblecheyapi*, literally, the Lamentation. Likewise, the questor is the "lamenter," who goes to fast and to pray alone, "crying for a vision." Sooner or later the quest brings one face to face with that stark emptiness. It is the same place that can bring suicidal darkness in one moment and transforming bliss the next. It is the place where we are changed forever. If one is not able to embrace that emptiness, they will not be able to cry for their vision. Vision comes only when we have emptied ourselves. And in that emptying, we find the lament, and in the lament, the water of the spring flows again. Colin wrote about that fierce place on his vision quest and read it to me as a part of his ceremony when he returned:

> *I came to find a place where there was nothing but a deep gnawing emptiness in the center of my abdomen. I recognized it as an emptiness I had spent my life trying to fill, with food, sex, achievements, money, success, woman...to no avail, in the end I always came back to it. This vast emptiness at the center of me, at the core. Then, in the middle of the night, with the night sky ablaze with starlight I found myself talking to the emptiness for the first time in my life. I knew it would consume me if I kept running, so I made a commitment to myself that night and spoke out loud into the cold north wind, "I will no longer run from you, I submit myself to learn from you. To no longer deny you, but to befriend you. O.K. my old friend emptiness, what truths can you whisper to me this dark night.*

He found his life changing significantly after that. To come home to ourselves means embracing the emptiness at the core of who we are. To not cover it up, deny it, or explain it away is to find out after the grieving that a rainbow appears and the emptiness turns into an opening; a clearing. Too often, we as a culture have lived in a denial of emptiness, a denial of multiplicity, a denial of uncertainty, a denial of unpredictability in each of which are veiled denials of mystery, which at the bottom is a denial of death. The orchestral self embraces the voice of death, for even as she whispers to us wordless words that bring terror, it is on the other side of that terror that we find she is also the bearer of truth, grace and joy.

The orchestral self embraces and is conscious of contingency, uncertainty, and impermanence and in so doing cleanses our jaded eyes of perception, our stale logic, and false posturing. By entering into our own internal orchestral world, we open ourselves to the deeper realms of what is and what can be. When the eyes of perception are cleansed in this way, then, as William Blake says, we will finally see the world as it truly is, "infinite."

THE ONE AND THE MANY

The creation of a thousand forests is in one acorn.
~Ralph Waldo Emerson

Can we hear the music? The song being played is not just our own story. The chorus that is singing when the many voices join is not only our individual journey towards wholeness and oneness, but the story of the whole world, Nature herself becoming conscious. When

I say nature I mean the whole cosmos, including the divine source, the Creator. The real challenge is to see that to work on ourselves is to be working on and for the good of *all-that-is*. If we do not learn to attend to hear and find harmony with the voices within, how can we ever hope to find harmony with the many voices without.

If the reader has followed our spiraling journey through the sacred tree of being, then the full impact of how the agony of the quest blossoms into the joy of the dance has become the clearing where we find the ever flowing on spring of love, at the edge of light and dark, day and night, joy and sorrow, emptiness and fullness, being and becoming. Further, that when we follow the life of any single one of us far enough and deep enough, we discover not only the story of "everyone", but of "all-that-is".

If we are able to shift from believing, we are alienated shipwrecked souls on earth, living in a weigh station after being kicked out of paradise and begin to see we are part of a grand dance of Being. Our lives cannot help but become consecrated and enchanted. Ever so slowly, we will become journeyers through the ceaseless adventures of time and space, and each of us can listen in rapture to the "truths our blood whispers to us." Making this shift always reminds me of a similar transition I went through as a child. Through the dark nighttime house I would step in silence terrified of the unknown. Then, I learned to over time, befriend the darkness and it gradually became a cocoon to me, in which I believed that if I could become still and quiet enough, I could hear God's heart beating.

As we begin to awaken to the experience of being part of Being, and in some way containing "all-that-is" within us, we tap into the ancient truth that mystics the world over have always known: "The One and the Many are two sides of the same coin." The Hindu's express this truth in the words, "as is the human body, so is the cosmic body," meaning that how we tend, explore and care for our own inner world and body, so, too, will it reflect the whole cosmos. Said another way, the insight we achieve will resonate with the whole cosmos. We have the Judeo-Christian saying, "as above, so below," referring to the reflection between the earthly and heavenly. There is a powerful passage from the Upanishads that describes this very simply. However, I have substituted the word Being for God, "When you see that Being acts through you at every moment, in every moment of mind or body, you attain true freedom." In contemporary biology, we have a similar understanding when biologists talk of ontogenesis recapitulating phylogenesis, that is that the cycle of a human life, from conception to birth, recapitulates, recycles, the evolution of our whole species. At first we are nothing but a small single cell being. Then as cell division takes place we evolve as our whole species did into more and more complex forms until the small embryo looks much like a polliwog, or fish which then begins to sprout arms and legs. We truly move from fish, to reptile, to amphibian to mammal. It is awe inspiring when we contemplate the fact that each one of us passed through these phases. *We live out the life of the cosmos in every single life.* What evolution took millions of years to accomplish, we attain in nine months. It is almost as if each one of us is playing the same melody, from the same pattern, with infinite variations. In our life cycle we both are on our own individual spiraling soul journey through this world, *and* in and through that we are also mirroring the processes of the cosmos itself. As we are becoming oneself, we are also always and forever becoming Oneself: from amness, through the fall, to the quest and finally blooming in the dance and all the while we are ever flowing on. Here resides fullness of purpose and intention. How could it be otherwise? For as we work on ourselves we are not only doing our own work, but the work of the cosmos. We are furthering the evolution of the divine spirit. We are on a never ending adventure where we court, engage and finally marry innocence to wisdom, energy to form, the circle to the line, spirit to soul, all this expressed so profoundly in the spiral.

To see a spiral is to see visual music, a symbol of the dance of creation and destruction. Our lives themselves incessantly spiral into ever new/old patterns, and we can learn to rejoice in the ecstasy of endless re-creation. Transformation, transfiguration, spreading out, moving in, receding, approaching, dancing to the rhythm of eternity, upon the vast wheel of timeless, spaceless, imageless Being.

From this day forward let us not forget that the earth's molten core is forever lapping at our feet, hungry for our own fiery presence. If we can just walk with eyes of our heart open, and the ears of our soul clear and wake up to this moment, then we can let our mouths sing the truths our blood whispers to us. We will embody and give voice to Being, singing new songs, and dancing the new dances. To sing and dance in this way is to move consciously upon the sacred *all-that-is*. We become aware that all things change when we do, and that through all of our striving and we realize that all along through these changes we have, like the water of life, both been being and becoming ourselves, in that awakening we come home. We blossom in our letting go, giving ourselves over to our being and becoming, our questing and our dancing; our never ending seeking and return-ing; the circle dance of life. Here is the glorious paradox, that in the farthest reaches of our quest, when we are so tired and worn out "trying" to get somewhere, we come to realize, much like Dorothy in the Wizard of OZ, that all the while we only had to say, "There is no place like home" and click the heels of our ruby red shoes and dance. For even if we are dancing the blues, we are dancing.

COMING HOME

Life is the flash of the firefly
in the night, the breath of the
buffalo in winter time.
~ *Old Blackfoot Saying*

We spend so much of our lives walking on the face of the earth with some strange yearning. We can't quite put our finger on what is missing, do we ever? I have seen a peace in the eyes of the dying that makes me wonder if in those final moments they find that gnawing something. Some have even told me they have. One of them being my grandmother. The day I held my grandmothers hand and I knew it would be the last time I would see her was the moment I beheld that kind of knowing. All of the endless unanswerable questions kept rising in my mind. Yet, in all of that seeming darkness she looked at me with eyes so tender, so loving, just beholding. In her eyes in that moment there were no more questions, no grasping; just radiance, like a little girl's wonder. In those endless eyes finally my mind found silence and my heart opened. Her presence always spoke the invisible language of the heart, if I would just listen. My heart told me that day that she knew she was going home. She did not grieve. She had done so much in her life that her soul had become smooth as silk, no snags. She prepared her bed, kissed her stuffed animals, talked to the sky, the trees, the grass, one more time, in her innocent child-like way, openly, unashamed. Then kissing the picture of her loved ones, straightening the flowers on her small side desk in her hospital room with her stuffed teddy bear, she said goodnight and went to bed for a long overdue rest, never again to awaken in that body she had grown to know so well. For she was going home, back to the place she had come from so long ago. Through all the suffering, pain and joy of living a life, she had made peace with letting go of everything here; perhaps made easier as she began to taste home again in vivid dreams and the special connection she had with plants and animals.

It is said in tribal culture the reason grandparents and grandchildren get along so well, is that the children have just come from the place the grandparents are preparing to go. They have a special bond. I always knew that connection with my grandmother. Even as I grieved, I felt deep down beneath the tears a remembrance of her embrace and a phrase she often whispered to me, *"death is nothing more then a mother's warm embrace."* Her name is Elizabeth, which means, gift of God, and so she was and is.

Though we suffer here, it is amazing how we continue to find the courage and energy to set out on our endless quests and somehow find our moments to dance. Through it all we are always growing older, growing ever closer towards death, the greatest and final vision quest, the last dance, the ultimate right of passage. We are always and forever leaving it all behind, ever letting go of all we have, all we have known. If we have the courage to cry all of our tears and laugh all of our laughter, we can perhaps finally, after it is all said and done find the courage to ever flow on as we ever let go into the great undiscovered country; and in our ultimate dissolution, find resolution. For Rumi dying was like melting into the river of the Divine, like sugar into water.

Our homecoming is announced by the miracle that we have journeyed from being unconsciously bathed in *amness* as an infant to growing a self, separate and apart, all the time yearning for home, gaining a strength apart and then to discover that our yearning and desire for separateness has brought us to the desire for union and surrender back to *amness*. Then, as if by a mysterious, impossible paradox, we realize how attached and in love we have become to these people, places around us that are so impermanent. The greatest strength the Iroquois say is gentleness, which is only found by keeping death over our shoulder, that is, the knowledge of our sure defeat in the face of death, that ultimately we give away all we came here to claim, to let go of all we have learned so painfully how to love and cherish. The gentle preciousness in my daughter's laughter, the sky blue of my wife's eyes, the twinkle in my father's dear smile. At the edge of night and day, life and death, grief and sorrow there lies a spring, and in that spring flow the waters of a love that is conscious of contingency, that is all too aware of impermanence, a loving that can heal the deepest wounds, the greatest grief, the darkest fear. Loving from this spring embraces the tears of joy and sorrow, for it is *ever flowing on* and reveals the hidden connection between all people, all places, all times and all beings. To be connected *and* to love openly, unselfishly all the time letting go.

The West has half the answer, to love deeply. The East has the other, to let go. It has been my experience on my very humble earthwalk, that I find there is a meeting between these two ways of living, one which for the time being I will call the *Indigenous* - the middle way, the deeper way, where letting go and loving deeply can abide together, and heaven and earth are embraced and we can finally add something to the heart of the West and the mind of the East, the Soul the indigenous cultures of the world have always known the dark feminine face of the divine, the Earth herself; for she is us, we are her; she is the old woman, the Great Grandmother of all of us, and ultimately being and becoming oneself is acknowledging our never ending vital rootedness in and through her.

Ultimately, there is no quick answer, no easy solution. There is no one book, one place, one person who will provide us with all the answers. Life is difficult. However, the good news that's afoot is that the pearl of great price, the sacred elixir that lies within the Holy Grail we have searched so long and hard for, has always and forever been right with us, each one of us, all along. All along. It is the miracle of each one of us, as a unique, special, one-of-a-kind, never to be repeated experiencing being that we have our own authentic first person experience of the world. That is our birth right, *our* fire, our sacred elixir. To pay attention, *really* pay attention, and be present to the miracle of this unfolding moment in our body, in our life, in our breath, then by some mysterious presence, some paradox that is beyond our wildest imaginings, we miraculously find ourselves linked and related to each other and to *all* things, all people, in all times, and all of creation under the sun. To know ourselves in this way is to move from my pain, my grief, my emptiness; to *the* pain, *the* grief, *the* emptiness of all the world; and likewise to *the great loving* that makes it all worthwhile and meaningful and allows us even in the briefest of moments to know we have lived, and we have loved and ultimately we have mattered. We have signified a moment of feeling, of being, of life and we have experienced the miracle of being conscious, even if just for a moment.

In that miracle, we can find repose and peace and our long sought for vital connection not despite our failures, but rather through our incessant failings, imperfections and deficits, we then may find a joyful song deep down in the recesses of ourselves, our voice. A voice that somehow transcends the impermanence of it all, even death, for in the very presence of this voice death is included not as an end but as a beginning. A light does shine in the depths of the darkest night, a star shining through the million light years of darkest space and flickers as it calls us forth to be who we truly are. Truly a fixed star to steer by even during the darkest night of the soul. Something opens within, perhaps, forgotten wings, and we find that the world all along has not been over and against us, fighting us, but flowing right through us, as us, and we rejoice.

Here is calm
so deep, grasses cease waving..
wonderful how completely
everything in wild
nature fits into us, as if truly part
and parent of us. The
sun shines not on us, but in us. The
rivers flow not past,
but through us, thrilling, tingling
vibrating every fiber
and cell of the substance of our
bodies, making them glide and sing.[13]

~John Muir

Notes

PART I: The Source

[1] Brooke Medicine Eagle, *Buffalo Woman Comes Singing* (New York: Ballantine, 1991) p. 44

[2] Marvin Meyer, Trans. *The Gospel of Thomas* (New York: Harper Collins, 1992) p. 35

PART II: The Abyss

[1] Hermann Hesse, *Demian* (New York: Bantam, 1965) p. 4

[2] Kahlil Gibran, *The Prophet* (New York: Alfred A. Knopf, 1934) p. 47

[3] William Blake, *The Complete Poetry & Prose* (New York: Doubleday, 1988) p. 470.

[4] David Elkind, *The Hurried Child* (Reading: Perseus Books, 1988)

[5] D.H. Lawrence, *Collected Poems* (New York: Viking, 1959) p. 144

[6] St. Francis de Sales, quoted in Aldous Huxley, *The Perennial Philosophy* (New York: Harper & Row, 1970) p. 293

[7] Joseph Campbell, *The Power of Myth* (New York: Doubleday, 1988) p. 37

[8] David Whyte, *Fire in the Earth* (Washington: Many Rivers Press, 1992) p. 8

[9] Louis B. Fierman, *Effective Psychotherapy: The Contribution of Helmuth Kaiser* (New York: The Free Press, 1965) pp. 36-37.

[10] Oriah Mountain Dreamer, *The Invitation* (New York: HarperCollins, 1999) pp. 1-2

[11] Joseph Campbell, *The Power of Myth* p

[12] Hermann Hesse, *Demian* (New York: Harper & Row, 1965) p. 140

[13] Luis J. Rodriguez, *Always Running: La vida loca* (New York: Simon & Schuster, 1994)

[14] Pablo Neruda, *Selected Poems* (New York: Dell, 1972) p. 457

PART III: The Quest

[1] Don Lathrop, *Letter to a friend*, 1995, American Academy of Psychotherapy web forum.

[2] Bart Kosko, *Fuzzy Thinking: The new science of fuzzy logic* (New York: Hyperion, 1993) p. xv

[3] Joseph Campell, *Hero With A Thousand Faces* (Princeton: Princeton University Press, 1972) p. 30

[4] Joseph Campbell, *Hero With A Thousand Faces*, p. 30

[5] Ruth Beebe Hill, *Hanta Yo* (New York: Warner Books, 1979) p. 15

[6] Rainer Maria Rilke, *Letters To A Young Poet* (New York: W.W. Norton, 1954) p. 35

[7] Jeff Salz, *Escape Magazine*, summer 1994

[8] Robert Johnson, *Owning Your Own Shadow: Understanding the dark side of the psyche*

(San Francisco: Harper Collins, 1991) pp. 75-78

[9] Robert Johnson, *Owning Your Own Shadow*, pp. 84-85

[10] Stephen Foster with Meredith Little, *The Book of the Vision Quest: Personal transformation in the Wilderness* (New York: Simon & Shuster, 1992) p. 216

[11] Stephen Foster, *The Book of the Vision Quest* p. 216

[12] James Dillet Freeman, *Of Time and Eternity* (Unity School of Christianity, 1981)

[13] Deena Metzger, *Writing For Your Life* (New York: Harper San Francisco, 1992), p. 49

[14] Rainer Maria Rilke, Tr. Stephen Mitchell, in *The Essemce of Wisdom* (New York: Broadway Books, 1998) p. 43

PART IV: The Dance

[1] Mickey Hart, *Drumming at the Edge of Magic,* (New York: HarperCollins, 1990) p. 81

[2] Black Elk, *The Sacred Pipe* (London: University of Oklahoma Press, 1989)   p. 92

[3] Carl Jung, *Memories, Dreams and Reflections* (New York: Random House,1965) p. 196

[4] Margaret Thompson Drewal, *Yoruba Ritual: Performers, Play, Agency,* (Bloomington: Indiana University Press, 1992) p. 47

[5] Black Elk, *Black Elk Speaks* (Lincoln: University of Nebraska Press, 1979) p. 34

[6] Timothy Freke and Peter Gandy, *The Wisdom of the Pagan Philosopher* (Boston: Journey Editions, 1998)

[7] Lao Tzu, *Tao Te Ching*, trans. By Gia-Fu Feng and Jane English (New York: Vintage Books, 1989) pp. 10, 34, 45, 68, 80

[8] Chaung Tzu, *Inner Chapters* trans. By Gia-Fu Feng and Jane English, (New York: Vintage, 1974) chapter 13 and 21

[9] Alan Watts, *Tao: The Watercourse Way* (New York: Pantheon, 1975) pp. 48-49

[10] Alan Watts, *Tao: The Watercourse Way,* p.94

[11] Dr. Seuss, *Oh, The Places You Will Go* (New York: Random House, 1990) pp. 2, 6

[12] Linnie Marsh Wolfe, *Son to the Wilderness: A Life of John Muir* (New York: Alfred A. Knopf, 1945)

[13] Joseph Cornell, *Listening to Nature: How to deepen your awareness of nature* (Dawn Publications, 1987) p. 42

67923222R00180

Made in the USA
Charleston, SC
25 February 2017